Play
THE REAL- LIFE
MONEY GAME
With Your Teen

SARAH WILLIAMSON

The Real-Life Money Game, LLC
Medina, WA
First Edition

To Michael

Acknowledgements

· ·

No one person creates a book. I enjoyed the support of a remarkable, diverse team. I am grateful to all who are involved in creating "Play *The Real-Life* Money Game With Your Teen."

My sister, Deborah, and my brothers, Martin and Chris, offered encouragement, love and support. My mother inspired my strength and tenacity. She passed along her remarkable insight, compassion, and empathy. She died earlier this year, but her spirit will always be with me.

Scott Driscoll, a gifted writer, teacher, editor, collaborator, and communicator, offered guidance and support through the entire project.

The case-study families, featured throughout this book, revealed their successes and their failures while putting *The Real-Life* Money Game into practice.

The parents who attended *The Real-Life* Money Game course gave me ongoing feedback and allowed me to share their lessons with you. My friends went above and beyond the call of duty to attend my courses, and at times, had more faith in my project than I did.

Dr. John Thompson patiently reinforced the "simple truths" of parenting and of life.

Drs. Lana and Lynn Staheli, founders of Global-Help, a nonprofit organization that produces health publications for developing countries free of charge, shared their invaluable wisdom, experience, and referrals in book writing, production, and marketing.

Paul Merriman of Merriman Capital Management, Inc. greatly influenced the key investment fundamentals found in chapter fourteen.

Carol Watson, CPA, reviewed all tax-related references.

The production team: Conie Blake provided meticulous proofreading; Jeff McCord of Freelancelot committed timely and concentrated efforts on book design and layout; Laura Fisher designed *The Real-Life* Money Game website; Debbie Mizrahi of Mizrahi Media and Lana Abrams of Nine Design created the exceptional logo and cover design.

The Spellman Company provided branding, packaging, and the book's public relation's launch.

Finishing the book is not the end, just a new beginning. I hope to continue working with such valued partners.

— *Sarah Williamson*

Table of Contents

Play *The Real-Life* Money Game With Your Teen

Part One

The Real-Life Money Game—What It's All About

Chapter 1 • *The Real-Life* Money Game and Why You Should Play It .. 3

Why You Need to Play the Game With Your Teen 3

Teaching Teens Tangible and Intangible Skills 4

A Scalable Financial Plan 6

The Real-Life Money Game Concept 10

The Real-Life Money Game Plan Overview 12

The Book's Promise 14

Chapter 2 • Who You Are and How You Fit Into *The Real-Life* Money Game 15

Player Profile Questionnaire 15

Scorekeeping Box 18

Chapter 3 • What You Need to Play *The Real-Life* Money Game 23

Accessories 23

How To Use the Personal Financial Binder 25

Scorekeeping Box 29

Chapter 4 • Where the Money Will Come From: Teen-Generated Income 31

Teen-Generated Income 31

Activities Pie-Chart 33

Playing the Game: Income Worksheet 49

Scorekeeping Box 51

Chapter 5 • Where the Money Will Come From:
Parent-Generated Income 53

Parent-Generated Income.. 53

Playing the Game: Family Fund Contribution Formula 56

Scorekeeping Box 72

Chapter 6 • Spending: The Mechanics 75

Cash Pockets.. 75

Savings Account and ATM Card.. 77

Checking and Debit Card Account 78

Investment Account... 80

Teaching Your Teen to Keep Track of Cash................................... 80

Scorekeeping Box 86

Chapter 7 • *The Real-Life* Money Game Playing Board—
A Spending Plan 89

Playing the Game: The Playing Board-Spending Plan (Column 1).............. 89

Scorekeeping Box 95

Chapter 8 • *The Real-Life* Money Game Rules 97

Rule One 97

Rule Two 100

Rule Three 102

Rule Four 103

Rule Five 104

Playing the Game: *The Real-Life* Money Game Contract 104

Golden Rule For Parents 106

Scorekeeping Box 108

Chapter 9 • *The Real-Life* Money Game Plan 109

Playing the Game: *The Real-Life* Money Game Plan.................... 110

Scorekeeping Box 118

Chapter 10 • Tracking *The Real-Life* Money Game Monthly Activity 121

Playing the Game: The Playing Board-Spending Plan (Column 2)............. 121

Scorekeeping Box 131

Part Two

Resource Management—From Home to the Bank and the IRS

Chapter 11 • Saving: Playing It Safe 135

Playing the Game—*The Real-Life* Money Game Three-Part Savings Plan: Now, Later, Never 138

Scorekeeping Box 150

Chapter 12 • Giving: Is It Worse Than a Shot? 151

Playing the Game: "Who Or What Matters Most to You?" 151

Scorekeeping Box 159

Chapter 13 • Borrowing and Lending: A Spendthrift's Nightmare or a Wise Money Manager's Hedge Against the Future? 161

Playing the Game: *The Real-Life* Money Game Borrowing Chart 165

Playing the Game: *The Real-Life* Money Game Lending Chart 166

Scorekeeping Box 168

Chapter 14 • Investing: Creating More Resource 171

Develop a Resource 172

Step One: Learn Investment Basics 172

Step Two: Understand the Market 174

Step Three: Identify a Strategy 180

Step Four: Evaluate Investment Alternatives 185

Step Five: Track and Manage Investments 187

Investing With a Traditional IRA or a Roth IRA............................190

Playing the Game: Putting the Five Steps to Investing Together..............191

Scorekeeping Box 194

Chapter 15 • Taxes: An Invisible Resource Depletion 197

What Teens Need to Know..197

What Parents Need to Know 199

Tax Computation Websites 203

Scorekeeping Box 203

Part Three

Playing the Game and Keeping Score

Chapter 16 • *The Real-Life* **Money Game Five-Step Instructions**......207

How I Play *The Real-Life* Money Game With My Son 208

The Real-Life Money Game Five-Step Instructions 211

Chapter 17 • Winning Strategies For Parents..............................217

Teaching Skills In Order of Priority..217

Seven Deadly Sins: The Seven Most Common Financial Mistakes Parents Make With Their Teens..220

Chapter 18 • Winning Strategies For Teens.............................239

Common Mistakes To Help Your Teens Avoid................................239

Developing a Teen's Financial "Instinct" 245

Chapter 19 • Resolving Conflict That Arises As *The Real-Life* **Money Game Is Played** 249

Common Problems Parents Can Anticipate 250

Four-Step Method For Problem Solving 250

Chapter 20 • **Special Circumstances: How *The Real-Life* Money Game Deals With the Three Disruptive "D's"**..................261

Divorce 261

Disability 263

Death..264

Chapter 21 • ***The Real-Life* Money Game's Word on Worth** 269

Income Versus Worth 269

Valuing the Resource 275

Chapter 22 • **Keeping Score**...277

Scorekeeping Box Totals: Gauging Your Teen's Progress...........278

Identifying Your Teen's Player Level....................................289

Appendix..291

Worksheets 292-320

Index..321-330

Introduction
Toys "R" Us "Showdown" Moment

You're in Toys "R" Us and you have fifteen minutes to get a birthday gift. Your twelve-year-old son insists he must have a $50 Nintendo game. Here's the rub: he just bought one two days ago with his allowance. What will you do? Ignore him? Reason with him? Scream and stomp your feet, as he does?

This showdown transpired between myself and my son Michael when he was twelve, leaving me to wonder what the world would be like if I never had to negotiate another penny with my child. But this is not the *real* world. The real world is filled with catchy musical tunes and flashy neon signs and hypnotic TV hypes and overspending and debt and bankruptcy. I was just as harried and hesitant and frustrated as other parents I knew who were caught up in this societal consumerism. So what *do* you do as a parent in a situation like this?

Later, after I'd had some time to reflect on the incident, I realized that the point wasn't to teach my son *not* to spend, the point was to teach him *how* to spend! Simply put: I realized it was time for my son to have some money, so he could practice making some independent spending decisions without his parents' intervention. He needed to be a participant, to make decisions for himself where he did the thinking and learned to live with his choices.

It was out of this realization that *The Real-Life* Money Game grew. In the first two years, as we both learned how it would work, Michael became a savvy money manager, and we, his parents, discovered the benefits of openly discussing our family's finances with him. Since then, we haven't experienced a single showdown with Michael over money.

I am an experienced CPA who has worked for a national accounting firm. I tend to pay attention to money gurus like Alan Greenspan, luminary former chairman of the Federal Reserve, who campaigned for the teaching of basic financial management skills to children beginning at a young age. Greenspan's call-to-action was in response to the country's low financial literacy rate among teens as reported by the Jump$tart Coalition for Personal Financial Literacy. An organization working with the Treasury Department, Jump$tart seeks to evaluate and improve the standards of financial literacy among children and young adults.

So when I mentioned this quote to another parent friend of mine and admitted that I was practicing money management with my child, he said with tongue in cheek, "Yeah. So are we. We just give it to them."

This approach will neither halt the tantrums nor prepare your child for a financially responsible future. The solution is *The Real-Life* Money Game that is both fun and effective as a tool for teaching teens the basics of money management.

Part One

The Real-Life Money Game—What It's All About

In part one you'll learn what The Real-Life Money Game is all about, why you should play it with your teen, and what accessories you need to get started. You will discover how to create a fund by pooling both teen-generated income, as well as, parent-generated income for your son or daughter to manage. Armed with a spending plan, you will see how you can shift payments on many regular expense items to your teen. With this in place, you'll be introduced to The Real-Life Money Game Rules, a set of guidelines that you and your teen are encouraged to follow. The Real-Life Money Game Plan then helps you establish money-management goals for your teen, and helps you track his or her monthly financial activity. To enable you to gauge your teen's on-going progress, The Real-Life Money Game provides handy scorekeeping boxes.

Chapter One
The Real-Life Money Game and Why You Should Play It

• •

Money is a renewable resource. For those who know how to manage it, money is like a groomed and productive forest. It grows as it's nurtured. For those who don't know how to manage it, when the money is spent, what's left resembles the barren ground of a clear-cut. This book is about how to help your teens prevent their own financial lives from becoming clear-cuts.

In order to do this, I like to follow what I call a *scalable plan*. Don't let the oddity of the term put you off. All it really means is a plan that can expand as your needs and proficiencies expand. Let's go back to our *renewable resource* example. A maturing forest changes as its needs change. Like the healthy forest, a scalable plan is a method of resource management that will adapt to your teen's changing financial needs. The plan expands to create new opportunities. You and your teen can learn to cultivate a scalable financial plan from the ground up, and in so doing, nurture it into a renewable resource, a money plan that will remain productive and useful in the years to come.

Why You Need to Play the Game With Your Teen

Money management is not taught in schools. You may think that because your son or daughter learns lofty subjects such as calculus and chemistry, that they would learn about personal finance. Surprisingly, our teens don't.

According to a recent survey, 85% of high school students receive no school-based personal-finance education whatsoever. What families often discover is that their teens end up graduating from high school without even the simplest, most pragmatic, *real-life* skills. When out in the *real world* for the first time, teens accustomed to acing academics find themselves suddenly expected to manage a resource they know nothing about. Studies indicate that many cannot so much as balance a checkbook.

By default, parents become the teachers. I discovered this through trials with my seventeen-year-old son, Michael. Many concepts in this book grew out of my experience teaching him the money-management skills I knew he would need if he were to become financially independent from his parents.

Consider a few alarming facts.

Statistically, teens spend the most and save the least of any other age group. Generation Y—the ten to twenty-four year-old children of baby boomers—spend $250 billion a year on clothes. That comes to $4,176 per person, per year, or $348 per month. The average adult has over $5,000 in credit card debt, and credit-card companies target college-entry-age teens. In a recent survey, the Jump$tart Coalition for Personal Financial Literacy, an organization working with the Treasury Department to evaluate and improve the standards of financial literacy among children and young adults, reported that high school seniors scored less than 50% on 31 multiple-choice questions about saving, spending, insurance, investing, and credit. And the trend is moving downward. Three years ago students' average scores were 57% percent.

Is any of this a reason to be alarmed? Consider. What this means is that today our teens have more money to spend than ever before, more pressure to spend it, and fewer skills with which to manage the resource competently. Now, more than ever, if you believe, as I do, that financial health is an essential component of your teen's future well-being, then you can't afford not to play *The Real-Life Money Game* (RLMG).

Teaching Teens Tangible and Intangible Skills

How do we help our teens acquire the skills they will need in order to manage money effectively? We start by identifying what skills they will need to learn if a healthy independence is our goal for them. These skills can be broken down into two categories: tangible and intangible. Think of tangible skills as a tool-kit that will allow teens to enjoy a hands-on connection to money management. The sidebar on this page lists these tangible skills.

Tangible Money-Management Skills

- Knowing how income is generated, learning how to earn money.
- Managing the mechanics of spending, creating a spending plan, and learning how to pay expenses.
- Understanding the concept of savings, including setting aside money for unanticipated costs.
- Instilling a mind-set for giving.
- Understanding borrowing and lending and learning how to use debt wisely.
- Learning how to invest.
- Understanding taxes.

Knowing how income is generated and managing the mechanics of spending—the first two tangible skills—lay the groundwork for developing the other tangible skills, the concepts of saving, giving, borrowing, investing, and taxes.

Learning how to generate income might mean, for example, receiving money as a gift, earning money from a job or teen-business or investing money that produces income or gains. Managing the mechanics of spending involves setting up a monthly spending plan that will identify your teen's income sources as well as the expenses you wish your teen to pay. Your teen will also learn how to handle cash, ATM withdrawals, a checking account and a debit card.

Confused? Unsure what I'm getting at? Let's look at an example. One family's sixteen-year-old daughter earns money babysitting. Most of what she earns, she saves. She is very good at saving, but for the wrong reasons. She is afraid to spend money. She needs to learn how to spend. To encourage her, the family set up a spending plan with two expenses, entertainment and gas, that she was responsible for paying out of her monthly babysitting earnings.

The family's thirteen-year-old daughter also earns money babysitting. Most of what she earns, she spends. She loves to spend money. In her case, the family set up a spending plan for entertainment expenses as well as a line item for clothing. With the expenses specifically identified, this daughter was encouraged to spend less frivolously and to take on more responsibility. In the process, she also learned to save.

When we teach our teens tangible skills, we lay a foundation from which to build intangible skills. A list of intangible skills could be as long as the roll-call of families who care about their teens' futures. For the sake of brevity, I will provide here the short list of learned behaviors and values an informal survey indicated were uppermost on parents' minds. The sidebar on the following page lists these intangible skills.

For the above-mentioned family's sixteen-year-old daughter, specifically identifying and limiting what expenses she would pay helped develop her spending skills and diminish her fears. As a result her self-confidence took a boost.

The family's thirteen-year-old daughter was developing spending skills similar to her sister's. Teaching her to curb her impulsive spending helped her learn to delay gratification.

The desired end result is up to you. Maybe you want a teen who is above all things magnanimous. Maybe you want a teen who is disciplined. Whatever your goal, my goal in writing this book is to help you help your teen fledge into adulthood on sound wings of financial responsibility and independence.

A Scalable Financial Plan

Now that we've identified the money-management skills we need to teach our teens, the next step is to learn how. This is where the scalable plan comes into play. But first, it's helpful to understand what setting up a scalable plan is intended to accomplish. The scalable plan offers the following four key benefits.

> ### Intangible Money-Management Skills
>
> 1. Valuing assets (what they have)
> 2. Delayed gratification (curbing impulses)
> 3. Differentiating wants from needs (and understanding the importance of contributing to both)
> 4. Problem solving
> 5. Personal responsibility
> 6. Self-discipline
> 7. Self-confidence
> 8. Self-motivation
> 9. Independent thinking
> 10. Strong work ethic

Transferring Control

The object of *The Real-Life* Money Game is to let your son or daughter take personal responsibility for money your household already spends on their behalf. A scalable plan will first and foremost assist you in transferring control of money to your teen. As challenging as this notion may seem—it was for me at first—by allowing your teen to participate in money decisions, you will be giving your son or daughter an opportunity to learn at what I call a *gut level*. They will experience first-hand how money works. We can do our teens a great service by showing them how to rise above the age-old "my money," "your money" dilemma. When they are in control, Mom and Dad are no longer the target of pressure and manipulation. Everyone in the end is happier. But more importantly for the long run, using a scalable money plan offers teens something of much greater value than cash to jam into their pocket, or, for that matter, to sock away into a savings bank. The power of a plan is that it becomes a lifetime, resource-management tool. Teens who learn to devise their own plan at a formative age will carry this management ability with them into the rest of their lives.

Specifically, here's how a scalable plan helps you transfer control of money to your teen. The key concept in this transfer process is called the Family Fund Contribution (FFC). This will be explained in detail in chapter five. The Family Fund Contribution provides a formula that will help you pool money contributed by both you from your household funds, as well as from money pulled from your teen's income sources. The Family Fund Contribution is designed to be flexible. It takes into account both you and your teen's needs as well as the financial resources your family has available. Once the fund has been established, your teen draws upon this pool to cover expenses you've agreed he or she should be responsible to pay. You determine the size of the pool, while your teen manages the actual earning, spending, saving, giving, borrowing or lending, investing, and taxes.

Here is an example of why your teen needs to be brought into the decision-making process. One mother planned to give her fourteen-year-old daughter $600 twice a year for clothes. This mother discovered later that her daughter was too fearful to buy clothes, because she didn't know how much they cost. Her daughter's concern, as she later admitted, was that she would run out of money too soon and not have enough left for items she might need later. When this mother and daughter went shopping, the daughter would *conveniently* leave her wallet at home. Her mother would end up paying for the clothes to avoid the hassle. Finally, when given an opportunity to participate in the decision, the daughter said what she really wanted, at least to start with, was a small fund of money to buy her friends gifts and for makeup and jewelry.

Teens learn by doing, but they also have to start within the boundaries of their comfort zone. It's better, for instance, to receive an overdraft fee of $30, as my son did, than to find themselves suddenly with several hundred dollars worth of charges on a credit card they thought they could max to the limit (never quite grasping where the money was to come from). My son's overdraft charge did happen once again. The damage was small, and through his repeated experience, he learned to keep a minimum balance in his account. The point here is that a scalable plan allows your teen to start at a level for which he or she is ready. With practice, they graduate into riskier territory.

Flexibility

A scalable plan provides flexibility. The amount of money available can change as needs change. A flexible scalable plan is designed to adapt to your family's evolving resources, values, and financial priorities.

Here's how a scalable plan provides that flexibility. A mother with two teen-age boys reported that each week her sons were devouring all the snack food and drink in the house. She couldn't keep up with consumption and it was costing her far more than her budget allowed for discretionary *junk* food. To teach her sons a lesson, she saved her grocery receipts for a month and showed them how much money she was spending on snacks. She rejoiced when one son said, "We spent that much money on snacks?" He told her he could think of better ways to spend the money. She decided to give him the opportunity.

In keeping with our scalable plan, she allocated a weekly snack food allowance that each of her boys would be responsible for purchasing. Once the snacks were gone, she would not purchase more. The family agreed that no one could eat the snack food each boy purchased for himself.

This mother claimed that snack food had amounted to thirty-five percent of the grocery bill. She aimed to cut that amount to ten percent. But she was not the only family member to have a say. Her boys now had a say in the plan. If they wanted more snack food, they could negotiate from their side. They had the option to come up with more resources. Feeling motivated by an upcoming soccer-team party for which he was to provide snacks, one son turned entrepreneur. Now that he had an understanding of cost, he did a candy-sale fundraiser, thus increasing the contribution to his plan from the supply side.

What makes a scalable plan flexible is that it allows for this process of negotiation. Rather than looking at money as a finite quantity, it becomes a resource that can grow as the need for more exists.

Money Equals Opportunity

Do you find yourself in confrontation with your teen over money? Does every argument turn into a defensive battle of wits? If your answer is "yes," you are in good company. Many families find themselves in this quagmire.

The scalable plan's third benefit—transforming money into opportunity—offers parents a way to escape the feeling that they're on trial every time the subject comes up. When your teen learns that money creates opportunity, he or she can view the subject in a positive way.

A single dad shared his experience with his sixteen-year-old daughter. Money in their household was chronically tight. Even though he allowed his daughter to have her own spending money, it bothered him that she "frittered it away" on CDs, most of which she quickly lost interest in. He couldn't understand why their mutual anger flared over spending choices. After much prompting, his daughter admitted she got the impression her dad thought she was stupid and incompetent. In essence, by complaining about her choices, or by arguing that it was money ill-spent, he was telling her that he knew better than she did what was best for her, that he was wiser and more experienced, and that her choices were inferior.

The scalable plan sets parameters for both parents and teens. What this dad discovered, once he learned to give up control over choice, was that his daughter learned to discipline her own spending. When she had mid-range and long-range goals thrown into the mix, she was even more inclined to limit herself. For instance, she and her dad were planning a trip to Italy the following year. He agreed to match her dollar for dollar for everything she could save toward her own entertainment expenses for the trip. Excited by the idea of shopping in Florence and Rome, she quickly learned to modify her own spending on CDs. In return for matching funds, he only asked that she agree that he could cut back on his contribution to the discretionary spending pool, so that he could divert more money to her college fund. She was okay with that. She learned to shop for clothes at off-beat discount stores instead of higher-priced department stores. With these parameters in place, the arguments stopped. She no longer felt criticized. And he learned to accept the validity of her right to make choices.

Spirit of Entrepreneurship

When I talk to my son about money, I catch myself using the word *money* to mean *income*, as though the words were synonymous. Often we talk to our teens about income, but rarely do we talk about *worth*. In simplified terms, financial worth is what you own, less what you owe. Income is what you earn. Once we learn to differentiate *worth* from *income*, a world of money possibilities can open up for our teens. They can learn how to use income to increase worth, in other words, to use money to create money. A scalable plan enables teens to embrace possibilities that go beyond frivolous spending or defensive hoarding. Sometimes that requires risk. This risk-taking is what I call the spirit of entrepreneurship—it means thinking like a risk-taking entrepreneur.

Here is how one family promoted this kind of thinking with their twelve-year-old son: He asked to borrow money to start a car-detailing business. He needed to purchase a power-vacuum, car-buffer, and carpet-shampooing equipment. Both he and his parents were taking a calculated risk that the idea would work. On sunny Sundays their son would sit outside at his local church parking lot and detail church-goers cars while they were inside.

It seemed like a sound idea, but the parents at first hesitated because they didn't like the idea of their son borrowing money. When it was explained to their son that his part of the Family Fund Contribution pool would cover the up-front costs, whether his plan worked or not, and when he agreed, they knew they had to let him try. Within two weekends he had made enough to cover the cost of the equipment and to pay back his parents. Later, to his parents' surprise, he took half his business earnings and bought used books, which he in turn sold for a small profit to retirement homes where residents had time to read, but little money to pay. All this was made possible through the flexibility of a plan that allows for entrepreneurial risk.

● ● ●

So, let's look at this once more. A scalable plan, as long as you agree to transfer decision-making to your teen, provides flexibility, encourages responsibility, transforms money from a punitive measure into an opportunity, and promotes creative thinking and disciplined risk-taking. The benefit to you and your teen can be enormous. All it requires is that you take a deep breath and prepare yourself to cede control. Ultimately, this is our goal anyway, isn't it? To help our teens responsibly take control of their own lives?

The Real-Life Money Game Concept

Here's how the concept of the scalable plan fits into *The Real-Life* Money Game you're going to play at home with your teen.

But first a few words about the plan's game-like nature. I call this a game because you *play* it with the kind of give-and-take that typically goes into a game. To help you along, this book provides you with game-like things. For instance, instead of an actual playing board, you'll receive what I call a spending plan. Instead of accessories in the form of dogs, lead pipes, or wrenches that move from room to room, in this game you'll learn to use *cash pockets*, a savings account with an ATM card, or a checking and debit card account with a checkbook. These accessories are intended for beginner and intermediate players. Ultimately, if your teen reaches the advanced player-level, he or she may progress to an investment account and a credit card. The reason I call it *The Real-Life* Money Game is that you will be applying these methods in your *real* lives.

In a nutshell, here are the game's key features.

- I'll start you off with a set of instructions. Each step will show you what you need to do. This will include: identifying information you need and things you need to have on hand; putting together a fund of money for your teen to practice with; signing a contract; understanding how to account for the fund; and setting aside time to talk about the results.

- Along with the instructions, you'll receive a set of ground rules. This will include an explanation of how to reach an agreement with your son or daughter. The rules will provide specific guidelines at the start of the game, so that your family will know what is expected.

- Once you've got all the parts in place, you'll be shown how to complete a Playing Board-Spending Plan. The spending plan is a three-column worksheet that identifies how much money your teen will have available at the beginning of the month and how the money will be used during the month. The spending plan is also used to help your teen calculate how much is available for savings, giving, borrowing or lending, investing, or taxes. The spending plan will have enough built-in flexibility to allow your teen to make independent choices. At month's end, the same spending plan will be used to show how the money was actually used.

- You'll be encouraged to fill out a worksheet that will help you define the desired end result and break the long-term goal into concrete, specific, achievable tasks. This is called *The Real-Life* Money Game Plan.

· Like most games that we enjoy, keeping score is part of the process. This game will prove no different, except insomuch as the object of this game will not be to best the competition. Instead, keeping score will allow you to establish benchmarks that will help you gauge your teen's progress. Each chapter ends with a Scorekeeping Box that summarizes key concepts and lists activities for which your teen earns points. Beginning-player-level activities are worth five points each, intermeditate-player-level activities are worth ten, and advanced-player-level activities are worth 20.

The Real-Life Money Game Plan Overview

The Real-Life Money Game Plan Overview, shown on the following two pages, offers a guideline to assist you and your teen in identifying your RLMG Plan goals over time. The objective, at each player-level, is to teach the tangible skill. As your teen becomes proficient with the tangible skill indicated, an associated intangible behavior can result.

As with any game, repetition and practice are the key to success. Believe me, even in my own household, best intentions went astray. The first time my son attempted to balance his checkbook, he forgot to record an ATM withdrawal. He transposed a $23 deposit as $32, and made a calculation error on his balance. With so many errors to reconcile, the process turned into a complete disaster. He wanted to quit the game altogether. We practiced letting go, a *Zen-like* attitude that in this case, at least, took the steam out of my son's resistance. It may be that the first month he needed rescuing. But he stayed with it. By the fourth month, when he balanced his checkbook, euphoria reigned. There was no going back.

Each time my son mastered new money-management skills, his scalable plan grew. More financial opportunities came his way as his proficiencies continued to build. Now, as his expanding supply of financial information allows him ever new decision-making opportunities, I am convinced Michael's forest will only continue to grow and flourish well into his adulthood.

The Real-Life Money Game Plan Overview: Tangible Skills

	Beginning Player	Intermediate Player	Advanced Player
Earning	Gets paid for house-hold tasks or chores.	Lands a job.	Starts a "Teen Business."
Spending	Uses "Cash Pockets" or Savings & ATM to distribute spending-plan funds.	Uses checking & debit card account to distribute spending-plan funds.	Uses investment account to distribute spending-plan funds.
Saving	Establishes one short-term savings target for "Now."	Establishes one long-term savings target for "Later."	Puts aside a fixed percent of monthly income for "Never."
Giving	Considers what cause or organization matters most.	Chooses one cause or organization to contribute to on a regular basis.	Chooses one cause or organization to contribute to or volunteer for on a regular basis.
Borrowing/ Lending	Understands and fol-lows all debt rules.	Borrows and lends responsibly following established guide-lines.	Has one major credit card used for emer-gencies, borrows from one lending institu-tion, and requests and understands a credit report.
Investing	Earmarks money to be matched for investing.	Invests with an in-vestment institution.	Invests on own using Internet research and books or sets up an IRA or Roth IRA account.
Taxes	Aware taxes exist.	Calculates tax ex-pense.	Prepares own tax return.

The Real-Life Money Game Plan Overview: Intangible Skills		
Beginning Player	**Intermediate Player**	**Advanced Player**
1. Valuing assets (what they have) 2. Delayed gratification (curbing impulses) 3. Differentiating wants from needs (and understanding the importance of contributing to both)	4. Problem solving 5. Personal responsibility 6. Self-discipline 7. Self-confidence	8. Self-motivation 9. Independent thinking 10. Strong work ethic

The Book's Promise

My promise to you?

Remember those angry, embarrassing confrontations over money? Those desperate negotiations, those peer-pressure demands that you felt powerless to counterbalance? Remember those times when you were in the mall or the grocery store, a target for the scornful looks and clucking tongues from other parents, whom you could tell had branded you, of all people, a failure? Remember how many times you've wished you could wave a magic wand and your teens would suddenly become mature, responsible, innovative managers of their own money?

Think of this as your magic wand. Okay, a magic wand that takes some work. Not much, but a little. A bit of set-up time at the start, then one-and-a-half hours a month. That's all. That's really all. And for this small investment of your time, you will have a teen who understands where money comes from, who appreciates the value of what is bought, and who learns how to manage financial resources so you can stand on the sideline and cheer your son or daughter on!

Chapter Two
Who You Are and How You Fit Into *The Real-Life* Money Game

· ·

When I teach *The Real-Life* Money Game course for parents with teens, one of the first things I have them do is interview each other. Part of the point is to get them to know one another. But you might argue that they could do that on their time. It's true, but left to themselves they'd never get around to asking the key questions. We don't like to talk about our money habits. The discussion comes off for many feeling too revealing. Yet, it's precisely for this reason that most parents who sign up for my course have no clear idea of how their behavior is subtly influencing their teen's feelings about money, and not always in a constructive way.

> ### Parent Player Profile Questionnaire
>
> - Part one helps you identify your teen's money habits.
> - Part two helps you identify your money habits.
> - Part three helps you identify your goals.

The questions in the interview allow participants to overcome their uneasiness and to simply discuss their money habits. Because we can't do an interview here, I've provided a Player Profile Questionnaire that in effect allows you to interview yourself regarding your money habits. Gathering this information is an important first step toward understanding the values you want to teach your teens. The Player Profile Questionnaire is designed to help you and your teen assess your priorities and identify your goals, once you've learned to recognize your typical money habits.

> ### Teen Player Profile Questionnaire
>
> With regards to managing money:
>
> - Lets your teen rate you.
> - Identifies what your teen would wish most to learn.
> - Determines how your teen would use money now.
> - Identifies your teen's future money goals.

Player Profile Questionnaire

The Parent Player Profile Questionnaire is divided into three parts. In part one, the questions will help you determine who pays for what and what spending limits your household can comfortably support.

Part two of the questionnaire is designed to help you identify your spending priorities. You'll be asked to examine habits, such as whether you save regularly, what your attitude is toward debt, how easy it is for you to invest, and what you invest in. The dominant patterns of your money use will be made clear. Knowing this will help you focus your future spending to take advantage of priorities—maybe investment for the future matters more than general saving. The information gleaned from your answers will help you decide what spending habits you really want to teach your teen.

Part three simply asks you to identify your goals. That is to say, what you hope to get out of playing this game. While teaching my course, I discovered several important things on parents' minds with regards to teaching their teens about money. Parents wanted to know where to begin. Secondly, they wanted a way to talk openly with their teens about their family's finances. Many families reported that their teens had no notion of how their parents managed their money. The Parent Player Profile Questionnaire provides a forum for opening the lines of communication in your family.

The Teen Player Profile Questionnaire, to be filled out by your son or daughter, helps your teen identify his or her money priorities. This is your young rebel's chance to say what she thinks she should be responsible for paying. She will also be asked to put down in writing exactly how she thinks the money should be spent, and to explain to her parents in no uncertain terms how she feels about her money.

As one family discovered with their twelve-year-old son, the answers can be surprising. Their son indicated that he would like to learn how to manage money so he could "make wise financial decisions when he becomes an adult." His dad rolled his eyes when he read his son's answer, and said that his son probably wrote what he thought his parents wanted to hear. His mother, delighted by her son's mature-sounding response, wasn't so sure. She encouraged her husband to give their son a chance. She suggested they offer their adolescent a semi-annual shoe expense to manage. To him, shoes mattered, and he had been nagging his mother to let him make his own shoe choices. The family decided to give him $175 to spend on his fall and winter shoes. They determined this amount would be reasonable by looking back on how much they had spent in the prior year, and further by double-checking prices both on the Internet and in shops. The money would need to cover regular daily shoes, soccer cleats, and cold-weather boots. He could not spend more than this amount. They helped him identify a reasonable price to pay for each, but he would have some discretion when he finally made his purchases. The Player Profile Questionnaire provided this family with a valuable communication tool. Without their son's input, he might have been less committed to the spending priorities his parents imposed on him. After filling out his profile, he was much more willing to follow-through buying the appropriate shoes, which was *his* priority.

You might be tempted to skip this exercise. Go straight to the game. Allow me a moment to counsel against this rush. If you take some time to identify your family's financial priorities, you will have a baseline upon which to build your scalable plan. Remember, the scalable plan allows room to expand as you and your teen's needs and proficiencies change. Let's look at how one family used the questionnaire to lay the groundwork for their daughter's scalable financial plan.

The Wilsons, one of the case-study families we will follow throughout this book, have three teenage daughters. Their oldest daughter Karen had just turned sixteen when they introduced her to *The Real-Life* Money Game. She wrote on her Teen Player Profile Questionnaire that she wanted to buy a car. Connie Wilson, Karen's mother, identified *teaching my daughter to save a portion of the cost of a car* as a tangible goal she hoped to reach by playing the game. She wanted her daughter to understand that if Karen wished to buy a car, she would need to make a contribution.

Using the information from the questionnaires, the Wilsons established their preliminary goal. They set forth a plan for Karen to earn some money toward her car purchase. Since Karen was an accomplished swimmer, the family agreed she could pursue a lifeguard job at a local pool. She would set aside half of the money she earned for the down-payment on a car. This was the baseline for their daughter's scalable plan. Over the next month, Karen got her driver's license. Once Karen started driving, the Wilsons reviewed with her the actual costs of owning and operating a car. The Wilsons realized that in their heart of hearts, they expected their daughter to not only pay for part of the car, but to pay for her gas and a portion of the car insurance as well. Her savings weren't adequate to cover both. The Wilsons agreed to kick in a higher percent of the up-front cost of the car because it was a higher value to them to teach Karen to make regular monthly payments toward expenses. Together, they agreed that $50 a month, earned from babysitting, would be fair. For the time being, the Wilsons agreed to cover the rest as they didn't yet want Karen working more hours. The family agreed to revisit this plan at the end of the semester.

Like the Wilsons, once you've identified your financial goals it will prove an easy next step to decide how much to provide your son or daughter. The information on the Player Profile Questionnaire helps you realize just how and in what amount you will comfortably be able to cede spending control to your teen. Have each family member complete a Player Profile Questionnaire as shown on the following three pages.

Scorekeeping Box

After completing the Player Profile Questionnaires, give your teen point credit below. Add the full score if your teen has successfully completed the activity. Add no score if your teen hasn't. Write down the date of the activity, make note of any discussions, problems or successes, and tally your teen's score. This score will be added to the final score at the end.

Key Concepts	Activity Point Value	Date Activity Completed/Discussion Notes	Point Value Earned
Assist your teen with the following to help him or her earn points:			
• Complete the Teen Player Profile Questionnaire.	5		
• Using the answers from the questionnaire as a guide, agree on one tangible money-management objective to achieve.	5		
Total Score	**10**		

Parent Player Profile Questionnaire
Family Member Player _____

Answer the following questions on the answer sheet provided using complete sentences and including the details.

Regarding your teen's money habits:

1. Have you ever discussed the subject of finances with your teen? If so, in what way?
2. How much money is currently available to your teen?
3. How would you describe how your teen handles money?
4. With regard to your teen's expenses, who typically pays for what?
5. How much money would you feel comfortable giving to your teen to manage?
6. What would be the primary reason your teen might want to learn money-management skills from you?

Regarding your current money habits:

7. Would you say you live within your means, or would you truly like to get spending under control?
8. Do you save money? If so, how do you use your savings? Do you use it to pay bills, or to make a major purchase or to take a family vacation, or do you leave it untouched?
9. How important is an emergency fund?
10. Are you saving for your teen's college? If so, how?
11. Are you saving for your retirement? If so, how?
12. Are you comfortable and confident using credit cards? (i.e. Do you pay them off monthly or do you keep a running balance for which you pay interest? Are you aware of the interest rate you pay?)
13. Are there reasons you consider using debt as worthwhile? If so, for what?
14. How do you feel about investing your money? What do you invest in?
15. How important is charitable giving to you and your family?

Identify your goals:

16. Why are you reading this book?
17. What is the primary tangible goal you hope to achieve by teaching your teen money-management skills?

A blank copy of this worksheet is provided for your use in the appendix on page 292.

Parent Player Profile Answer Sheet
Family Member Player _____

Regarding your teen's money habits:

1.

2.

3.

4.

5.

6.

Regarding your current money habits:

7.

8.

9.

10.

11.

12.

13.

14.

15.

Identify your goals:

16.

17.

A blank copy of this worksheet is provided for your use in the appendix on page 293.

Teen Player Profile Questionnaire
Family Member Player _____

Ask your teen to answer the following questions regarding his or her own and parents' money habits. Answers should use complete sentences and include details.

1. How would you describe the way your parents handle money?

2. What would you like to learn most about managing money?

3. If you had money to manage, what would you want to do with it right now?

   • What things would you buy?

   • Would you save? How much? What for?

   • What things do you think you should be able to buy versus what things you think your parents should buy?

4. What are your future money goals?

   • Have enough to buy a _____

   • Save for _____

   • Give to _____

   • Invest in _____

   • Work for _____

A blank copy of this worksheet is provided for your use in the appendix on page 294.

Chapter Three
What You Need to Play *The Real-Life* Money Game

. . . .

On the first night when I teach my course, I place on the table a coin jar, a wallet, a three-ring binder open to display clear plastic sheet protectors with pockets, an ATM card, a debit card, a checkbook, and a calculator. Before we start—well, before we do the Player Profile Question-naire—I ask everyone to pass by the table and mentally catalog what they see. This, I tell them, is everything you'll need to play the game. Invariably, they look perplexed. This seems too simple. All you're lacking, I explain, is the *system of organization* you are about to learn. But the needed accessories, with the possible exception of the binder and clear plastic sheet protectors, are nothing more than ordinary items already available at home.

Accessories
• Coin Jar or Coin Counter—Clear Glass or Plastic
• Wallet, Money Clip, Coin Purse, Back-Pack Pouch, or *Reliable* Pocket
• 1" White Binder With Clear Insert Cover
• Index Dividers
• Clear Sheet Protectors
• Calculator
• Bank Savings Account With ATM Card
• Checking and Debit Card Account
• Investment Account

Accessories

A summary list of the accessories is provided in the sidebar above. Let's look at how each of these items will be used. The last three items—the bank savings account with ATM card; the checking and debit card account; and the investment account—are optional at the outset. The game's intermediate to advanced-level players, suitable for teens more practiced at handling money, suggests that you add these accounts later.

Please forgive me for making the prescriptive instructions sound like an operator's manual. Feel free to modify this in any way you see fit. What I'm sharing here is the game kit I've found, through trial and error, to work for most families. Still, innovation is a wonderful asset, so modify where appropriate.

Coin Jar or Coin Counter—Clear Glass or Plastic

The first accessory on the list is a large glass or plastic jar or a see-through coin counter used to accumulate small earnings and spare change. An oversized mayonnaise or peanut butter jar works well. Clear plastic coin counters sold at office supply stores are also great because they stack coins by denomination for easy counting. Clear jars or coin counters work best especially for young teens who need to see their money growing and depleting. This may not be the most efficient method for saving, but that's okay. In the early going, it's important for teens to see tangible evidence of their money accumulating.

One mother reported her two sons' poignant experience using their collected coins. Together the boys had been saving them in a clear, denominated coin bank. Once full, they rolled their coins up to cash them in at their local bank. The young bank teller asked the boys what they were planning to do with their money. They told him they wanted to buy a Game Boy. The teller smiled and told them that today was their lucky day, adding he had a "mint condition" Game Boy and some games he was going to sell. The boys were ecstatic. So was the mother. Beyond finding a bargain, the boys were able in a very concrete way to connect the coins they'd collected to the reward. Subtly, they were learning the value of time and labor.

Wallet, Money Clip, Coin Purse, Back-Pack Pouch, or Reliable Pocket

Your teen needs a regular, safe and portable place to carry cash and to collect receipts. A reliable pocket or a coin purse or back-pack pouch works well. Routines matter. Encourage your teen to keep his or her cash in the same place each day.

1" White Binder With Clear Insert Cover

The next item needed is a 9 ½" wide by 10 ½" length by 1" deep, white (to recognize easily) binder with a clear insert cover. This will become your teen's "personal financial binder" that will hold everything relating to his or her financial goings-on, such as: receipts for purchases; monthly bank and investment account statements; earnings information pertaining to a job; and tax returns. The binder will also hold all *The Real-Life* Money Game worksheets, such as the monthly spending plan and the income and expense summaries.

Index Dividers

In order to organize the binder, you will need to have index dividers with clear tabs that can be labeled for each month's financial activity. The index dividers may also prove useful in creating separate sections for earning, saving, giving, borrowing or lending, investing, and taxes. More experienced players like to use the dividers to set up sections devoted to contracts, investment account information, and securities' confirmations.

Clear Sheet Protectors

Parents are also encouraged to place several dozen clear sheet protectors in their teen's binder. These are plastic "see-through" envelope style pouches designed to hold important items such as cash, bank deposit slips, and mailing envelopes.

How To Use the Personal Financial Binder

Once the binder, index dividers, and sheet protectors have been gathered, I encourage parents to help their teens assemble them in the following manner:

- Create a personalized cover. The clear insert cover is intended for your teen to personalize the binder. Your son or daughter might stencil his or her name, include a school photo, or personal artwork. Popular items with many teens are magazine pictures of something they are saving for, such as a computer or a car.

- Label an index tab for each month of the year. Put several clear sheet protectors behind each tab to hold cash, deposit slips, or monthly receipts.

- Label an index tab for earning, saving, giving, borrowing or lending, investing, and taxes. Insert these tabs behind the twelve, monthly tabs. Put several clear sheet protectors behind each tab to hold information related to these activities.

- Label a tab for contracts.

- Label a tab for bank and investment accounts. Put a clear sheet protector behind the tab to hold deposit slips and mailing envelopes.

- Identify the year on the inside cover. Each year start a new binder to get your teen in the habit of cutting off his or her financial information at year-end.

One mother, Laura, described the financial binder as a way to organize her teen's "financial world." She attended my course and admitted she'd started too late teaching her son, a nineteen-year-old college student, about money management. He was not as organized as he could be in keeping track of his checking and debit account transactions. As a woman carrying a purse, it was much easier for her to carry a register and keep meticulous records. She needed a way to help her son get organized.

Setting up a teen's personal financial binder is the first thing I teach parents in my course. In Laura's case I recommended that her son keep all of his money and business related information in one personal financial binder. The binder can be organized with index dividers and clear-sheet protectors to hold job paycheck stubs and W-2s, bank statements, credit and debit card statements, and tax returns. I suggested that he put this binder in a safe place, such as a locked file cabinet, for instance. Her son should carry only the cash he needs, his debit card, and one or two checks in his wallet, pocket, or back-pack pouch.

Calculator

Calculators are an essential tool. I encourage parents to have their teens keep a small hand-held calculator in their binders for updating their check register on a regular basis. When first starting out with *The Real-Life* Money Game, you'll find, I suspect, that a large ten-key style calculator with a printed tape is indispensable. The printed tape makes it easy to check calculations for errors, an essential part of the early-learning process.

• • •

A key component of the scalable plan is flexibility. One way I bring this into the game is by showing you and your teen how and when to use spending options. These include what I call "cash pockets," a basic savings account with an ATM card, a checking and debit card account, and an investment account. In chapter six we will talk about these four options in great detail. Some, you will already be familiar with. For now, I want to introduce you to the unfamiliar notion of cash pockets.

Cash Pockets

The clear sheet protectors, among other uses, can be turned into a pouch in which to store cash. For beginning-level players, cash at the beginning of the month is inserted in the clear pockets, one for each expense your teen will be responsible for paying.

The concept of cash pockets came to me after Connie Wilson lamented that she didn't know how to teach her three teen daughters to handle cash more responsibly. She commented that, the other day, she pulled six pairs of jeans from the washing machine. Her girls all wore the same size, and one of them had left ten dollars in the pocket. She didn't know whose jeans were whose, so she claimed the laundered bill as hers.

Cash pockets were the answer for the Wilson family. They provided a simple and easy way for Connie Wilson to teach her daughters how to keep track of their cash and account for their spending. Once the money in a cash pocket was gone, they would see they had no more money left to spend on that particular expense item.

I encourage parents to make a note on each cash pocket, indicating how much money the pocket contains for each expense. As teens spend the cash on a predetermined expense item, they then put their receipts back in the same pocket. This way, as they spend the cash, they can see how much is left. Clear cash pockets provide an easy-to-grasp, visual form of record-keeping.

Many families I work with, such as the Wilsons, tell me they have two predominant concerns. The first is that their son or daughter is wary of spending money. What usually underlies this reticence is their teen's fear of running out of a limited resource. If it's not that, the parents are concerned about the opposite: their teens spend money as fast as it hits their hands. What's usually at the bottom of both problems is that their teen doesn't have any method for keeping track of cash.

The beauty of cash pockets is that they provide a visual way for teens to watch their cash ebb and flow. By actually being able to see the supply of money on hand, teens learn that money is a renewable resource. And like any renewable resource, it must be managed if it is to fulfill its purpose.

Cash pockets is the first of four spending options. The other three spending options include using a bank savings with ATM account for beginner players who've had some experience using cash pockets. A checking with debit card account is reserved for intermediate players. And an investment account awaits the more advanced players.

Parents can open a savings with ATM, checking with debit card, or an investment account as a guardian or custodian for a minor teen either under the Uniform Gift to Minors Act (UGMA) or the Uniform Transfer to Minors Act (UTMA) with their son or daughter named as the beneficiary.

The Uniform Gift to Minors Act (UGMA) allows for transfers of irrevocable gifts of money and securities to minors. This act gives the power of management to the custodian until the teen reaches the age of majority, which depends on the state of residence.

The Uniform Transfer to Minors Act (UTMA) has been adopted by most states, replacing the UGMA. The UTMA account provides more flexibility over the period of time control passes to a minor. Again, this depends on the state of residency, but can be eighteen, twenty-one, or even twenty-five for the funds to revert to the teen.

Whichever account you open with your teen, the following sidebar provides a useful checklist of information. Go through each point with your son or daughter at the bank or investment institution.

> ### Bank and Investment Account Information Checklist
>
> - Rules and restrictions
> - Fees and/or commissions
> - Minimum balance requirements
> - Minimum investment requirements
> - Age restrictions
> - Interest rates
> - Account features – ATM, debit card, credit card
> - Per check charges, overdraft charges, minimum balance charges, and ATM fees
> - Direct deposits allowed
> - Online services

Bank Savings Account With ATM Card

The RLMG Plan Overview in chapter one suggests that beginning players manage their spending using cash pockets. Once they become proficient using cash pockets, parents can help their teens open a bank savings account with an ATM card. Usually this is the first introduction most teens will have to banking. Teens can open a savings account with a parent as a cosigner at any age.

Checking and Debit Card Account

You also have the option to open a bank checking account, with or without a debit card, for your teen. I recommend to parents that they save this option for teens who have more experience handling money. These are considered intermediate players. Teens can have a checking and debit card account with a parent as a cosigner at any age. However, age fourteen is usually the youngest age recommended. This is when teens can legally work. Encourage your teen to select checks that create carbon copies. If your son or daughter forgets to enter a check in his or her register, the carbon copy acts as a reminder.

Parents in my coarse often report how exciting it is to watch their teen's eyes light up the first time they fill in a check for a purchase. For many, it's a major right-of-passage into adulthood.

Investment Account

The ultimate goal, reserved for advanced players, is opening an investment account. This may or may not have a checking with debit card feature. Like a one-stop-shop, teens can use an investment account like a checking account, where purchases are automatically debited from the account like a debit card, have access to a major credit card when they turn eighteen, and have any funds not used for Playing Board-Spending Plan expenses already available in the account to invest. No need to transfer funds.

Scorekeeping Box

After helping your teen gather the accessories and organize his or her personal financial binder, give your teen point credit below. Add the full score if your teen has successfully completed the activity. Add no score if your teen hasn't. Write down the date of the activity, make note of any discussions, problems or successes, and tally your teen's score. This score will be added to the final score at the end.

Key Concepts	Activity Point Value	Date Activity Completed/Discussion Notes	Point Value Earned
Assist your teen with the following to help him or her earn points:			
• Gather the accessories.	5		
• Design a personal binder cover.	5		
• Organize the personal financial binder.	5		
• Open a Savings Account with ATM Card.	5		
• Open a Checking Account with a Debit Card.	10		
• Open an Investment Account.	20		
Total Score	**50**		

Chapter Four
Where The Money Will Come From: Teen-Generated Income

· ·

Should I give my teen an allowance? If so, how much? Should I pay my teen for household chores? Should I expect my over-scheduled teen to earn money from a job? If my teen earns money or I pay my teen an allowance, whose money is whose? These are the questions parents who sign up for my workshops most frequently ask.

Their concern boils down to this: parents want to know how much money to make available, and they want to know where that money is supposed to come from. Money—*currency* your teen will use to practice developing money-management skills—comes from two sources: teen-generated income and parent-generated teen income. In this chapter, we'll look at the various ways your teen can generate income and explain how their income fits into *The Real-Life* Money Game. In chapter five, we'll talk about your contribution, how you can provide your teen with a renewable resource. As you may recall, we're working from a flexible formula that you can tailor to suit you and your teen's personal needs. In the course of these two chapters, we'll address parents' oft-asked questions.

Teen-Generated Income

How many times have you heard your teen say this: "It's my money, not yours! I can spend it on whatever I want!" Do you respond by saying words like, "Yes, that's true," and watch with tight lips as he or she spends it indiscriminately? Or conversely, do you say to them, "It's your money to spend, so spend it however you wish," and then criticize them for their decision? Parents attending my course confess they aren't sure how to resolve the age-old conflict surrounding whose money is whose and whose preferences should prevail.

In *The Real-Life* Money Game, teens pool their income with their parents to create a large enough resource to make discretionary choices. Through this choice-making they can contribute to their wants and needs, take responsibility for paying some of the expenses their parents are already paying on their behalf, have enough money to track, and to make financial decisions that promote independent thinking. Parents who've taken my course report that once their son or daughter has had time to practice pooling their resource, they tend to become less possessive, more open-minded, and less confrontational.

Having said all that, let's look at some common sources of income your teen can generate in the following sidebar.

Collected Coins

Remember the coin jar accessory I mentioned in chapter three? You'd be amazed at how much money can accumulate in a jar over the course of a month or a year. If you contribute $1 in quarters, dimes, nickels, and pennies each day, by year's end your teen has $365 to add to his or her savings.

> **Teen Income Sources**
>
> • Collected Coins
> • Gifts: Birthday or Holiday
> • Earnings From:
>   Household Tasks or Chores
>   A Job
>   A "Teen Business"
> • Savings and Investments
> • Borrowed Funds

Without operating from a deliberate plan, Sam Sanchez, a single dad and another case-study family we will follow throughout the book, found that his daughter, Maria's jar averaged between $170 and $220 each year, a painless boost to her savings that carried them over times when he couldn't contribute any cash beyond her allowance. Encourage your teen to be more systematic. A dollar a day should be a realizable goal. But remember, this money doesn't count as income on your teen's spending plan until it's been rolled and counted.

Gifts: Birthday or Holiday

Parents *and* grandparents love to give money for birthdays and holidays. Many families I've interviewed say they feel it's an appropriate way to hand over cash *with no strings attached*. Now we're going to change that thinking, just slightly. Birthday or holiday money is a valid source of income for teens. Money that has been gifted must be accounted for as income and become incorporated into the spending plan. This will, of course, place restrictions on that money's use, an unhappy situation for teens who want immediate gratification. I have two answers to this objection. First, teens do have a valid point—they should be allowed to spend an agreed-upon percentage of that money on what they want. But, parents, take heart. Once you've ceded control over spending to your teen—once they understand the true cost of clothes, snacks, and entertainment—they will willingly defer their own spending in order to pursue goals.

I gave my son, for example, a $200 gift certificate good at any store in his local shopping mall. I wrote on the certificate, "for clothes." He shared with me how much he spent on each clothing item he purchased. He exercised his own discretion as to what to spend the money on, and he made a contribution to his own annual clothing expenses. Progress for both teen and parent.

Earnings

There are primarily three ways your teen can earn money: getting paid for household tasks and chores; earning money from a job; or launching a "Teen Business." What I tell parents in my course about their teens earning money —*and I cannot stress this point enough*—is that what we are doing here is teaching our teens a "bundle" of tangible, financial skills. Not just one or two in isolation. Earning money is included in that bundle as a tangible skill.

The Real-Life Money Game encourages you and your teen to choose one of these three methods as a way to develop the skill of earning money. Whichever method you select, remember that the biggest benefit—aside from generating income—is the boost that comes to your teen's pride with their feeling of accomplishment and self-reliance.

Before we talk about the three specific earnings options, we need to assess how much time your son or daughter might have available to earn that money.

Activities Pie-Chart

If you are like most families, your teen is busy. Busy with school, friends, family, extracurricular activities and homework. Today's families are faced with the difficult task of prioritizing time. To help harried parents understand these demands and make the best choices, I've devised a tool called the "Activities Pie-Chart" shown on the following page.

The Activities Pie-Chart represents 100% of a teen's time and is sliced up into percentages of daily activities. Activities include: school, homework, household contributions, computer, TV, socializing with friends, family time, volunteerism, and, of course, what teens seem to like and need most—sleep.

Activities Pie-Chart
Family Member Player _____

1. Make a separate list of the eleven activities noted on the Activities Pie-Chart worksheet.
2. Beside each one, assign an average daily amount of time your teen spends on this activity.
3. Divide the day into 100%. Now assign a percentage of that day to each activity and draw them into your circle as wedges of the pie, their relative size based on their percentage of the day.

- Sleep
- School
- Homework
- Extracurricular Activities
- Household Responsibilities
- Family Time
- TV
- Computer
- Job
- Volunteer Work
- Free time

A blank copy of this worksheet is provided for your use in the appendix on page 295.

Parents who attend my course take this exercise home to solicit their teen's input. They invariably report back how much they *love* this pie-chart! It's visual! It's revealing! It's teen-friendly! It's a simple way for them to talk to their teen about how they are using their time and, if need be, to reestablish priorities.

Here's how my son used his pie-chart shown on the following page to talk about his time commitments.

One warm summer day, Michael, who was fourteen at the time and would start his freshman year of high school in the fall, sat with me on a park bench sharing a picnic lunch. The setting was peaceful and relaxing and he was particularly contemplative. He said to me, "Mom, you know that pie-chart with all

Activities Pie-Chart
Family Member Player ___*Michael Williamson*___

1. Make a separate list of the eleven activities noted on the Activities Pie-Chart worksheet.

2. Beside each one, assign an average daily amount of time your teen spends on this activity.

3. Divide the day into 100%. Now assign a percentage of that day to each activity and draw them into your circle as wedges of the pie, their relative size based on their percentage of the day.

- Sleep
- School
- Homework
- Extracurricular Activities
- Household Responsibilities
- Family Time
- TV
- Computer
- Job
- Volunteer Work
- Free time

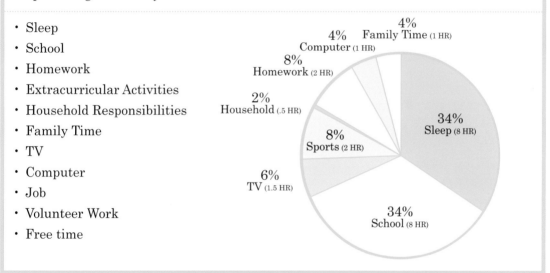

4% Family Time (1 HR)
4% Computer (1 HR)
8% Homework (2 HR)
2% Household (.5 HR)
8% Sports (2 HR)
6% TV (1.5 HR)
34% Sleep (8 HR)
34% School (8 HR)

A blank copy of this worksheet is provided for your use in the appendix on page 295.

my activities you had me fill out? Well, I don't think I want to work while I'm in high school. I've thought about how much time I use up studying. I want to follow through with my commitment to sports, and I really want to have free time to spend with my friends. So I was wondering if you wouldn't mind that arrangement for now?" Then he said, "But I could still work for you or for Dad when I need extra money, and I like umpiring baseball which is only two hours a month."

There was something magical to me in what my son was saying. *He* was doing the thinking and setting his priorities. All I did was offer him a simple tool to encourage him to start thinking for himself. Would I have preferred he work more hours? Possibly. But the main thing for me was that he had grasped the concept of time as a manageable resource.

Your teen can modify the Activities Pie-Chart whenever his or her schedule changes. Many families I've worked with have their teens complete the Activities Pie-Chart for weekdays and another one for weekends. Once the Activities Pie-Chart is done, you may find, as I have, that smarter decisions on how to use time, a precious commodity, follow. And, you have some idea of how much time your teen has available to earn money. Great. Let's look at our three options.

Earnings From Household Tasks or Chores

This question comes up at least once in every course I teach: "Should I pay my teen for chores?" The concern is that their teen might expect to get paid for every task he or she does. Of course, every family has individual needs and values and will have to make a personal choice. Keep in mind that paying your teen for household jobs provides better scheduling flexibility than working for an employer, while still giving your teen an opportunity to practice *earning* money.

A recent poll offers our country's sentiment on the subject. Of those families who pay their teens an allowance, 75% say the money is tied to performing chores. Psychologists, on the other hand, warn that parents who insist on job performance for allowance run the risk that their teens don't learn to contribute to the well-being of others or of their family.

They suggest, instead, that allowances should be used for learning about money-management. It's a good idea to pick one or two tasks or chores that are "paid" jobs and differentiate them from "expected" contributions at home.

The Real-Life Money Game offers a worksheet, shown on the following page, that includes a list of household tasks and chores you might pay your teen for, such as washing the family car, feeding family pets, mowing the lawn, or vacuuming.

Here are some helpful guidelines you might follow if you decide to pay your teen for chores:

- When tying money to housework, make sure your teen has at least one "regular" household responsibility or job that he or she is not paid for. In this way, you are reinforcing that a contribution is expected, so not all jobs are paid.

The Real-Life Money Game Household Tasks and Chores
Family Member Player

Household Chores:	Sunday	Monday	Tuesday	Wednesday	Thursday	Friday	Saturday	Amount Earned
Cooking								
Laundry								
Ironing								
Cleanup								
Garbage								
Beds								
Shopping								
Pet Care								
Yard								
Car Wash								
Other								
Financial Tasks:								
Sort Mail								
Pay Bills								
Filing								
Computer								
Research								
Total Due:								

A blank copy of this worksheet is provided for your use in the appendix on page 296.

- Let your teen choose the jobs. This can help your son or daughter stay motivated, since they are making the choice. Sam Sanchez had this experience with his daughter. He tried to get Maria to wash his car. She so hated washing the car, she'd go without money rather than do it. When your teen is stubborn and uncooperative, keep in mind that the idea is to transfer some choice-making control to your son or daughter. The consequence of their action is small, but important, as they learn to live with the choices they make.

- Include the chores you don't have time to do yourself. For example, cleaning out the garage, grooming family pets, or folding and putting away clean laundry.

- Select jobs that provide some flexibility for when they are carried out. Washing the car, for example, might be a good option, but only if the flexibility ensures the job will eventually get done. Consider paying for the bigger jobs or the ones that recur less often. For example, Connie Wilson paid Karen to clean the pool. If her daughter didn't do it, Connie would have to hire the job out. She would rather give her daughter the money.

Try to tie some earnings into money-management related activities such as filing, banking, or bill-paying jobs. Once, my son organized our insurance policy binder and from this day forward he remembers that we have insurance for many different things: our home, earthquake, auto, medical, disability, and life. Good training for his future.

Pay your teens to do the research on an item you intend to purchase, such as a car, a computer, a home appliance, a bike, or even a pet. If your son or daughter is eager to learn more, you can have them create a set of cost-comparison schedules so they might practice using spreadsheet software, as well as learn to research on the Internet.

When using *The Real-Life* Money Game Household Tasks and Chores worksheet you can base the number of chores on the number of hours your teen has available. Or you can assign a dollar value to each job. Find out what the going-rate is in your area. It's better to pay by the job, not by the hour, because you can control the standard of performance. Make a space by each chore to record time or check-mark done. Set a regular pay day. For younger teens just starting out earning money, I suggest to parents that they pay when the job is completed. At least for the first month or two. This reinforces the concept of earning rewards commensurate with the job done. For older teens, a monthly payday is appropriate. An added benefit: this will help keep your recordkeeping to a minimum.

Here's how the Wilson family arranged payment for weekly chores. With three teenage girls, Connie Wilson wanted to keep her system simple and effective. She made a list of all the weekly chores that needed to be done. Instead of a dollar amount assigned to each, she assigned time—an hour for each chore. Most jobs, such as vacuuming the family room, cleaning out the cat litter, making a bed, washing a load of laundry, did not require more than an hour. Each of her daughters was required to contribute a minimum of two hours per week, with ten hours of activities by month's end.

In three months time, Connie Wilson wanted each of her daughters to have made a contribution of thirty total hours at $10 each to their spending plans. By month three, each Wilson daughter would have earned enough to pay for her Disney World vacation park entry ticket, a major item on her spending plan.

Connie got great results. She discovered that her youngest teen was quick to select the easiest jobs and get them done, before her sisters caught on. "Those are the rules of the game," Connie told her other two daughters when they complained. The other sisters had an epiphany, as did Connie, who was amazed at how many jobs were getting done without her constant nagging. Using the game approach, Connie taught her daughters to strategize without them even being aware they were learning a lesson.

I am no longer surprised at how much time I spend talking about *The Real-Life* Money Game Household Tasks and Chores worksheet with parents attending my course. It seems especially ideal for younger teens—those age twelve and thirteen. Yet even parents with teens fourteen and older, old enough to land a *real* part-time job, are equally interested in this worksheet. I've discovered that the need to acquaint teens with the give-and-take process of performing a job, coupled with the need to keep a household functioning and the desire to have everyone make a contribution, seems almost universal. If I may indulge a preachy moment, I think it's worth reminding parents that teaching your teens to work—*to get the job done*—begins at home!

Earnings From a Job

Another way your teen can earn money is by getting a job. There are specific tangible and intangible skills your son or daughter can learn on the job that will be different than those they learn by earning money for tasks at home. The sidebar identifies the set of tangible job skills they can learn, which in turn can lead to developing a set of intangible skills.

Before your teen can set out to find suitable employment, you need to consider a few basic federal and state labor laws.

Teen Labor Laws

The table on the following page summarizes the federal labor law and gives an example of a state labor law that effects your teen's employment. Review the law with your son or daughter. Once you know that your teen is qualified to work, consult *The Real-Life* Money Game's tick list of tips on page 42 to help him or her select, land, and keep a job. Some of these might seem elementary to adults, but remember, for many of our teens, these are new and unfamiliar skills that need developing.

You will find a list of general job areas on page 43 usually reserved for teens from age fifteen through eighteen. Review this list with your teen. A space is provided at the bottom of the worksheet for discussion notes. Write down any comments, so you can track your teen's interests and help focus his or her search.

Sam Sanchez worked out a plan for his daughter's employment. Sam teaches and supplements his income with writing. He supports Maria with very little financial help from her mother.

Tangible and Intangible Job Skills

Learning this set of tangible job skills…

- Finding and keeping a job
- Managing job earnings
- Prioritizing time among activities
- Learning how business works
- Learning how to get along with other people
- Taking orders from supervisors

…will lead to these intangible skills:

- Contributing to personal wants and needs
- Personal responsibility
- Self-confidence
- Independent thinking
- Strong work ethic

Teen Labor Laws

Federal	• The minimum age for employment is 14 years old. There are some exceptions such as delivering newspapers; performing in radio, television, movie, or theatrical productions; and working for parents in their solely-owned non-farm business (except in manufacturing or in hazardous jobs).
	• Fourteen and 15-year-olds may be employed outside of school hours for a maximum of 3 hours per day and 18 hours per week when school is in session and a maximum of 8 hours per day and 40 hours per week when school is not in session. This age group is prohibited from working before 7 a.m. and after 7 p.m., except during summers when they may work until 9 p.m. (from June 1 through Labor Day).
	• Sixteen and 17-year-olds may be employed for unlimited hours. There are no federal laws restricting the number of hours of work per day or per week.
Washington State Example	• Teens under age 16 are prohibited from working in manufacturing and in certain food processing operations.
	• Minors under age 18 must obtain a parent or guardian authorization form for employment and employers who hire them must have a minor work endorsement on their master business license.
	• State law allows employers to pay minors under age 16 only 85% of the state minimum wage.
	• During the school year, students under age 16 may work a maximum of 16 hours a week. During school vacations, they may work 40 hours a week.
	• Sixteen and 17-year-olds may work a maximum of 20 hours a week during the school year and 48 hours a week during school vacations.
	Above is an example of Washington State's labor law. To find your state's labor laws, you can access information on the Internet at <u>*www.dol.gov*</u> *(U.S. Department of Labor website).*

Teen Jobs: Select, Land, and Keep

Select
- Brainstorm ideas with your teen.
- Investigate jobs that are a good personality fit.
- Identify your teen's interests, hobbies, and talents.
- Cut out articles about jobs and industries.
- Collect pamphlets, catalogs, brochures and directories.
- Do a "jobs search" on line.
- Speak to people working at jobs your teen might enjoy.
- Use your teen's working friends as contacts.
- Use school teachers and counselors as contacts.
- Assess transportation needs.
- Start job search early, at least one to two months lead-time.

Land
- Detail on paper what it will take to land selected jobs.
- Prepare a resume.
- List specific places to contact.
- Follow up with people you know.
- Make phone calls.
- Find out the dress requirements.
- Learn and practice successful interview techniques.
- Review hourly pay rates and minimum wage laws.
- Understand the tax rules.

Keep
- Be on time to work once you have a job.
- Each day challenge yourself to solve a problem.
- Do every job to your potential best.
- Be business-like and professional.
- Be enthusiastic for your work, even if the tasks are dull.
- Respect co-workers and supervisors.

Job Areas For Teens
Family Member Player _____

- Athletic or Service Clubs
- Child and Daycare Assistant
- Computer Data Entry Assistant
- Department Store Inventory
- Entertainment: Movie Theaters, Fairs, Amusement Parks
- Factories and Industry
- Fast Food Restaurants
- Parks, Camps, and Recreation Facilities
- Small Business Retail Sales
- Sports: Lifeguard, Umpire, Golf Caddy, Assistant Coaching
- Tutoring
- Working at Parents' or Relatives' Business

Note other job interests or ideas:

A blank copy of this worksheet is provided for your use in the appendix on page 297.

One of Sam's biggest concerns was how to keep up with the expense of owning and maintaining a car as she approached driving age. Sam ascertained that his budget could not withstand additional costs for insurance, repairs, and gas. So he struck a deal with his daughter. If she would pay the additional cost of insurance for the second car, and half of her own gas, he would pay for any repairs or maintenance. The problem was how to help her save $500 every six months—over and above her other expenses—while giving priority to school and time with friends.

She wanted to work in a late night café. Sam thought that was a bad idea. They compromised. She took a job as a courtesy clerk at a supermarket that allowed variable hours. She worked an average of twelve hours per week, which was her agreed-on limit during the school year.

With that goal in mind—knowing she could not have her car until she'd earned enough money to pay the additional burden to Sam's insurance policy—she restricted spending on other items. For the remainder of her high-school years they continued this arrangement, Maria adjusting her hours as needed, and moving, finally to the Internet café in the second semester of her senior year when Sam felt she was old enough to prioritize her own time.

Earnings From a "Teen Business"

A highly underrated and oft misunderstood source of teen income is the "Teen Business." Many families think that when their sons or daughters baby-sit or mow a neighbor's lawn that they have a job. But in fact this qualifies as a teen business. Their teen is considered "self-employed" (the formal term for being in business for oneself). The idea of a teen business can conjure up some lively and innovative pursuits, however.

Before your teen embarks on a business idea to earn money, here are some important questions to consider: Is your teen old enough to work? Does he or she have that follow-through, stick-with-it brand of maturity being in business for oneself requires? Has your son or daughter made an attempt to utilize his or her strongest ability or talent? Does your teen have resources to commit to the project? If not, are you willing to kick-in the up-front costs? Have you discussed a realistic time-frame within which your teen either succeeds or stops? Have you determined your teen's available hours to run the business? Does your son or daughter have sufficient financial motivation to persist when customers are few? Have you considered what your community needs? What environmental opportunities, such as recycling, clean up, etc., are available? Have you looked into the legalities for starting a business? Have you reviewed the federal and state labor laws as to the age and the number of hours your teen can work? Have you investigated the federal, state, and local taxes your teen will need to pay? (More about taxes in chapter fifteen). Phew! Well, that's what it takes!

Much time and money are often sunk into unsound plans before they've really been tested. *The Real-Life* Money Game offers the "Teen Business" Plan to stimulate your teen's thinking about the business and to help ensure that he or she will gather the information needed to determine if the idea is sound.

"Teen Business" Plan
Family Member Player _____

Organization Plan	Business Name and Description: Product or Service: Target Market/Primary Customers: Rate or Price Charging: Weekly Time Commitment: Other Assistance Needed:
Financial Plan	Start-Up Capital and Available Sources: Cash-Flow Projections: Profit and Loss Statement: Taxes Required:
Marketing Plan	Competition Within the Target Market: Advertising: Selling:
Implementation Plan	Establish and Set Up Base of Operation: Contact Target Market/Primary Customers: Analyze and Evaluate Results:

A blank copy of this worksheet is provided for your use in the appendix on page 298.

"Teen Business" Ideas	
Business Type	**Service Provided**
Auto	• Car wash • Detailing
Computer	• Teach Software • Create Web sites
Crafts	• Clothes • Jewelry • Home Décor • Gift Wrapping
Entertainment and Food	• Parties • Specialty foods
"Sales"	• eBay selling • Garage Sales • Concession Stands
"Sitting"	• Children • Houses • Pets • Elderly
"Skills"	• Tutoring • Golf Caddy • Baseball Umpiring • Horseback Riding • Piano Lessons • Housecleaning
Yard	• Gardening • Mowing and Cleanup

The Real-Life Money Game offers a list of potential "Teen Business" ideas shown on the preceding page that can offer you and your teen some fun, while pursuing income opportunities. You can refer to www.reallifemoneygame.com for more information on how to complete the "Teen Business" Plan details.

Here is an easy idea my son pursued. In our community we have a large annual arts and crafts fair. Observing that success, his school decided they had plenty of talented teens who could produce and sell hand-made crafts similar to items popular in the fair. My son was painting watercolors at the time. Birds, flowers, mountains and sunset scenes. With my financial assistance up-front, we had the art reduced and color copied to make note cards and bookmarks. We had the bookmarks laminated. He sold them for $1 apiece. Teachers and students alike bought the assortment of cards and bookmarks for personal use and as gifts. On the first day of the school fair, he ran out of inventory. Cheered by this success, and eager to earn enough to buy more art supplies, my son decided to try again.

Savings and Investments

Wisely managing savings and investments is a skill that takes time and practice to develop. We will talk in upcoming chapters in more detail about tools you can use to develop these skills in your teen. For now, let's look at how the money your teen may be receiving from savings and investments can provide an income source for your son or daughter. What we're talking about here would be interest, dividends, or gains on the sale of marketable securities such as stocks, bonds or mutual funds.

Consider a case in point. One mother specifically attended my course to find out how she might encourage her fifteen-year-old daughter to work. Her daughter's primary source of spending cash came from dividends on stocks she received as gifts from her ex-husband's parents. Her daughter was well aware of the money, and told her mother that she didn't see the need to work. Her mother, who had a successful, well-paying career as a lawyer, thought her daughter needed a better work ethic. Her daughter, on the other hand, felt that because she was using her dividends to pay for part of her personal spending, she didn't need to contribute money from a job, too. By the end of the course, this mother realized that a bigger concern than worrying over her daughter's work ethic, was whether or not her fifteen-year-old perceived the fundamental difference between spending dividends versus investing. Once they started playing *The Real-Life* Money Game together, the daughter learned how to track her dividend income versus her spending activity. In this way her daughter was able to know whether she was spending beyond her dividend income. Once she gained this awareness, both she and her mom agreed to a plan. If her daughter needed more spending money than she received in dividend income, her daughter would work at her mother's law office, filing and doing computer input at $10 an hour, to make up the difference. What this family learned by playing *The Real-Life* Money Game was to use teen-generated income to teach independence and responsibility.

Borrowed Funds

Borrowed funds can also provide a source of income for your teen. We will talk about legitimate uses for debt extensively in chapter thirteen. For now, here is an example of how my son included borrowed funds as an income source when he was putting together his resource.

My son was excited about getting a new computer. His old one had become outdated faster than I could have imagined. He did all the research, we talked over the features with a computer consultant, then we agreed Michael would contribute $300 to the total. He didn't want to take it out of his savings. Instead, he wanted to borrow the money. I told him that I didn't want to do that because he needed to learn how to delay his gratification. He didn't know what that expression meant, so he attempted to look it up in a dictionary. It wasn't there. When I explained to him that it meant he would have to "wait" before he got his new computer, until he had his $300 saved up, he said he was sorry, but "delayed gratification" would have to wait! He needed the computer now. So we set up a plan. We looked at his Activities Pie-Chart to see how many hours he had available to work for me. We came up with an hourly rate. And we agreed I would loan him the money with an interest charge tacked on, payable timely each month. With this plan in place, not only was my son practicing how to use borrowed funds for a valid need, he also learned how to prioritize his time.

Playing the Game: Income Worksheet

The "Income Worksheet" is *The Real-Life* Money Game's way of providing a means of teaching your teen how to keep track of money he or she receives throughout the month. Recall that teen income sources can include collected coins and gifts from birthdays or holidays. Also, consider all your teen's earned income, whether from household tasks or chores, from a job, or a from a "Teen Business." If your son or daughter receives income from savings or investments be sure to record amounts received throughout the month. Finally, should your teen have borrowed funds or have income from money he or she lent, record any amounts received on the Income Worksheet.

Don't worry if your teen has not generated any income from the sources we have discussed in this chapter. What matters for now is that you familiarize yourself with the worksheet. By the end of the next chapter when we talk about income *you* generate, your teen will have a potential fund of money to record.

• •

Income Worksheet

1. Compute your teen's current month's income using the Income Worksheet provided in the appendix on page 299.

• •

Let's look at how the Wilson's daughter, Karen, records income she receives from a gift, from babysitting, and payment for washing the family cars on the following page. We will continue adding to Karen Wilson's Income Worksheet in the next chapter when we include her allowance and a Family Fund Contribution amount she receives from her parents.

Income Worksheet

Family Member Player Karen Wilson   **Month:** September

Date	Coins	Gifts	Earnings: Chores, Job, "Teen Business"	Allowance	Family Fund Contribution (Includes Rainy-Day Fund)	Savings & Investment	Savings & Investments Matched Funds	Borrowed Funds	Other Income	Week's Income
Week 1		20	Babysitting 30							50
Week 2			Babysitting 30							30
Week 3			Chores 20							20
Week 4										
Total Income		20	80							100

A blank copy of this worksheet is provided for your use in the appendix on page 299.

Scorekeeping Box

After helping your teen fill in the Activities Pie-Chart, discussing ways your teen can generate income, and helping your son or daughter complete the Income Worksheet, give your teen point credit below. Add the full score if your teen has successfully completed the activity. Add no score if your teen hasn't. Write down the date of the activity, make note of any discussions, problems or successes, and tally your teen's score. This score will be added to the final score at the end.

Key Concepts	Activity Point Value	Date Activity Completed/Discussion Notes	Point Value Earned
Assist your teen with the following to help him or her earn points:			
• Complete the Activities Pie-Chart for both weekday and weekend.	5		
• Identify available time to earn money.	5		
• Earning: Get Paid for Household Task or Chore.	5		
• Earning: Land a Job.	10		
• Earning: Start a "Teen Business."	20		
• Record money received during the month on the Income Worksheet.	10		
Total Score	**55**		

Chapter Five
Where the Money Will Come From: Parent-Generated Income

· ·

Often I am asked why I conduct workshops for parents instead of for teens. I tell people my motivations are two-fold. First, most parents I have interviewed hold strong attitudes about money. Secondly, more often than not, parents are the primary source of money—*currency*—that teens will use to practice developing tangible money-management skills. Because it's the parents who feel they have most at stake where money-matters are concerned and who are most likely to persist, I've found that the most effective way to reach teens is through parents who are taking a view to their teens' futures. Plus, there is an added benefit: this way the whole family learns.

In the last chapter, we explored the ways teens can generate income for themselves. Now it's time to talk about how parents will contribute to their teen's income. That done, we'll look at how both teen-generated income and parent-generated income pool together to create a resource your son or daughter can learn to manage.

Parent-Generated Income

While two predominant methods exist for parents to contribute to their teen's resource base as indicated in the sidebar, most of it will come through what I've labeled the "Family Fund Contribution." Both methods deserve a look.

> **Parent-Generated Income Sources**
>
> - "Allowance"
> - Family Fund Contribution

Allowance

In this country, paying "allowance" is the most widely practiced method parents use to give money to their teens. Volumes have been written and compiled on allowance statistics that record everything from how much parents give and at what age teens receive allowance, to what teens are required to do in exchange for the money, and how they typically use the cash.

Here is a recent example: A Harris Interactive Poll surveyed 736 families across the United States to determine who pays an allowance, how much they pay, and what percent of families expect something from their teens in return. Only about one third of parents pay an allowance, and the average nationally is $9.65 per week. Two-thirds pay nothing at all. Of those families who pay, 75% require chores, 29% require good grades, 18% expect the allowance to be earned in other ways, and 18% require nothing.

With so much emphasis being placed on allowance statistics, I like to read them out loud in my workshops. Parents, myself included, want to know what *every other parent is doing out there*. I see the relief in parents' faces when someone else shares how much allowance their family is giving and how their teen is spending the money. It seems to either reinforce their notion that what they're doing is right, or, conversely, it further convinces them that they're on the wrong track. I like to push parents out of that confining "right versus wrong" box. In a scalable plan, there is no right or wrong. All that matters is what's appropriate for your needs at the present time. I do this by sharing with them the concept of the Family Fund Contribution, which, from my experience, is the more effective way to generate a flexible resource plan for your teen.

Family Fund Contribution

So what is the Family Fund Contribution and how does this differ from an allowance?

The Family Fund Contribution is an amount of money you make available for your teen to manage each month. It is different than an allowance in that it is calculated by using a formula that takes into consideration your teen's income, the expenses you want your teen to be responsible for, as well as your family's resources. This formula is designed to be flexible. The numbers that go in will change to suit your family's needs.

> **Family Fund Contribution**
>
> An amount of money you make available for your teen to manage each month. The amount takes into consideration:
>
> • Your Teen's Income
> • Expenses Your Teen Pays
> • A Rainy-Day Fund for Unplanned Expenses
> • Your Family's Resources

When I first bring it up in workshops, I often get quizzical looks. "Isn't it still just allowance?" those confused looks seem to say.

No, it is not the same as allowance. An allowance is a fixed sum, pocket-money, cash your teen will usually squander immediately on items you'd consider frivolous. The Family Fund Contribution provides a growing and changing fund resource that allows your teens to become both independent money managers and caretakers of their own financial needs within predetermined parameters, of course.

In my workshops, I usually precede the discussion of the Family Fund Contribution with these two suggestions: I ask parents to consider how much money they would be willing to commit over and above what they are providing now, and to think about areas in which they would be willing to give more spending control over to their teen.

Family Fund Contribution Questionnaire
Family Member Player _____

1. How much money, if any, are you paying your teen?

2. Generally, how does your teen use the money?

3. Choose one thing you would like your teen to be responsible for paying.

A blank copy of this worksheet is provided for your use in the appendix on page 300.

For example, in my household, when I first started teaching my son about money, he never stopped nagging me for video games. I decided to give him $25 a month, over and above his $5 weekly allowance, that he could spend on video games. I was determined to turn spending control over to him, so he could make the decisions and learn to live with his choices. The best way to start down this path of ceding control is to choose one expense item to begin with, usually an item that causes conflict.

Okay. If you have done this questionnaire, you now have an idea of how you might use the Family Fund Contribution to fulfill you and your teen's *specific* needs. You will have a chance to use this information after we work through an example. Let's look at the formula:

Family Fund Contribution Formula

$$\underline{\text{Family Fund Contribution}} = \left(\underline{\text{Expenses Teen Pays}} + \underline{\text{Rainy-Day Fund}} \right) - \underline{\text{Teen's Income}}$$

To help reinforce the idea, again, the formula is calculated using your teen's current income; if any, expenses your teen either pays or you wish for him or her to pay; and a Rainy-Day Fund intended for unplanned expenses. These numbers are plugged into the formula to compute a Family Fund Contribution amount.

Let's go through the steps in detail to see how an actual calculation works.

Playing the Game: Family Fund Contribution Formula

Income Worksheet

1. Compute your teen's current month's income using the Income Worksheet provided in the appendix on page 299.

As you may recall from chapter four, you were introduced to the Income Worksheet and encouraged to fill in your teen's current month's income. To assist you in completing it, we looked at an example of Karen Wilson's Income Worksheet that included her teen-generated income from birthday money she received from her grandparents, babysitting earnings, and payment for washing the family cars. In addition to the income Karen generated, her parents gave her a $10 weekly allowance. This was the minimum amount of cash they wanted her to have on hand each week. Let's look at Karen's Income Worksheet on the following page with the allowance added.

If we look at the figure on the bottom right-hand corner of the Income Worksheet, we can see Karen's total income for September is $140. This is the amount

Income Worksheet

Family Member Player _Karen Wilson_ **Month:** _September_

Date	Coins	Gifts	Earnings: Chores, Job, "Teen Business"	Allowance	Family Fund Contribution (Includes Rainy-Day Fund)	Savings & Investment	Savings & Investments Matched Funds	Borrowed Funds	Other Income	Week's Income
Week 1		20	Babysitting 30	10						60
Week 2			Babysitting 30	10						40
Week 3			Chores 20	10						30
Week 4				10						10
Total Income		20	80	40						140

A blank copy of this worksheet is provided for your use in the appendix on page 299.

the Wilsons will include for "Teen's Income" in their Family Fund Contribution Formula calculation. If you pay your teen an allowance, include the amount in the Income Worksheet. If your teen has no income at this point, the amount you will plug into the Family Fund Contribution Formula for your teen's income will be zero. If your teen does have income, show your son or daughter how to add up the amounts on their worksheet, as in Karen Wilson's example.

• •

Expense Worksheet

2. Calculate your teen's expenses using the Expense Worksheet provided in the appendix on page 301.

• •

Now we need to come up with an amount to include in the formula for "Expenses Teen Pays." At this point in my workshops, I see parents pull out pens and sit up straight in their chairs. Of the tangible money-management skills I introduced to you in chapter one, teaching teens about spending seems to be at the top of most parents' lists.

These days, our teens are bombarded with advertising and marketing both from the TV and the Internet. Parents are anxious for their teens to become wise consumers. But they also don't have the time or the desire to supervise their son or daughter every time they want to buy something. The Expense Worksheet is easy to fill out and allows your teen to keep track of the money he or she spends throughout the month. You will use this worksheet to calculate your teen's *first* Family Fund Contribution amount.

Let's continue our example with the Wilsons to see how they completed Karen's Expense Worksheet on the following page. Then we'll go from there to see how the Wilsons calculated Karen's first Family Fund Contribution amount.

The Expense Worksheet lists common expense items typical for families with teens. There are two parts to the computation for "Expenses Teen Pays." In part (a.), you identify all the expenses you are paying on your teen's behalf for the current or previous month and record them on the Expense Worksheet. In part (b.), you tally up all the expenses your teen is currently paying for the same month. Then you add these two amounts together on the Expense Worksheet. Let's look at the parts in detail following Karen Wilsons' example.

Expense Worksheet

Family Member Player _Karen Wilson_   **Month:** _September_

Date	Food & Eating Out	Car Expense	Trans-portation	Enter-tainment	Books, Music, Movies	School Expense	Clothes & Accessories	Toiletries & Haircuts	Gifts Given to Family or Friends	Estimated Projected Expenses	Other Expenses	Week's Expenses
Week 1		Gas 25		Movie 15	CD 20	Sports 25 Lunches 20	Necklace 15					120
Week 2						Lunches 20						20
Week 3		Gas 25		Movie 15		Lunches 20	Top 40					100
Week 4				Movie 15		Lunches 20		30	25			90
Total Expense		50		45	20	105	55	30	25			330
Total Expense Teen Pays												

A blank copy of this worksheet is provided for your use in the appendix on page 301.

(a.) Record the expenses you are paying on your teen's behalf for the current or previous month.

In class, I usually get a bewildered look from parents when I ask them to take the worksheet home and fill in all the expenses they are paying on their teen's behalf. They ask, "*All* the expenses, even household stuff like doctor's bills and utilities?" If completing this worksheet for the first time, I advise them to include only the expense items listed under each column description. These items are the most common. They can add household items later if they wish their teen to eventually be responsible for a portion of them.

What I've discovered over the course of teaching is that many parents don't know how much they are spending on their teen. When parents come back the following week with their completed worksheets in hand, they often report that the exercise was an eye-opener. Mostly, they are shocked to discover how much they have been spending. Once you have completed this part, I encourage you to share the information with your son or daughter, too. This is a first step toward transferring responsibility for managing those expenses.

Let's continue with our example. To fill in expenses the Wilsons paid on behalf of Karen, Connie Wilson looked through her check register and Visa credit card statement for September to come up with dollar amounts for the necklace and the top, the CD, and the gift Connie bought for Karen to give to a friend. Connie estimated the cost of gas to get Karen to and from school and to after-school sports. Connie estimated school lunch, sports, and movie expense, since she usually gave Karen cash to pay for these items.

Be sure to take time to summarize the current or previous month's expenses that you pay on your teen's behalf and record them on the Expense Worksheet. Be as accurate as you can. Guess where you don't have receipts or charge card records.

(b.) Record the expenses your teen is paying in the current or previous month.

What you do here is simple. Record any expense that your teen is responsible for paying. For example, if your son or daughter contributes money towards the cost of gas to use the family car, then that amount should be included on the Expense Worksheet under car expense. You will probably have an amount listed on the worksheet for the gas expense already, if you have incurred this cost on behalf of your son or daughter. You can include your teen's gas expense below the amount you have recorded.

Parents in class frequently ask me where they are supposed to record such items as car insurance, for which their teen pays a portion, but that is only paid every six months. I tell parents to list the actual or an estimate of one month's worth of the insurance expense under the column "Projected Estimated Expenses," even though the amount has not yet been paid. We will look at a supplemental expense worksheet that you and your teen can use to help you estimate expense amounts for items not paid on a monthly basis. The worksheet is explained in detail in step three when you *select* expenses your teen is either paying or you wish your teen to pay.

Before the Wilsons started playing *The Real-Life* Money Game with Karen, they never formally expected their daughter to be responsible for paying expenses. Every time Karen wanted something, she had to ask her parents for it. On-the-spot decisions were time-consuming with three daughters, and Connie had no consistent way of pre-determining who should pay for what. As a result, Connie inevitably paid. Therefore, on Karen's September Expense Worksheet, the Wilsons listed no expense items that their daughter was responsible for paying for herself.

At this point, you should have an Expense Worksheet that reflects a month's expenses both paid by and for your teen. By completing the worksheet you now have a summary of how much is being spent on your son or daughter. Accurate financial information will help you prepare the case you are going to present to your teen. Based on the expenses recorded on the worksheet, you will now *select* or *choose* certain expenses you want your teen to pay.

Teen Responsibilities

3. Select Expenses Your Teen Pays.

Earlier, I asked you to complete the questionnaire and jot down one expense item you've been haggling over with your son or daughter. At this point you can formally *select* that as one expense you will turn over to your teen. Using the

Family Member Player _____ **Expense Worksheet** _____ **Month:** _September_

Karen Wilson

Date	Food & Eating Out	Car Expense	Trans-portation	Enter-tainment	Books, Music, Movies	School Expense	Clothes & Accessories	Toiletries & Haircuts	Gifts Given to Family or Friends	Estimated Projected Expenses	Other Expenses	Week's Expenses
Week 1		Gas 25		Movie 15	CD 20	Sports 25 Lunches 20	Necklace 15					120
Week 2						Lunches 20						20
Week 3		Gas 25		Movie 15		Lunches 20	Top 40					100
Week 4				Movie 15		Lunches 20		30	25			90
Total Expense		50		45	20	105	55	30	25			330
Total Expense Teen Pays		50		45	20		55	30	25			225

A blank copy of this worksheet is provided for your use in the appendix on page 301.

Expense Worksheet just completed, choose those specific items you wish your teen to pay, and mark them, for example, with a yellow-highlighting pen.

I encourage you to sit down with their son or daughter and have an open discussion about this selection. This is a wonderful way to get your teen involved in the process. You may discover, as many families I've worked with report, that when your teen is included in the choice, they tend to be more willing to accept the responsibility you're handing them.

Let's look at Karen Wilson's Expense Worksheet for September on the preceding page to see what expenses she and her parents agreed Karen would be responsible for paying, shown as the highlighted expenses.

To help you select expenses, I have summarized some time-tested guidelines in the following sidebar. Below is my list of items parents most frequently decide their teens should be responsible for:

- Expenses your teen incurs on a regular basis. These are the ones your teen is constantly having to ask for cash from you to pay for: movies, school lunch, school supplies, toiletries.

- Expenses you are constantly negotiating with your teen: video games, DVDs, music CDs, clothes.

- Subjective items that are better for your teen to decide: birthday and holiday gifts, music, books, or clothes.

> ### Selecting Expenses Your Teen Pays
>
> *Choose:*
>
> - Expenses your teen incurs on a regular basis.
> - Expenses you are constantly negotiating with your teen.
> - Subjective items that are better for your teen to decide.
> - Small-cost or frivolous items.
> - Expenses that help your teen distinguish between needs and wants.

- Frivolous expenses: These are items that satisfy your teen's immediate wants, items you might consider unneeded, or a waste of money. They can be extras of anything. For my son, it was baseball caps and t-shirts. For the Wilson daughters it was cosmetics and tops. For Maria Sanchez it was yet more music CDs.

- Expense items that ask your teen to distinguish between needs and wants: A shoe fund, for example, may be broken down into categories, such as mandatory spiked track shoes, versus a discretionary pair of athletic shoes.

To help you make these choices, *The Real-Life* Money Game offers two supporting worksheets. These are called the "Estimated Projected Expenses" and the "Estimated Projected Clothes Expense." The first worksheet is designed to help you and your teen project upcoming expenses that are not paid each month. The second worksheet provides a way to project how much money to set aside for a clothing fund. Let's look at these worksheets in detail.

Estimated Projected Expenses

When teens are first learning how to manage money, it's important that they understand the need to put funds aside to pay for future expenses. You can teach your teen how to strategize for upcoming expenses by helping them complete the Estimated Projected Expenses worksheet on the following page.

The worksheet lists common expenses teens are often asked to pay, but that do not come due on a monthly basis. You can help your teen manage these expenses by computing the total estimated amount that will be due at a future time, and then dividing that cost into regular payments.

The easiest way to estimate an expense is to consider what you have paid over the past year. If the amount usually stays the same from month to month, then you can add up the previous year's expenses and divide by twelve. If the expense fluctuates, such as for birthday gifts, you can make a projection of when the events will come up and attach an amount to them. For practice, try having your teen go online to research costs of common gift items in catalogs.

The information recorded on the Estimated Projected Expenses worksheet is then transferred to the Expense Worksheet for the specific month the expense is due under the column heading "Estimated Projected Expenses."

Estimated Projected Clothes Expense

Entire books have been written on how to manage money spent on clothes. You might remember that statistic I shared with you in chapter one. Generation Y spends on average $348 per month on clothes. With that much money at stake, teaching our teens to manage a clothing fund requires they pay close attention to effective planning.

Estimated Projected Expenses
Family Member Player _____
From _____ To _____

Expense Item	Month Needed	Projected Amount
School Expenses:		
• Tuition		
• Special Events: Homecoming, Winter Ball, Sports Tournaments		
• Music, Drama, Clubs		
• Other		
Car Expenses:		
• Insurance		
• Maintenance		
• Repairs		
• Other		
Summer Activity Expenses:		
• Camp		
• Sports		
• Vacation Spending Money		
• Other		
Other Expenses:		
• Taxes		
Total Projected Expenses		

A blank copy of this worksheet is provided for your use in the appendix on page 302.

Giving your teen too much money and responsibility all at once can have unintended consequences. The MacLeans, who gave their daughter a lump sum and told her she was responsible for her wardrobe, discovered their fourteen-year-old wouldn't buy *any* clothes. Because she didn't know how much each item cost, she was fearful she would run out of money for items she knew she would need later, such as a costly winter coat.

Giving your teen too little responsibility and money can be equally disastrous. The Delaney family gave their daughter access to the family credit card for clothes thinking she would understand how to spend appropriately. But their daughter had never been given responsibility or money for clothes shopping before. When her mother reviewed the month-end credit card statement, she realized her daughter had gone wild, spending over $1,000 in one weekend's shopping spree.

The key to managing a clothing fund is to start by selecting one or two items your son or daughter can be responsible for paying. Once they become proficient, you can add more items until eventually you've assigned an entire season's clothing fund. *The Real-Life* Money Game provides the Estimated Projected Clothes Expense worksheet on the following page to help you show your teen how to anticipate clothing expenses.

Parents in my workshops report that they've found the inventory column extremely helpful in getting their son or daughter organized. Encourage your teen to check out costs using catalogs, the Internet, or by browsing store prices in advance of purchasing.

The information recorded on the Estimated Projected Clothes Expense worksheet is then transferred to the Expense Worksheet for the month the expense is projected under the column heading "Clothes and Accessories."

• • •

The Wilsons, after completing the Expense Worksheet and then highlighting certain items, added the total of the highlighted expenses to come up with "Expenses Teen Pays." The total expense amount for one month came to $225 as shown on page 62. This is the amount the Wilsons will plug into the Family Fund Contribution Formula calculation.

Estimated Projected Clothes Expense
Family Member Player _____
From _____ **To** _____

Clothing Item	Inventory of What I Have	Description of What I Need	Month Needed	Projected Amount
• Coat				
• Shoes				
• Shirts/tops				
• Pants/shorts				
• Dresses/skirts				
• Underclothes				
• Accessories				
• Swimsuit				
• Special Occasion				
• Other				
Total Projected Expense				

A blank copy of this worksheet is provided for your use in the appendix on page 303.

• •

Rainy-Day Fund

4. Compute a Rainy-Day Fund.

• •

Parents attending my workshop will inevitably ask, "How will my daughter pay for a party gift she doesn't know about?" Or, another parent will say, "My son has to buy spiked athletic shoes he didn't know he needed, since he made the track team. Who's supposed to pay for those?"

Setting aside money for an unanticipated event is an important skill your teen can learn. Adults usually label this an *emergency* fund. Since our teens don't typically worry about "survival," they can develop the same skill by earmarking cash for unplanned expenses. In *The Real-Life Money Game* I call this the Rainy-Day Fund. The sidebar details how the Rainy-Day Fund works.

A fund set aside for unanticipated circumstances can help teach teens to have foresight and to plan, and can often diffuse family conflict before it explodes.

Let's run through an example. Following the Rainy-Day Fund guidelines, the Wilsons agreed that the $225 expenses that Karen would be responsible for paying represented an average month. They discussed with their daughter whether to put the entire amount aside all at once, but felt it would be a strain on their resourc-

Rainy-Day Fund

An amount set aside for unanticipated costs or emergencies. Follow these guidelines:

- Calculate an average monthly expense amount and put one month's aside, or set aside a fixed contribution amount each month until an average month's expenses have been reserved.

- Set the money aside in a clear sheet protector labeled Rainy-Day Fund kept in the personal financial binder or deposit in a Savings, Checking, or Investment Account.

- Decide what the fund will be used for and agree that this money cannot be used to cover spending-plan shortfalls except under special circumstances.

- Make note on *The Real-Life* Money Game Plan worksheet of the Rainy-Day Fund amount and the circumstances in which it will be used.

- If the fund is used, the replacement amount needs to be included in the following month's Family Fund Contribution Formula calculation.

es. Instead, they agreed to contribute $30 each month until they accumulated sufficient funds to cover one month's expenses of $225. They agreed the fund could be used on school expenses such as special events or activities. The money would be deposited into Karen's bank account for safekeeping. If the money was used, Karen and her parents agreed to contribute up to $30 each month to replenish the fund. Connie Wilson noted this arrangement on *The Real-Life Money Game Plan* worksheet which will be discussed in detail in chapter nine.

Using the guidelines, calculate an amount you think would be appropriate for your son or daughter to set aside for a Rainy-Day Fund.

• • •

We've now gone through all the steps necessary to calculate a Family Fund Contribution. Using Karen Wilson as an example, we can plug in the appropriate numbers and come up with her parents' Family Fund Contribution.

Family Fund Contribution Formula
Family Member Player _____*Karen Wilson*_____

1. Compute your teen's current month's income using the Income Worksheet.
2. Calculate your teen's expenses using the Expense Worksheet.
   a. Record the expenses you are paying on your teen's behalf for the current or previous month.
   b. Record the expenses your teen is paying in the current or previous month.
3. Select expenses you want your teen to pay.
4. Compute a Rainy-Day Fund to set aside expenses for unanticipated costs.

Family Fund Contribution	= (	Expenses Teen Pays	+	Rainy-Day Fund	) –	Teen's Income
$115	= (	$225	+	$30	) –	$140

A blank copy of this worksheet is provided for your use in the appendix on page 300.

As it turns out, Karen's income is insufficient to cover the expenses her parents want her to take responsibility for. This shortfall—the difference—represents the Family Fund Contribution amount they will contribute to Karen's monthly fund.

Now it's your turn. Follow the steps below to calculate your Family Fund Contribution amount.

Family Fund Contribution Formula
Family Member Player _____

1. Compute your teen's current month's income using the Income Worksheet.
2. Calculate your teen's expenses using the Expense Worksheet.
   a. Record the expenses you are paying on your teen's behalf for the current or previous month.
   b. Record the expenses your teen is paying in the current or previous month.
3. Select expenses you want your teen to pay.
4. Compute a Rainy-Day Fund to set aside expenses for unanticipated costs.

$$\frac{\text{Family Fund}}{\text{Contribution}} = \left(\frac{\text{Expenses}}{\text{Teen Pays}} + \frac{\text{Rainy-Day}}{\text{Fund}} \right) - \frac{\text{Teen's}}{\text{Income}}$$

$$\underline{\qquad} = \left(\underline{\qquad} + \underline{\qquad} \right) - \underline{\qquad}$$

A blank copy of this worksheet is provided for your use in the appendix on page 300.

Most likely your teen's income will not be enough to cover all the expenses plus the Rainy-Day Fund. Parents do occasionally ask, "What happens if your teen's income is more than the expenses plus the Rainy-Day Fund? Does that mean you make no Family Fund Contribution?" Other parents have admitted that their financial circumstances don't allow them to make the entire Family Fund Contribution calculated by the formula.

Herein lies the exciting flexibility of this formula. If your teen's income is more than their expenses plus the Rainy-Day Fund, select additional expenses you wish your teen to pay. But also bear in mind that if needs are being met, this doesn't have to be a zero sum game. You might simply agree that the additional income could be spent at your son's or daughter's discretion, though reserve the right to have its use accounted for. I would consider this circumstance an excellent reason to save for a future outlay, or to invest. I will talk about these options in upcoming chapters.

If money is tight, you can first calculate how much you're able to contribute. From the known Family Fund Contribution, you can add your teen's income, then determine, given how much cash is available, what teen expenses can be covered. If, on the other hand, your financial circumstances do not allow you to make a Family Fund Contribution, you can use the formula to teach your teen the need for cutting expenses, or, better yet, the need to find other ways to generate income. Remember, your Family Fund Contribution reduces the money you would otherwise spend on your teen's behalf.

• • •

Having come up with the Family Fund Contribution, parents should stand back and look at the amount they have calculated and ask themselves: Is the amount realistic? Does my son or daughter have enough experience handling money to start with this fund? Does the amount fit within our family's resources?

One way you can determine if the amount is reasonable is to compare it to a national average by referring to the Bureau of Labor Statistics at <u>www.bls.gov</u>. While this information provides a benchmark, it's only a guideline. Don't worry if you find that your needs stray from the average statistical trends. The contribution formula is designed to be flexible, to address your individual family's needs, resources, and values.

• • •

Once you've calculated the Family Fund Contribution, have your teen record the amount on his or her Income Worksheet. Try this amount with your teen for six months. It takes time for teens to practice. If your teen is taking responsibility, great, you can maintain the Family Fund Contribution amount or even add to it. Each time new expenses are added, go back and highlight the original worksheet to remind your teen of the progress he or she has made. If your son or daughter is struggling to manage their fund, try pulling back on some of the expense items. Eliminate those that seem to cause the most worry. Keep the items that your teen seems to manage best.

Maria Sanchez, at the outset, was very good about setting money aside to prepare for upcoming big-ticket items—such as car insurance or a prom dress or spending money for a vacation—but she couldn't seem to control her impulse buying when it came to music CDs. Sam and Maria used to get into protracted fights over this. One day, Sam simply agreed that he would not monitor her CD purchases as long as she agreed to stop asking him to increase his Family Fund Contribution. It took her only a month or two to realize that her CD binges were causing her to come up short on other expense items, and so she learned to monitor herself.

• • •

Let's see where we are in *The Real-Life* Money Game. You now know how your teen can generate income, and how you can provide your teen with a resource, as well. These two sources of income, pooled together, make up the fund your son or daughter will use to pay expenses during the month. The next question to consider is how that fund will be distributed. In the upcoming chapter we will go over the four spending-mechanic options available to you and your teen. Once you've selected a spending-mechanic option, we will talk about how all the Income and Expense Worksheet information you and your teen have gathered comes together on the game's "Playing Board." The goal of all this fun is to ultimately come up with a "Spending Plan."

Scorekeeping Box

After you and your teen have gathered the information to compute the Family Fund Contribution Formula, give your teen point credit using the scorekeeping box on the following page. Add the full score if your teen has successfully completed the activity. Add no score if your teen hasn't. Write down the date of the activity, make note of any discussions, problems or successes, and tally your teen's score. This score will be added to the final score at the end.

Key Concepts	Activity Point Value	Date Activity Completed/Discussion Notes	Point Value Earned
Assist your teen with the following to help him or her earn points:			
• Record any allowance received on the Income Worksheet.	5		
• Complete the Income Worksheet using current month's information.	5		
• Complete the Expense Worksheet and agree on *selected* expenses to be paid.	10		
• Project estimated expenses using the supplemental worksheet.	10		
• Project estimated clothes expense on the supplemental worksheet.	10		
• Follow the guidelines to determine a Rainy-Day Fund amount.	10		
• Calculate the Family Fund Contribution and record the amount on the Income Worksheet.	20		
Total Score	**70**		

Chapter Six
Spending: The Mechanics

• •

At this point, we have calculated how much money to make available to your teen, and we've identified where that money will come from, both as teen-generated income, and from parent-generated income sources. Now we need to decide how your son or daughter will actually distribute his or her funds. In chapter three, you were introduced to the concept of cash pockets and to three bank and investment account-types. In this chapter, you and your teen will decide which spending option to use. Let's consider the four options identified in the sidebar list.

Cash Pockets

In my courses, I derive much pleasure watching parents' eyes light up when I show them how cash pockets work. I hold up for viewing a clear sheet protector with a twenty dollar bill inserted inside along with a handwritten note that says "Lunch Money-$20." The clear sheet protector enables teens to see and count how much money they have at any one time to pay for a particular expense. The same pockets are also used to track spending. Every time your teen pulls cash out of a particular cash pocket, they replace the cash with a receipt.

Okay. I imagine what you're thinking. My son? My daughter? Remember to keep a receipt? You must be joking! Learning to keep receipts should be a life-long habit, even if they eventu-

---

Spending Options

1. **Cash Pockets**
   For teens with little or no experience handling money or who are struggling to handle money.

2. **Savings Account & ATM Card**
   For teens with some experience handling an allowance or small earnings and who are eager to handle money independently of their parents.

3. **Checking & Debit Card Account**
   For teens who have a regular source of earnings or income and who are in need of a mechanism to manage their money.

4. **Investment Account**
   For teens who have had a few year's experience handling earnings or a fund of money and who are eager to learn more about saving and investing.

ally end up in the garbage. Here is why. The purchase price of an item is documented. The items often can be returned with a receipt. The Internal Revenue Service often requires verifiable information such as a receipt for tax returns. And they are an excellent and simple way for teens to track spending. Receipts can also be used to reconcile bank-account-statement information. At any rate, the point is, without receipts there is no accurate way to track the money being spent. And guesswork often leads to deliberate fudging, or worse, forgetting.

Cash pockets are kept in your teen's personal financial binder under the index tab for a given month. For example, if "Lunch Money" pertains to the month of September, then the cash pocket will be kept behind the September index tab. Your son or daughter can use as many cash pockets for a month as they have expense items. For example, one sheet protector might be labeled "Lunch Money." Another might be, "Gas and Insurance." Another might be "Pizza and Snacks." At month's end your teen totals up his or her receipts and remaining cash, if any, to determine how much was spent for each expense category.

Cash pockets are an ideal spending-mechanic option for teens with little or no experience handling money. I developed the concept of cash pockets as a way to prompt teens to think ahead about what they'll need money for, instead of routinely relying on their parents as a stop-gap measure. Families report that cash pockets work especially well for those teens who tend to spend their money the minute they receive it. This way they have a visual record of their diminishing resource. In most cases, they quickly learn to pace their spending rather than face an empty pocket through the bulk of the month.

One mother who attended my course reported her success using the cash-pocket method of spending with her sixteen-year-old son. He was great at earning money. He provided pet-sitting services to neighbors throughout the year. Usually, he would put his earnings into a savings account. But once he started driving and purchased a car, he struggled to know how much money to set aside each month for his gas and a portion of his insurance. His mother set up two cash pockets. One for "Gas" and one for "Car Insurance." She helped him estimate fuel costs based on prices at the local gas station pumps. Together they determined he would need $50 each week, and encouraged him to put this amount of his earnings aside in a cash pocket. Then his mother helped him calculate how much to set aside monthly for his portion of the family's semi-annual auto insurance, which came to $100 a month for six months, until the insurance came due. If her son didn't earn enough money for both his gas and insurance during any given month, he knew he would have to forgo savings, or make up the short-fall in earnings the next month. Of course, this only works if the insurance payment is due in the month of the short-fall. Her son soon learned he had two options when this happened: to use less gas in order to divert more of his funds toward auto insurance, or to buy cheaper gas. Cash pockets not only provided him with a visual means of tracking his expenses, it also helped him to reorganize his spending priorities.

Savings Account and ATM Card

A savings account with an ATM card offers a spending option suitable for teens with experience handling an allowance or small earnings. Many teens yearn for something *plastic*, which seems to symbolize their induction into the adult world.

Unlike cash pockets—where the resource is visible, tangible—with a savings account teens have to be prepared to work with a layer of abstraction. They can't touch the resource with their senses. Because of this, you may encounter some resistance when you insist that they deposit their funds into their savings account at the beginning of each month. Walk them through it. Introduce them to the account manager at the bank. Take them to the ATM (Automated Teller Machines) with their new card and watch while they punch numbers and look on in amazement when money—their money—all but falls into their hands. Explain to your son or daughter the importance of safeguarding their "PIN" number (Personal Identification Number) which enables them to access the ATMs and get cash. Reports abound that teens are frequently approached at shopping malls and asked if they want to sell their ATM and "PIN" for money.

Remind your teen to keep his or her ATM receipts and put them into a clear sheet protector in their binder at home. When the bank statement comes in, you will need to help your teen review the statement to show how to compare deposits and ATM transactions made throughout the month to the bank statement. Teaching your teen to reconcile his or her transactions with what the bank shows on the statement will help your son or daughter understand how much cash he or she has on hand and to confirm that the cash balance per the bank is correct. Quickly, your teen will learn that his or her resource has not been diminished simply because it disappeared into the bank.

I started teaching my son at age twelve about spending beyond a simple allowance. At the time, we had agreed to a Family Fund Contribution of $90 for expense items he would be responsible for paying. We based this amount on what we had actually spent over the last year on the following expense items for one month: $10 for entertainment; $25 dollars for t-shirts; $35 for games; and $20 for books. Michael was so excited when I took him to the bank to open his first bank savings account with an ATM card that he wanted to try his card at every ATM he saw.

Michael was thrilled to have the opportunity to start making spending decisions for himself. I took him to the mall to shop, and showed him how to use the ATM card to get cash. When he was at the mall with friends, he learned to browse first, so he had a better idea of how much cash to withdraw for an item he might wish to purchase.

Michael's newfound financial independence was not only a first big step for him, it was for me, as well. Within three months, Michael stopped asking me for cash handouts every time he went shopping. The sense of responsibility had been shifted to him in direct proportion to the degree of control I was willing to relinquish.

Each month, I showed him how to take his savings account deposit slips and his ATM withdrawal receipts and compare them to the bank statement. Of course, at age twelve, he invariably forgot to keep his ATM cash withdrawal slips. He usually tossed them in the garbage at the mall or wadded them up in his pocket. The same with his purchase receipts. But over time, as he realized he couldn't reconcile his records with the bank's, he accepted the need to keep track of his cash and his spending. He learned why this mattered when, two months into it, he'd emptied his account of spending money by mid-month and had nothing left for movies, snacks, or CDs. He only had to learn this lesson once.

Checking and Debit Card Account

A checking and debit card account is ideal for teens who have a regular source of earnings or income. A check register is the best mechanism for managing money. This tool enables teens to learn to record every transaction they make in a given month: all deposited income; all expenses, whether from checks written or from debit card purchases; and all cash withdrawals.

Now you might be saying to yourself, as some parents have told me, "My son would never keep track of all of his transactions," generally objecting on the grounds that their teen is not that interested, or not that organized or doesn't have the time. Or you might object, saying, "I would never give my daughter a debit card. It looks too much like a credit card." This is a big concern expressed by parents in my course.

Before I address these concerns, let me explain how this spending option works. Each month your teen will deposit all monthly funds into a checking and debit card account, or, alternatively, deposit funds into a savings account set up for telephone or online transfers to checking. Throughout the month, your son or daughter will write checks or use his or her debit card to pay for expenses. Your teen will record checks written and debit card transactions, as they occur, in the check register. Purchase receipts are kept in a clear sheet protector in the binder. Deposit slips and ATM receipts are also kept in a clear protective sheet. When the bank statement comes in, your teen reconciles his or her check register transactions with the bank statement transactions. *The Real-Life* Money Game provides a bank reconciliation worksheet, shown on page 83, that keeps this business appropriately simple for your teen's use. I will explain this in greater detail later in this chapter.

Okay. Now I'll share with you what I tell parents in my workshops to help alleviate their concerns and to encourage them to take this step with their teens. From my experience as a CPA, there is one thing I see happen with people struggling to handle their personal finances: they do not have enough recordkeeping information to make effective financial decisions. Teens who have income need some way to capture the information and to match it up with their spending. A check register is the easiest and most informative tool available. And it's portable. Your teen can collect receipts and record them when they have a few moments to spare. Teens who are not organized often aren't, because they don't have a tool to help them get organized. Even teens who aren't very interested become interested when they are given the responsibility to manage a Family Fund Contribution that has been set forth in a spending plan. The efficacy of this method depends, of course, on your willingness as parents not to bail them out by forking over additional funds when they've depleted their account prematurely.

Yes, debit cards do look like credit cards. All the more reason to expose our teens to them. Most research supports that teens will be confronted with a "paperless society." *The Real-Life* Money Game attempts to provide as many visual tools as possible, before teens advance to a less visual tool, such as the debit card. By the time you are ready to make the decision to set your teen up with a checking account and debit card, you hopefully will have helped them practice keeping track of their income, expenses, and cash.

As mentioned in chapter three, encourage your teen to order checks that come with a carbon copy. When teens are first learning how to record checks, they frequently forget one or two. The carbon copy becomes a handy reference.

Investment Account

Setting up an investment account works best for teens who have had a few years experience handling a checking and debit card account. Here is how this spending option works. Each month, funds earmarked for your teen's spending plan will be deposited into an investment account that has been opened with a bank or brokerage institution. Throughout the month, your son or daughter will write checks, use a debit card, or ATM cash withdrawals to pay expenses. Your teen will keep his or her purchase receipts in a clear sheet protector, as well. At month's end, your teen will reconcile the check register balance with the investment account statement using *The Real-Life* Money Game Bank Reconciliation Worksheet on page 83. Keeping funds in an investment account makes the money readily available for investing. No need to transfer funds.

Teaching Your Teen to Keep Track of Cash

If you teach your teen no other skill before he or she goes to college, teach your son or daughter to keep track of his or her cash as summarized in the sidebar on the following page. Teens don't like to find out the hard way that they've depleted their resources. And banks charge $25 to $30 per check when there are insufficient funds in the account to cover them.

Keep Track of Your Cash

- Know how much cash you have in your account, so you can decide if you have enough money to cover checks you write and debit transactions you make.
- If you write a check, and you don't have enough money in your account, the bank will charge you a significant fee.
- The way you determine whether your cash balance is correct is by comparing it to your bank statement. The monthly bank or investment statement balance usually ends on a different date than your check register balance.
- Use *The Real-Life* Money Game Bank Reconciliation Worksheet to reconcile your checking and debit card account register to your bank or investment statement, which means to find out if the cash balance you show in your check register *today* is correct.
- The bank or investment statement provides a valuable way to make sure that all the deposits you make, all the checks you write, and all the debit transactions you have for the month are the same as yours. That way if you or the bank, or the brokerage institution makes a mistake, the worksheet helps you find any errors.

Sam Sanchez confessed that when, as a senior in high school, his daughter opened her first checking account with a debit card, Maria struggled to keep track of her cash balance. She wrote checks occasionally, but most often she would withdraw cash from an ATM to cover her weekly expenses. Toward the end of the year, she started writing checks and making purchases with her debit card for upcoming college expenses. At the same time, she was phasing out of her part-time job, knowing she was leaving for college, and thus her deposits into her account were smaller. She soon discovered when she received her bank statement that she had made a mistake in her check register and she was short by $17. Unfortunately, four checks came in after the shortfall was detected. By the time her next deposit was recorded by the bank, she had been charged check fees amounting to $120—thirty dollars for each check that cleared after the shortfall.

When Sam talked with Maria about the problem, his daughter admitted that instead of recording all her transactions in her check register, she relied on the balance she got from her last ATM withdrawal receipt. The balance didn't reflect four outstanding checks. She told her dad she had "guessed" at how much was left in her account.

Sam wanted to say "I told you that you needed to keep your check register current," but he didn't. He bit his tongue instead and let his daughter take responsibility for her own actions. She called the bank, pleading for sympathy, but to no avail. Her college savings were reduced by $120, a shortfall Sam refused to make up in order to teach her a lesson. As you can imagine, this was a lesson she did not need to learn twice.

Use *The Real-Life* Money Game Bank Reconciliation Worksheet, shown on the following page, to help your son or daughter balance his or her checkbook. In this way, your teen will learn how to check his or her entries in the check register against the statement the bank or brokerage institution sends every month. Use the worksheet in the appendix, monthly, to help your teen go through each step until he or she can do it on his or her own. Insert the completed worksheet in the binder for that month, behind the bank statement that it pertains to.

In step one of the worksheet, the bank's cut-off date, that is the last day the bank shows any activity in your teen's account, will most likely be different than the last date shown in your teen's check register. These checks and debit transactions have cleared the bank which means the bank has recorded them. If the bank shows any checks or debit transactions that your teen has not recorded in his or her check register, help your teen record them now. Your teen will also need to subtract them from his or her check register balance. Put a circle next to any checks or debit card transactions that the bank doesn't show. These are called outstanding transactions, items not shown on your teen's bank statement.

If the bank shows any deposits that your teen does not show in his or her check register, you will need to add these to the register now. You will also need to add these to your teen's check register balance. Put a circle next to any deposits that the bank doesn't show. These are called outstanding deposits.

In step three, be sure to include any deposits you noted on your teen's bank or investment statement that he or she forgot to record. Make sure that your teen has recorded all the checks written through today's date. Also include any checks, debit transactions, or ATM cash withdrawals you noted on your teen's bank or investment statement that he or she forgot to record. Your teen should have receipts for these transactions. Calculate the balance in your teen's check register now that all the activity has been recorded through today's date. This is how much money your teen has on hand today.

The Real-Life **Money Game Bank Reconciliation Worksheet**
Family Member Player _____
From _____ **To** _____

Step One:

- From your current month bank statement, write down the amount of money the bank shows you have in your account. Don't worry that the bank's date is different than your date. Write down the bank's ending balance here: _____

- Go to your check register. Put a check mark next to all the checks, and debit transactions in your check register that the bank shows on the statement. Add up all the outstanding checks and debit card transactions that have a circle by them and put the total here: _____

- In your check register, put a check mark next to all the deposits that the bank shows on the statement. Add up all the outstanding deposits that have a circle by them and put the total here: _____

Step Two:

- Take the ending bank balance from step one and subtract your total outstanding checks and debit card transactions from it; then add the total outstanding deposits and put the number here:
_____

Step Three:

- Update your check register by recording all the deposits you have made into your account through today's date. Write down your check register balance here:
_____

Step Four:

- Compare the number you computed in step two _____ with your check register balance in step three _____. If they are the same, congratulations! You have reconciled your check and debit card account register. This means that the cash balance you show today is correct.

- If the bank balance you computed in step two _____ is different than the check register balance you computed in step three _____, you will need to determine what the difference between them is and write it here _____.
You will then need to go back through steps one through three to recheck your work for errors. Check also for the following: Recheck the addition in your check register balance or check to see if the bank charged any fees you have not yet recorded.

A blank copy of this worksheet is provided for your use in the appendix on page 304.

The following is an example of how Michael records his checks and debit card transactions and reconciles his check register with his bank statement. The "B" represents his reconciled balance.

NUMBER	DATE	TRANSACTION DESCRIPTION	PAYMENT/DEBIT (-)		CODE	FEE (-)	DEPOSIT/CREDIT (+)	$ 136 . 61	
—	11/3	Bartells Drugs	7	38				129	38 23
—	11/5	Starbucks	6	12				123	12 11
—	11/8	Overlake subway	6	33				116	33 78
—	11/9	Starbucks	6	56				110	56 22
~	11/10	Athletic Supply	9	74 (B)				100	74 48
⌐	11/13	Casa D's	6	45 ✓				94	45 03
—	11/14	Entertainment weekly	29	95 ✓				64	95 08
—	11/17	Quiznos	6	— ✓				58	00 08
—	11/17	Johnny Rockets	7	55 ✓				50	55 53
→	11/19	Starbucks	4	32 ✓				46	32 21
—	11/20	Subway	6	77 ✓				39	77 44
—	11/21	Teriyahi bowl	6	50 ✓				32	50 94
⌐	11/21	B of A Withdrawl	10	00 ✓				22	10 — 94
—	11/24	Family Ford car		✓			470 —	492	470 — 94
\031	11/24	New/oil Car	150	00 ✓				342	50 — 94
—	11/24	Pallino Pasteria	7	65 ✓				335	65 29

To reorder call **1.800.652.1111**. Thank you for banking with Bank of America

The following table summarizes each spending option and the monthly instructions you can help your teen complete.

> ### *The Real-Life* Money Game Spending-Option Instructions
>
> **Cash Pockets**
>
> 1. Put monthly funds in clear protective sheets labeled for each expense item and amount.
> 2. Throughout the month, use the cash earmarked for each expense and insert a receipt, if available, as the money is used.
>
> **Savings Account and ATM Card**
>
> 1. Deposit monthly funds into a savings account.
> 2. Throughout the month, access cash using the ATM card to pay monthly expenses.
> 3. Put receipts for purchases in clear protective sheets labeled for each expense item and amount.
> 4. Keep deposit and ATM receipts in a clear protective sheet.
> 5. Review the bank statement to make sure all deposits and all ATM transactions have been recorded and the cash balance is correct.
>
> **Checking and Debit Card Account**
>
> 1. Deposit monthly funds into a checking and debit card account, or alternatively, deposit into a savings account set up for telephone or online transfers to checking.
> 2. Throughout the month, use checks and the debit card to pay for expenses.
> 3. Record checks written and debit card transactions as they occur in a check register.
> 4. Put receipts for purchases in a clear protective sheet.
> 5. Keep deposit and ATM receipts in a clear protective sheet.
> 6. Reconcile the check register balance with the bank statement using *The Real-Life* Money Game Bank Reconciliation Worksheet.
>
> **Investment Account**
>
> 1. Deposit monthly funds into an investment account.
> 2. Throughout the month, use checks or debit card, or ATM cash withdrawals to pay expenses and record the transactions as they occur in a check register.
> 3. Put receipts for purchases in a clear protective sheet.
> 4. Keep deposits and ATM receipts in a clear protective sheet.
> 5. Reconcile the check register balance with the investment account statement using *The Real-Life* Money Game Bank Reconciliation Worksheet.

• • •

The goal of *The Real-Life* Money Game is to enable your son or daughter to move from Cash Pockets, to the Savings Account with ATM Card, to a Checking with Debit Card Account, and finally to the Investment Account. After working with a number of families, however, I've discovered that not all teens have an interest in the investment option, and for some even the debit card option is a bit scary. Fine. The important point is to introduce your teen to each method so he or she can be aware of the options, but let your son or daughter decide what feels comfortable. In my experience, it takes between six months to a year for a teen to become proficient with a given spending option. It's best not to rush them. When they're ready, and as their needs change, shift to another spending method. This is all part of that scalable plan—a plan that is flexible enough to meet your needs.

Scorekeeping Box

After reviewing the spending options with your teen, and showing your son or daughter how to keep track of his or her cash, give your teen point credit on the following page. Add the full score if your teen has successfully completed the activity. Add no score if your teen hasn't. Write down the date of the activity, make note of any discussions, problems or successes, and tally your teen's score. This score will be added to the final score at the end.

Key Concepts	Activity Point Value	Date Activity Completed/Discussion Notes	Point Value Earned
Assist your teen with the following to help him or her earn points:			
• Select Cash Pocket spending option.	5		
• Select Savings Account and ATM Card spending option.	5		
• Select Checking and Debit Card Account spending option.	10		
• Select Investment Account spending option.	20		
• Keep track of cash on hand.	5		
• Balance the check register with the monthly bank statement.	10		
• Keep a minimum balance in the bank or investment account.	20		
Total Score	**75**		

Chapter Seven
The Real-Life Money Game Playing Board—A Spending Plan

· ·

A playing board anchors the activity in many games. In *The Real-Life* Money Game, the *spending plan* is the equivalent of a playing board. Think of the spending plan as the "board" upon which the game's activity takes place.

Prior to this I've introduced the steps to set up a monthly fund your son or daughter can manage. We've discussed how you can help your teen complete an Income Worksheet. I've encouraged you to identify expenses you want your son or daughter to start paying on the Expense Worksheet. Now you and your teen need a place to collect this information.

The Real-Life Money Game Playing Board-Spending Plan offers your teen a way to see in one place a complete itemization of his or her income and expenses, as well as a description of who pays for what. The spending plan is used to establish how much money your teen projects to have on hand at the beginning of the month, and what expenses that money will cover. Within the spending-plan parameters, there is enough built-in flexibility to allow your teen to make independent choices. At month's end, the same spending plan will be used to record how much income your teen actually received and how he or she actually spent the funds. Finally, the spending plan reflects how much money is earmarked for savings, giving, borrowing or lending, investment, or taxes, concepts that will be discussed in detail in part two.

Playing The Game: The Playing Board-Spending Plan (Column 1)

· ·

Income Worksheet

1. Transfer the totals from the Income Worksheet to the Playing Board-Spending Plan, provided in the appendix on page 305, under column one labeled, "Income amounts I have projected at the beginning of the month."

· ·

Let's look at how the Wilsons transferred the information from their daughter, Karen's Income Worksheet to her Playing Board-Spending Plan.

Income Worksheet

Family Member Player _Karen Wilson_   **Month:** _September_

Date	Coins	Gifts	Earnings: Chores, Job, "Teen Business"	Allowance	Family Fund Contribution (Includes Rainy-Day Fund)	Savings & Investment	Savings & Investments Matched Funds	Borrowed Funds	Other Income	Week's Income
Week 1		20	Babysitting 30	10						60
Week 2			Babysitting 30	10						40
Week 3			Chores 20	10						30
Week 4				10	115					125
Total Income		20	80	40	115					255

A blank copy of this worksheet is provided for your use in the appendix on page 299.

The Real-Life Money Game Playing Board-Spending Plan
Family Member Player _____*Karen Wilson*_____ **Month:** _*October*_

Income	Income amounts I have projected at the beginning of the month	What I actually received during the month	Difference between income I project in column one with the actual amount received in column two
• Coins			
• Gifts	20		
• Earnings	80		
• Allowance	40		
• Family Fund Contribution	85		
• Savings & Investment Income			
• Investments: Matched Funds			
• Borrowed Funds			
• Rainy-Day Fund	30		
• Other			
Total Income	**255**		

Expenses	What I expect it to cost	What it actually costs	Difference between expected cost in column one with the actual cost in column two
• Food & Eating Out			
• Car Expense			
• Transportation			
• Entertainment			
• Books, Music, Movies			
• School Expense			
• Clothes & Accessories			
• Toiletries & Haircuts			
• Gifts Given			
• Rainy-Day Fund			
• Other			
Total Expenses			
Total Income Minus Total Expenses			

A blank copy of this worksheet is provided for your use in the appendix on page 305.

On Karen's Playing Board-Spending Plan, shown on the previous page, the Wilsons helped her record $20 for gifts, $80 in earnings, $40 allowance, and $115 Family Fund Contribution which includes the $30 Rainy-Day Fund. Her total income on her Income Worksheet matched the total income on her Playing Board-Spending Plan, as it should. They both show a total income of $255. This is the amount of income Karen will be responsible for managing in October.

• •

Expense Worksheet

2. Transfer the highlighted "Total Expenses Teen Pays" from the Expense Worksheet to the Playing Board-Spending Plan, provided in the appendix on page 305, under column one labeled, "What I expect it to cost."

• •

The Wilsons helped Karen record expenses from her Expense Worksheet, as shown on the following page: $50 for Car Expense, $45 for Entertainment, $20 for Books, Music & Movies, $55 for Clothes & Accessories, $30 for Toiletries & Haircuts, and $25 for Gifts. Her expenses for the month total $330, but the expenses that she agrees she's responsible to pay total $225. The shortfall simply remains part of her parents' responsibility. The Wilsons also helped Karen record $30 to be set aside for the Rainy-Day Fund. These amounts are recorded on her Playing Board-Spending Plan as shown on page 94.

At this point in my workshops, parents usually begin to smile and nod. They are starting to see the big picture. It's much clearer to them how they can convey this broader view of money to their teen. Typically, they will start asking specific questions: What if my son doesn't always have the same amount of income each month? What if my daughter's expenses vary?

When you and your teen fill out the Income and Expense Worksheets for the first time, you need a starting point. Experience has shown that it's best to choose either the current or the previous month's income and expenses. This will provide actual numbers you can use to calculate the initial Family Fund Contribution amount. In all subsequent months, the income and expense numbers you transfer from the current month's worksheets will be used to fill out the next month's Playing Board-Spending Plan.

Family Member Player _Karen Wilson_   **Expense Worksheet**   **Month:** _September_

Date	Food & Eating Out	Car Expense	Trans- portation	Enter- tainment	Books, Music, Movies	School Expense	Clothes & Accessories	Toiletries & Haircuts	Gifts Given to Family or Friends	Estimated Projected Expenses	Other Expenses	Week's Expenses
Week 1				Movie 15	CD 20	Sports 25 Lunches 20	Necklace 15					95
Week 2		Gas 25				Lunches 20						45
Week 3				Movie 15		Lunches 20	Top 40	30	25			130
Week 4		Gas 25		Movie 15		Lunches 20						60
Total Expense		50		45	20	105	55	30	25			330
Total Expense Teen Pays		50		45	20		55	30	25			225

A blank copy of this worksheet is provided for your use in the appendix on page 301.

The Real-Life Money Game Playing Board-Spending Plan

Family Member Player _____ *Karen Wilson* _____ **Month:** *October*

Income	Income amounts I have projected at the beginning of the month	What I actually received during the month	Difference between income I project in column one with the actual amount received in column two
• Coins			
• Gifts	20		
• Earnings	80		
• Allowance	40		
• Family Fund Contribution	85		
• Savings & Investment Income			
• Investments: Matched Funds			
• Borrowed Funds			
• Rainy-Day Fund	30		
• Other			
Total Income	**255**		

Expenses	What I expect it to cost	What it actually costs	Difference between expected cost in column one with the actual cost in column two
• Food & Eating Out			
• Car Expense	50		
• Transportation			
• Entertainment	45		
• Books, Music, Movies	20		
• School Expense			
• Clothes & Accessories	55		
• Toiletries & Haircuts	30		
• Gifts Given	25		
• Rainy-Day Fund	30		
• Other			
Total Expenses	**255**		
Total Income Minus Total Expenses	**0**		

A blank copy of this worksheet is provided for your use in the appendix on page 305.

For example, the Wilsons used September, the first month of school, as their starting point. They then transferred September's information to Karen's Playing Board-Spending Plan for the month of October, assuming her income would stay the same. They also planned that her expenses would be approximately the same for both months. Realistically, Karen's income and expenses varied.

Accounting for that variation is a key part of managing this resource base. If in October she doesn't earn as much for babysitting or washing the family cars, she will be short funds to cover expenses, unless her expenses go down. She needs to then figure out how she might generate more income, or spend less on her expenses. She might also have to dip into savings, though she's generally reluctant to do that. These are the discretionary choices that lead to money-management problem solving.

Karen's example raises a question we need to discuss. What happens if your teen runs out of money before the month is out? Similarly, what happens if your teen doesn't spend all the money he or she receives? In the next chapter we will learn the rules, and consider options to address these questions.

Scorekeeping Box

Help your teen transfer Income and Expense Worksheet information to the Playing Board-Spending Plan (Column One). Give your teen point credit on the following page for successfully completing the activity. Add no score if your teen hasn't. Write down the date of the activity, make note of any discussions, problems or successes, and tally your teen's score. This score will be added to the final score at the end.

Key Concepts	Activity Point Value	Date Activity Completed/Discussion Notes	Point Value Earned
Assist your teen with the following to help him or her earn points:			
• Transfer the information from the Income Worksheet onto the Playing Board-Spending Plan in column one under the heading "Income amounts I have projected at the beginning of the month."	5		
• Transfer the information from the Expense Worksheet onto the Playing Board-Spending Plan column one under the heading "What I expect it to cost."	5		
• Record any Rainy-Day Fund amount on the Playing Board-Spending Plan in column one.	10		
• Add up column one income and fill in the total. Add up column one expenses and fill in the total. Calculate Total Income minus Total Expenses and fill in the amount on the Playing Board-Spending Plan in column one.	10		
Total Score	**30**		

Chapter Eight
The Real-Life Money Game Rules

Games have rules the way a playing field has boundaries. Without the rules, the nature of the play becomes vague, the outcome uncertain at best. *The Real-Life* Money Game is no exception, though I've found that keeping the rules few and brief is the best way to promote enjoyment of the game. I actually prefer to call the rules *understandings*—established parameters—between you and your teen that can help you play the game more effectively. As an added benefit, sitting down and reviewing the rules with your son or daughter can open lines of communication.

I developed these five rules through trial and error while teaching money skills to other families. The following sidebar lists *The Real-Life* Money Game's five rules. Let's go through them one by one.

The Real-Life Money Game Rules

Rule One: If your teen has a shortfall of funds in a given month, you cannot bail your teen out by adding money that wasn't part of the original fund. Your teen either comes up with more funds or forgoes an expenditure.

Rule Two: If your teen has an excess of funds in a given month, you and your teen need to agree on how this excess will be used. Parents retain veto power over discretionary spending.

Rule Three: Teens agree to take on no harmful or illegal expenditures.

Rule Four: Teens agree that all debit or credit card Internet purchases require parent approval.

Rule Five: You and your teen agree in advance on what sanctions will be applied if the game is not played according to the instructions and the rules.

Rule One

If your teen has a shortfall of funds in a given month, you cannot bail your teen out by adding money that wasn't part of the original fund. Your teen either comes up with more funds or forgoes an expenditure.

In the last chapter, I mentioned that we would talk about what happens if your teen runs out of money before the month is out. Expect this to happen repeatedly in the first six months. For inexperienced teens, a small fund of money may seem like a green light to spend. Rule one is the stop-gap. And though you discuss this with your teen in advance, still expect it to happen. In fact, I'm hopeful it does, at least once, so your teen can experience at a gut level what it feels like to run out of money. It's always tempting for parents—I count myself as no exception—to bail our teens out. Resist the urge. Your teen needs to learn how to solve his or her own problem. As long as your son or daughter keeps within the spending-plan parameters, your teen will discover two potential solutions. They can either generate more income or forgo an expense. That's how it works in *real life,* and that's how it works in the game.

The Wilsons reminded their middle daughter, Casey, age thirteen, of this rule for the first three months. Casey loved to spend money. She loved to spend money so much, that she often went shopping with her friends or with her sisters and helped them spend their money, too. Before the Wilsons set Casey up with her own fund to spend, she would show up at the movies with no money, mooch off her sisters, then her sisters would expect repayment from their parents after the fact. Connie grew very weary of Casey's excessive spending, so she set her up with a fund for movies, snack food, and one small clothing or accessory item each month. Then she shared rule one with Casey.

Even so, for the first three months Casey kept running out of money before month's end. Casey would be invited to go to the movies with her sisters or friends. Since she didn't have the money to go, she'd end up staying home, watching TV. Not a pleasant prospect for the Wilson's very social daughter.

Around the fourth month, Connie reported a change in her daughter's behavior. Casey had gone shopping with friends and came home with two new $40 skirts. She wiped out her total monthly spending fund, again! Her mom suspected that Casey had acted out of peer pressure; her friends bought skirts, so she bought skirts. She'd seen Casey succumb to impulsive shopping under peer pressure before.

Exasperated though she was, Connie held her tongue. She watched and wait-ed to see what her daughter would do. The day after Casey bought the skirts, Connie noticed them laying on top of her daughter's dresser, folded neatly with the tags still on. She was amazed. Usually her daughter would have ripped the tags off her new skirts and worn them immediately. Was Casey leaving her option open to return the skirts? Connie knew her daughter had no money left to go to the movies and that she didn't want to baby-sit on weekends to earn more. She much preferred to go out with her friends. Was Casey finally catch-ing on? Connie would later find out that Casey exercised the only option that made sense. She returned the expensive skirts she purchased impulsively. Had Connie bailed Casey out every time she ended up short of funds, her daughter would have missed an opportunity to solve her own problem.

By following rule one, you enable your teen to experience first-hand the con-sequences of running out of money. It encourages teens to become resourceful and effective problem solvers.

If your teen ends up with a shortfall of funds, the following sidebar lists some options to consider. Not every option will be perfect for your family. Many parents tell me they do not want their son or daughter to borrow money. Though there are legitimate uses for debt, we'll save that discussion for chapter thirteen.

It's usually the case that when teens find themselves short of funds, their parents bail them out. No strings attached. This is a rule violation. Instead, parents need to set up funding shortfalls as problem-solving or skill-building opportunities. I deliberately avoid identifying *ideal* options, because every family's needs are different.

> **If your teen has a shortfall of funds, he or she can:**
>
> - Generate more income.
> - Spend less or forgo an expense to keep expenses in line with the spending-plan parameters.
> - Adjust projected income and/or expense amounts with more accurate numbers.
> - Use the Rainy-Day Fund.
> - Dip into savings.
> - Borrow from family, relatives, or a friend.

- -

Rule Two

If your teen has an excess of funds in a given month, you and your teen need to agree on how this excess will be used. Parents retain veto power over discretionary spending.

- -

I also mentioned in the last chapter that I would address what happens if your teen doesn't spend all the money he or she receives. Rule number two asserts that if your teen doesn't spend all the money he or she has available for expenses, the money isn't just up for grabs. You and your teen need to sit down and decide together how the excess funds will be used. Because our teens are just learning how to manage money, it's appropriate and necessary for parents to retain veto power over discretionary spending.

If your teen ends up with an excess of funds, the following sidebar lists some options he or she can consider. Again, not every option will be perfect for your family.

Families report much excitement the first time their teens end up with funds left over. Unspent funds provide options. But this means parents must also overcome the consternation the first time their teen says, "Wait a minute. That's not fair. That should be my money." If your teen refuses to see reason, simply explain to your son or daughter that you will reduce his or her Family Fund Contribution by the amount of the overage. When they see that their expenses will go up by that much every month, they'll stop squawking.

> **If your teen has an excess of funds, he or she can:**
>
> - Spend now.
> - Keep to pay upcoming month's expenses.
> - Set aside for a Rainy-Day Fund.
> - Give to a charitable organization.
> - Save for a future goal.
> - Start a "Teen Business."
> - Set aside for investing.
> - Pay back borrowed funds, if any.
> - Lend funds with interest.
> - Set aside for taxes.

At this point in my workshops, parents often say to me, "I'd like my daughter to give money to our church before she spends money on her clothes." Or, "My son is already saving most of what he earns, so what more does he need to do?"

These are legitimate points. First, I think it's important to acknowledge that developing the skills to give and save are as important as learning to generate income. They are part of the "bundle" of skills our teens need to learn to help them manage their resource. But there are two drawbacks to introducing these skills before your teen can understand them. First, teens need to know where money comes from and how it is used before they can comprehend giving it away or putting it aside. Secondly, while parents often require their teens to set aside money to give to their church or a charity, or to save money for a car or college, *The Real-Life* Money Game provides more comprehensive tools that your teen can use to actually understand the concepts behind the activity. And they will be given more discretion over their spending, which translates into taking more responsibility for outcomes. Beyond having money in the bank, they will have acquired a methodology that they can take with them to college and beyond.

The following is an example of how we handled this problem in our household: Since Michael has limited time to earn money during the school year, his primary goal is to learn how to manage his spending within a limited resource. We agreed that any money he didn't spend for a given month he could use in one of three ways: he could accumulate the money in his checking account for school expenses he was responsible to pay later, such as baseball shoes; he could contribute the excess, which we would match towards saving for his car; or, he could invest the money—again with parental matching funds—with one proviso. He must invest the entire amount under the guidelines we helped him establish with his broker.

Let's consider how Karen Wilson used the options. Karen had $98 more at the end of October than she projected at the beginning of the month. Her parents reviewed the options with her, and they decided together she would put an additional $50 towards her Rainy Day Fund amount. And since she had done such a great job keeping her expenses in line with her spending plan, her parents agreed she could decide what to do with the additional $48. Giving consideration to future expenses, she put the remaining $48 into her savings account.

. . . .

Rule Three

Teens agree to take on no harmful or illegal expenditures.

. . . .

Recently, I read a disconcerting survey. "More than half (52%) of teens are at risk for substance abuse if they have any one of three risk factors: stress, frequent boredom or too much spending money, according to a study from the National Center on Addiction and Substance Abuse (CASA) at Columbia University." The poll of 1,987 teens ages 12 to 17 finds that teens with $50 a week in spending money are much more likely to have tried cigarettes, alcohol or marijuana than those with $15 a week. The author suggests that the risks run throughout "mainstream America," not just among the poor.

How do we deal with "excess" spending money and the risk of substance abuse? Is it enough to simply tell our teens that they can't spend money on anything harmful or illegal?

The author of the study reinforces my premise, "What parents say does *not* fall on deaf ears. Children listen." He says, "The bottom line for parents is to stay involved in your teen's life…" The author suggests engaging in frequent conversations with your children on these issues. Appropriate discipline measures need to be agreed on and used. For our purposes it's enough to keep in mind that if you've done your spending plan carefully, your teen won't have discretionary money to squander on illegal substances.

The Real-Life Money Game provides three safety nets: spending money is limited to the agreed upon expenses; teens are held accountable each month; and *spending money stops if rule three is violated.*

Two months from Michael's sixteenth birthday, when still a sophomore in high school, he said something that reinforced my certainty that he understood this rule. Over the years in which he'd developed money-management skills, he'd done a remarkable job of achieving his long-term savings goal to buy a car. As the time approached to buy the car, he picked out expensive wheels, an additional cost to him. I asked him, pointedly, "Are you sure this is how you want to spend your savings?" He said, "Mom, at least I'm not spending money on drugs." I tried to take some consolation in his being straightforward. Bottom line, the purchase of the wheels fit within the parameters of his spending plan. He'd established and achieved his long-term savings goal. Even if the wheels were something he *wanted* rather than *needed*, the fact remained that he'd played by the rules of the game. And for that, he felt he should be rewarded.

Rule Four

Teens agree that all debit or credit card Internet purchases require parental approval.

I love the Internet for research, shopping, information. But one-finger shopping can prove a powerful temptation for many teens. Parents often tell me they want their son or daughter to use the Internet as a resource, but they also want the process to be safe.

Even if you are not computer savvy, your teen most likely is. He or she has access at the library, at school, at friends' houses. It's important to talk with your teen, honestly, about the potential hazards associated with using the Internet to buy things. Rule number four helps ensure that sensitive personal information is not given out over the Internet without your permission.

In the sidebar, I have summarized the most common ways your teen can use the Internet as a safe resource. Share with your son or daughter these acceptable guidelines. Talk to your teen about why it's important to follow rule four. Many illegal items can be purchased over the Internet without teens necessarily understanding that they are illegal. And with the proliferation of identity theft, now more than ever, you need to establish Internet safeguards with your teen.

> ### Using the Internet as a Resource
>
> - Investigate prices to comparison shop.
> - Design WEB sites for teen business.
> - Sell on eBay.
> - Give to charities.
> - Research investments.
> - Use for tax estimates and information.

Rule Five

You and your teen agree in advance on what sanctions will be applied if the game is not played according to the instructions and the rules.

Families have different needs. It's important to talk with your son or daughter, and decide in advance what happens if your teen doesn't follow *The Real-Life* Money Game instructions or the rules. I suggest that you write out a contract, promising compliance and spelling out the consequences. All parties involved in the agreement should sign it.

Playing the Game: *The Real-Life* Money Game Contract

To help promote compliance, *The Real-Life* Money Game provides you with a very simple, general contract shown on the following page. The contract calls for you and your teen to review and agree that you understand all the instructions and will abide by the rules of the game. For the contract to have any meaning, everyone involved in the agreement should sign it.

A word about contracts. At first I was hesitant to use contracts. They seemed too formal and contrived. But I can tell you honestly that from my experience teaching my son *real-life* skills, contracts work like magic! When it comes to money, expect fuzzy memories to lead to arguments. To avoid misunderstandings, I use contracts for all important "agreements" with my son, especially if they extend over a long period of time. Contracts are a part of the *real* financial world. By signing a contract, teens have an opportunity to learn how to commit to an agreement.

I encourage you to prepare subcontracts in addition to *The Real-Life* Money Game's general contract. The following subcontracts have proven effective with my son to stop arguments. We have a subcontract that identifies what contributions Michael will make to the household tasks and chores without payment. We have a subcontract for the amount we agree to pay towards the purchase of his car when he turns sixteen. The contract includes the down-payment he is responsible to contribute as well as his payment for any additional options he wishes to add to his car.

The Real-Life Money Game Contract
Family Member Player _____
From _____ **To** _____

General Contract

The foregoing family members agree to play *The Real-Life* Money Game in accordance with the instructions and the rules. If any rules are broken or instructions not followed, these specified sanctions will be applied:

_____

_____

_____

Subcontract

The family members further agree to the special terms listed below:

_____

_____

Signed: _____ _____ _____

Date: _____ _____ _____

A blank copy of this worksheet is provided for your use in the appendix on page 306.

We even have a subcontract for Michael's agreement to wear his headgear for the required six months. When he was twelve, he proved to be somewhat lazy about wearing his retainer. No amount of prodding, pleading, or insisting from his parents changed the situation. By the time he turned fourteen, he never received the benefit from his retainer, nor did we with the cost of the mouthpiece and the trips to and from the orthodontist.

Reality hit when we learned that he had to wear headgear at night, and for even more money than the retainer. I wasn't sure if he had matured enough to handle the commitment, so I put it in writing. He signed and agreed to the following: If he was not able to follow through with his commitment to wear the headgear, he would need to pay the expense back out of his car fund. To this day, I am convinced it was the subcontract that helped him comply.

Sam Sanchez worked out this agreement with his daughter, Maria, when she started driving the second-hand car. They agreed in advance that if Maria broke the rules, Sam would take the car away. To make certain that was a real negotiating chip, Sam kept the car title in his name. Suffice it to say, by Sam using the car as collateral, Maria was very careful to stay within the agreement.

The Golden Rule For Parents

Silence is golden. Or rather, as Lewis Carroll is quoted as saying, "Where one is hopelessly undecided as to what to say, there silence is golden."

Silence, I've discovered, is one of the most effective, rewarding, and even surprising tools available in our parenting toolbox. Following the "Golden Rule" means practicing *hands-off* parenting. Parents have to sometimes sit back, observe, make mental notes, and listen actively to their teens—without judgment or interference—until month's end. At this time, the results can be discussed openly and questions asked. How did you do with your spending plan? Did you save receipts? Did you remember to reconcile accounts? I encourage you to use *The Real-Life* Money Game Plan worksheet, discussed in the next chapter, to write down notes.

Sometimes, though, our son or daughter will ask for our input. While silence is the important point of the Golden Rule For Parents, I've also grown fond of the English author, Samuel Butler's interpretation: "It is tact that is golden, not silence." Tact does not mean telling your teens what they should do, ought to do, or have to do. To do so defeats the goal of helping them learn to think for themselves. Instead, tact means sharing experiences, exchanging information, or suggesting ideas. I continue to make surprising discoveries that reinforce my commitment to following this guideline. When I first started playing the game with Michael, I had the following experience with him when we were shopping at Barnes and Noble.

My son's monthly spending plan includes $20 for book expenses. I let him know that I thought it was a good idea for him to pick up a book he could read over the summer. He lingered in the music section with store headphones on, jiggling his body to a tune only he could hear, while I searched for a book. When I tapped him on the shoulder and suggested *The Hobbit*, he received the idea with a typical teenager brush-off. I wanted Michael to look for summer reading, and he wasn't cooperating. As we proceeded to the check-out counter, he eyed a table filled with magic books. In less than a minute, Michael selected *Magic For Dummies* at $19.99. I said nothing as we paid.

At home, I broke the Golden Rule For Parents. I told Michael that I didn't think that *Magic For Dummies* was appropriate summer reading. He ignored me, and a few days later he sat me down to show me a magic trick.

He placed a quarter on the table. "I'm going to make this quarter disappear through the table," he said, "and I'll use this saltshaker to help me." He held up a rectangular glass saltshaker and carefully wrapped a heavy paper napkin, so it took on the same form and shape and covered it completely. He placed it upright, on top of the quarter and chanted, "Abra cadabra alla kazam, make this quarter disappear, bam! bam! bam!" He lifted the saltshaker off the quarter. The quarter was still there.

"Oops." He looked at me and smiled sheepishly.

He repeated his chant and lifted the saltshaker, but again the quarter was still there. He looked at me bewildered. I felt badly for my son. He had wasted his money. Determined to try again, he placed the covered saltshaker over the quarter on the table and repeated, "Abra cadabra alla kazam, make this quarter disappear, bam! bam!..." and on the last "bam!" he slapped his hand on the covered saltshaker, the napkin flattened completely. I heard a thud; something dropped to the floor. The money was still on the table, but the saltshaker had disappeared!

My mouth hung open like a sea bass. "How'd you do that?"

"The author says that 98% of all saltshakers are designed to not break when they're dropped from a table." My son was referring, of course, to the saltshaker he had just dropped on the floor from who-knows-where he had slipped it. "The other two percent that break," he continued, quoting from the author, "should be thrown out anyway!"

We shared a rare spontaneous moment of joy between a parent and a teen. If I had forced upon Michael my book choice, we would have missed the "magic" of that moment. The book fell within the parameters of his spending plan. He'd remained true to our contract. It was up to me to fulfill my end of the bargain and allow him to make his own choices.

Scorekeeping Box

After discussing The RLMG rules, give your teen point credit using the scorekeeping box below. Add the full score if your teen has successfully completed the activity. Add no score if your teen hasn't. Write down the date of the activity, make note of any discussions, problems or successes, and tally your teen's score. This score will be added to the final score at the end.

Key Concepts	Activity Point Value	Date Activity Completed/Discussion Notes	Point Value Earned
Assist your teen with the following to help him or her earn points:			
• Learn and follow *The Real-Life Money Game Rules*.	5		
• Understand the Golden Rule For Parents.	5		
• Agree to what sanctions or consequences (penalty for noncompliance) might occur if the game is not played according to the instructions and the rules.	10		
• Sign the general contract agreeing to the terms of *The Real-Life Money Game*.	10		
• Agree to one subcontract that requires a long-term commitment.	20		
Total Score	**50**		

Chapter Nine
The Real-Life Money Game Plan

. . . .

The object of *The Real-Life* Money Game is to assist you in transferring control of money to your teen and in helping your son or daughter take more responsibility for his or her own finances. With that goal in mind, I like to remind parents, at this point in my course, that by shifting this responsibility, they gain an opportunity to teach their teens a set of tangible, *hands-on* money-management skills.

> **The object of *The Real-Life* Money Game**
>
> To assist you in transferring control of money to your teen and helping your son or daughter take more responsibility for his or her own finances.

Money-Management Skills	
Tangible Skills	**Intangible Skills**
• Knowing how income is generated, learning how to earn money. • Managing the mechanics of spending, creating a spending plan, and learning how to pay expenses. • Understanding the concept of savings, including setting aside money for unanticipated costs. • Instilling a mind-set for giving. • Understanding borrowing and lending and learning how to use debt wisely. • Learning how to invest. • Understanding taxes.	1. Valuing assets (what they have) 2. Delayed gratification (curbing impulses) 3. Differentiating wants from needs (and understanding the importance of contributing to both) 4. Problem solving 5. Personal responsibility 6. Self-discipline 7. Self-confidence 8. Self-motivation 9. Independent thinking 10. Strong work ethic

Using tangible skills, of course, strengthens intangible skills—behaviors and values—your teen can use for a lifetime. I have recapped both the tangible and intangible skills, shown in the table on the previous page, to assist you in completing *The Real-Life* Money Game Plan.

Playing the Game: *The Real-Life* Money Game Plan

The Real-Life **Money Game Plan**
Family Member Player _____
From _____ **To** _____

1. Identify at least one result/goal or tangible skill you wish to teach your teen.
2. List the steps your son or daughter can follow to accomplish the task.
3. Write down any notes with progress or items to be discussed at the scheduled meeting time.
4. Determine the time frame—the estimated period of time it will take to complete the goal—and write down the start and finish dates at the top of the worksheet.

Identify goal:

Detail tasks to accomplish the goal:

Discussion notes:

A blank copy of this worksheet is provided for your use in the appendix on page 307.

Let's look at the worksheet on the previous page and consider how to complete each step. As the name suggests, the worksheet is designed to help you develop a *game plan*—to define a goal and break it down into concrete, specific, achievable tasks. The worksheet offers a place to list the steps your son or daughter can follow to accomplish the goal, along with space for notes regarding his or her progress.

The first step asks you to select a goal you hope to accomplish by teaching your teen how to play *The Real-Life* Money Game. So how do you select the goal?

Recall that in chapter one*, The Real-Life* Money Game Plan Overview, shown on the following pages, identifies both tangible and intangible skills for each player-level: beginning, intermediate, advanced. As your teen becomes proficient with each tangible skill at each player level, you can select a new tangible skill at a higher level. For each tangible skill at each player-level an associated intangible behavior is identified. *The Real-Life* Money Game Plan Overview offers a guideline to assist you and your teen in identifying your goals over time.

The next step is to break the goal down into *specific* achievable tasks—small steps your teen can follow to accomplish the goal. For hints, refer to the chapter that relates to the tangible skill you are trying to teach. Each chapter provides tools to help your teen develop the tangible skill. Write down the tool and the specific steps that relate to it. Check each chapter's scorekeeping box, which lists the activities your teen can do to practice each skill-building concept.

Step three provides a place for you to jot down any observations you make as your teen attempts to accomplish the goal. You can discuss these notes at the regularly scheduled monthly meeting time.

Step four suggests deciding on a reasonable time frame to accomplish the goal. Time frames act as deadlines, and deadlines, in my experience, are necessary to keep your teen on task. You can assist your teen by identifying when a specific task can be accomplished. Discuss the times with your teen and allow his or her needs to influence your choice. Then, remember to follow-up regularly on your son or daughter's progress. Modify the plan if necessary.

The Real-Life Money Game Plan Overview:
Tangible Skills

	Beginning Player	Intermediate Player	Advanced Player
Earning	Gets paid for household tasks or chores.	Lands a job.	Starts a "Teen Business."
Spending	Uses "Cash Pockets" or Savings & ATM to distribute spending-plan funds.	Uses checking & debit card account to distribute spending-plan funds.	Uses investment account to distribute spending-plan funds.
Saving	Establishes one short-term savings target for "Now."	Establishes one long-term savings target for "Later."	Puts aside a fixed percent of monthly income for "Never."
Giving	Considers what cause or organization matters most.	Chooses one cause or organization to contribute to on a regular basis.	Chooses one cause or organization to contribute to or volunteer for on a regular basis.
Borrowing/ Lending	Understands and follows all debt rules.	Borrows and lends responsibly following established guidelines.	Has one major credit card used for emergencies, borrows from one lending institution, and requests and understands a credit report.
Investing	Earmarks money to be matched for investing.	Invests with an investment institution.	Invests on own using Internet research and books or sets up an IRA or Roth IRA account.
Taxes	Aware taxes exist.	Calculates tax expense.	Prepares own tax return.

The Real-Life Money Game Plan Overview: Intangible Skills

Beginning Player	Intermediate Player	Advanced Player
1. Valuing assets (what they have)	4. Problem solving	8. Self-motivation
2. Delayed gratification (curbing impulses)	5. Personal responsibility	9. Independent thinking
3. Differentiating wants from needs (and understanding the importance of contributing to both)	6. Self-discipline	10. Strong work ethic
	7. Self-confidence	

The Real-Life Money Game Plan worksheet can be completed monthly, quarterly, or when the need arises. The main thing is to be consistent. Establish a pattern. If you choose to revisit the plan on a monthly basis, choose the same approximate day and time each month to complete the worksheet, and to follow up on the results. The purpose of the worksheet is to prompt financial discussions with your teen on an ongoing basis. In our household, for example, we usually talk just before the end of the month on a late Sunday afternoon, the time when my son settles down to do homework.

Let's see how the Wilsons used *The Real-Life* Money Game Plan worksheet shown on the following page to address their daughter Karen's specific needs. Shortly before Karen's sixteenth birthday, she expressed to her parents that she wanted to buy a car. The Wilsons were reluctant. Their daughter's only source of earnings was an occasional babysitting job and one or two paid household chores. They were concerned she wouldn't have enough money to contribute toward the cost of purchasing and operating a car. At the same time, however, the Wilsons wanted Karen to learn how to earn money, so she could make a contribution toward her wants and needs. The Wilsons agreed to help Karen buy a car if their daughter would agree to find a summer job.

The Real-Life **Money Game Plan**
Family Member Player _____*Karen Wilson*_____
From ___*July 1*___ **To** _*August 31*_

1. Identify at least one result/goal or tangible skill you wish to teach your teen.
2. List the steps your son or daughter can follow to accomplish the task.
3. Write down any notes with progress or items to be discussed at the scheduled meeting time.
4. Determine the time frame—the estimated period of time it will take to complete the goal—and write down the start and finish dates at the top of the worksheet.

Identify goal:

• Get a summer job and earn money to make a contribution towards the purchase of a car.

Detail tasks to accomplish the goal:

• Project how much will be needed in earnings to contribute toward a car down payment and gas, maintenance, and insurance.
• Complete the Activities Pie-Chart to determine available summer hours to earn money.
• Put together a weekly summer schedule with available hours, blocking out vacation weeks.
• Go through "Teen Jobs: Select, Land, Keep" bulleted list to find a summer job.

Discussion notes:

• Called local pool to inquire about a lifeguard job.
• Scheduled swim test needed before hiring.
• Called pool manager to set up an interview.

A blank copy of this worksheet is provided for your use in the appendix on page 307.

Karen was hesitant. She'd never held a job before. She told her parents she didn't know how. From previous experience, Connie Wilson knew her daughter tended to be fearful of new situations. So the Wilsons completed *The Real-Life* Money Game Plan worksheet to break the goal down into easy steps. In this way, they hoped to minimize their daughter's fear.

The Wilsons helped Karen complete the Activities Pie-Chart from chapter four, so she could assess how much time she had available to work. Then they helped Karen put together a summer calendar from July 1 through August 31. They had family vacation scheduled, so as part of the plan, Karen needed to mark out the dates she would not be available to work. They also went through each step of the "Teen Jobs: Select, Land, and Keep" list from chapter four to help her begin her summer job-search. They agreed to follow up on *The Real-Life* Money Game Plan at the end of two weeks.

Connie reported that after filling out *The Real-Life* Money Game Plan, Karen actually accomplished several specific tasks toward her goal. At the end of two weeks, Karen had inquired about a lifeguard job at her local pool, had scheduled to take the required swim test to qualify for the job, and had talked with the pool manager to schedule an interview.

Here is how I used *The Real-Life* Money Game Plan worksheet shown on the following page to teach my son how to manage his spending on clothes. Because Michael had experience managing a resource, he was eager and ready to try his hand at a clothes fund. Together, we went through the steps needed to accomplish his goal. He completed the Estimated Projected Clothes Expense worksheet from chapter five. He priced out clothes both on the Internet and at two retail shops in the mall before we deposited the money from his Playing Board-Spending Plan into his checking account. He found, for example, polo-style golf shirts priced between $25 and $60. I reminded him that this clothing fund needed to last for four months.

From the get-go, Michael purchased his clothes from an expensive clothing store. He discovered that in doing so, he was only able to buy one shirt instead of three. We agreed that the number of items listed were only an estimate, and that what he actually ended up with should be based on his discretion. He started paying close attention to how much things cost, and to where he might find bargain clothing sales.

Michael continues to manage his clothing fund, now, twice yearly. He completes a Estimated Projected Clothes Expense worksheet, one for winter and one for summer. Only once did we prepare *The Real-Life* Money Game Plan worksheet for managing his clothes fund. After that he knew what steps to follow to achieve his goal.

The Real-Life Money Game Plan
Family Member Player ___*Michael Williamson*___
From _*September 1*_ To _*December 31*_

1. Identify at least one result/goal or tangible skill you wish to teach your teen.
2. List the steps your son or daughter can follow to accomplish the task.
3. Write down any notes with progress or items to be discussed at the scheduled meeting time.
4. Determine the time frame—the estimated period of time it will take to complete the goal—and write down the start and finish dates at the top of the worksheet.

Identify goal:

• Buy own clothes for fall, first year of high school.

Detail tasks to accomplish the goal:

• Clean closet and set aside clothes too small or too worn.
• Determine how much of each clothing item needed for the season.
• Complete Estimated Projected Clothes Expense worksheet.
• Look in catalogs and on the Internet for estimate of cost for each item.
• Decide what period of time the clothes fund covers.
• Keep all purchase receipts and clothing tags in a clear sheet protector in case something needs to be returned.

Discussion notes:

• Checked out sales at two retail stores in mall.
• Agreed to time frame.
• Deposited projected funds for clothes into checking account based on projected worksheet.

A blank copy of this worksheet is provided for your use in the appendix on page 307.

Here's what *The Real-Life* Money Game Plan worksheet looked like for the Sanchez family. At the beginning of the school year, Sam wanted Maria to think about how she would pay for her Winter Ball dress. The previous year, Sam was unprepared for the request of additional money from his daughter to fund her outfit for the event. He decided to use the opportunity to teach his daughter how to project and save for her outfit before this year's event arrived.

The Real-Life Money Game Plan
Family Member Player _____*Maria Sanchez*_____
From *September 1* **To** *December 31*

1. Identify at least one result/goal or tangible skill you wish to teach your teen.
2. List the steps your son or daughter can follow to accomplish the task.
3. Write down any notes with progress or items to be discussed at the scheduled meeting time.
4. Determine the time frame—the estimated period of time it will take to complete the goal—and write down the start and finish dates at the top of the worksheet.

Identify goal:

• Spend within savings limits over a period of time to buy a Winter Ball dress.

Detail tasks to accomplish the goal:

• Project amounts needed for Winter Ball dress.
• Match funds up to $40. Beyond that, any shortfall comes from savings.

Discussion notes:

• Spent double the allotted amount on Winter Ball dress. Made up the difference by shorting lunches and extras and not buying coffee and snacks for friends.

A blank copy of this worksheet is provided for your use in the appendix on page 307.

I can't emphasize enough how important it is to establish a tangible, skill-building goal. Over time, as you offer your son or daughter money-management tools, they become more confident and responsible. But the best part is, they're far less prone to blaming you when they don't get what they want.

Remember, they are just learning how to use the tools available to them. Don't be afraid to talk about their progress. Ask questions. Have the necessary steps been completed to accomplish the goal? Has the entire goal been accomplished? If not, why not? Change the time frame if it makes sense. But don't lose sight of the tangible skill you wish your teen to develop, ultimately.

We've looked at several families' plans used to address their specific needs. The Wilsons developed a plan to help their daughter overcome her fear of getting a job, so she could earn money to buy a car. My son's plan helped him manage his spending on clothes and shoes. Sam Sanchez helped his daughter, Maria, project a savings goal and manage her spending over a longer block of time than she'd been accustomed to.

• • •

The Real-Life Money Game Plan, together with the Family Fund Contribution, create a flexible, scalable plan designed to accommodate you and your teen's changing needs. Next, as part of managing their resource, your son or daughter needs to learn how to track his or her monthly activity. Your teen will do this by completing column two of the Playing Board-Spending Plan.

Scorekeeping Box

After looking over the Money-Managment Skills list, reviewing *The Real-Life* Money Game Plan Overview, and completing *The Real-Life* Money Game Plan worksheet, give your teen point credit using the scorekeeping box below. Add the full score if your teen has successfully completed the activity. Add no score if your teen hasn't. Write down the date of the activity, make note of any discussions, problems or successes, and tally your teen's score. This score will be added to the final score at the end.

Key Concepts	Activity Point Value	Date Activity Completed/Discussion Notes	Point Value Earned
Assist your teen with the following to help him or her earn points:			
• Agree on one general money-management skill-building goal.	5		
• Review the specific steps to accomplish the goal.	10		
• Discuss progress. If making progress toward the goal, continue following the detailed steps. If not, agree to modify the plan based on the initial efforts to achieve the goal.	20		
Total Score	**35**		

Chapter Ten

Tracking *The Real-Life* Money Game Monthly Activity

• •

At this point in *The Real-Life* Money Game, your son or daughter has a fund of money to manage, and together you have chosen a spending option he or she will use to distribute the funds. Your teen has recorded projected income on his or her Playing Board-Spending Plan under the first column heading, "Income amounts I have projected at the beginning of the month." Under the column, "What I expect it to cost," your teen has also recorded his or her projected expenses for the month. It's now time to track *actual* income received and *actual* expenses paid out. The *actual* amounts will be compared to the projections to find out where mistakes have been made and to better prepare for upcoming months. Don't worry. It may sound like work, but this is really when the fun comes in. You will now be shown how to compare what you expected your teen to earn and spend with what actually happened.

When I first introduced you to the Playing Board-Spending Plan, I explained that this is the place where all the financial activity happens. Plainly put, the goal of the Playing Board-Spending Plan is to summarize your teen's financial activity each month in a manner that makes it easy to access and use.

Let's look at how your teen tracks his or her actual monthly income and expense activity to come up with the information that will be recorded in column two of the Playing Board-Spending Plan.

Playing The Game: The Playing Board-Spending Plan (Column 2)

• •

Income Worksheet

1. Track income by filling in amounts actually received throughout the month on the Income Worksheet provided in the appendix on page 299.

2. Transfer the totals from the Income Worksheet to the Playing Board-Spending Plan, provided in the appendix on page 305, under column two labeled, "What I actually received during the month." Add up column-two income categories and put the total in the space provided for "Total Income."

• •

Income Worksheet

Family Member Player _Karen Wilson_ **Month:** _October_

Date	Coins	Gifts	Earnings: Chores, Job, "Teen Business"	Allowance	Family Fund Contribution (Includes Rainy-Day Fund)	Savings & Investment	Savings & Investments Matched Funds	Borrowed Funds	Other Income	Week's Income
Week 1			Chores Cleaned Pool 10	10	115					135
Week 2			Chores Vacuum 10	10						20
Week 3			Baby-Sitting 25	10						35
Week 4			Baby-Sitting 100	10						110
Total Income			145	40	115					300

A blank copy of this worksheet is provided for your use in the appendix on page 299.

Recording income as it is received is an important skill teens need to learn. Generally, teens are not accustomed to keeping track of money once they get their hands on it. If my son is any example, he forgets when he received it, why he received it, and how much he received. And, too, he never knows where to put it.

The Income Worksheet provides a place for your teen to record income as it's received. The worksheet can be kept in your son or daughter's personal financial binder, along with the cash or checks accumulated, until such time as the money can be divided into cash pockets to pay for expenses, or to be deposited in a savings, a checking with debit card, or an investment account.

Let's look at how the Wilson's daughter, Karen, recorded the income she actually received throughout October on her Income Worksheet shown on the previous page.

At the beginning of October, the Wilsons helped Karen open her first checking account to deposit the first installment of her $115 Family Fund Contribution. Karen's parents were particularly interested in teaching her how to use this checking account, since she would be heading off to college in little over a year. October would be the first month Karen would account for her funds.

Each week her parents helped her record amounts on her Income Worksheet as she received her earnings for babysitting and household chores and her allowance. Karen's total recorded income for October came to $300. She kept this ongoing Income Worksheet in her binder under the index tab labeled for October, along with the cash and checks she inserted into a clear sheet protector. At month's end Karen deposited the money she received in October, along with the November Family Fund Contribution of $115 given to her by her parents, into her checking account.

On her Playing Board-Spending Plan, shown on the following page, in column two under the heading, "What I actually received during the month," Karen transferred $145 from both her babysitting and household chores, $40 in allowance, and $115 from the Family Fund Contribution which included the $30 Rainy-Day Fund. All very neat and simple. Her resource on hand had been accounted for.

The Real-Life Money Game Playing Board-Spending Plan

Family Member Player _____*Karen Wilson*_____ **Month:** *October*

Income	Income amounts I have projected at the beginning of the month	What I actually received during the month	Difference between income I project in column one with the actual amount received in column two
• Coins			
• Gifts	20		
• Earnings	80	145	
• Allowance	40	40	
• Family Fund Contribution	85	85	
• Savings & Investment Income			
• Investments: Matched Funds			
• Borrowed Funds			
• Rainy-Day Fund	30	30	
• Other			
Total Income	**255**	**300**	

Expenses	What I expect it to cost	What it actually costs	Difference between expected cost in column one with the actual cost in column two
• Food & Eating Out			
• Car Expense	50		
• Transportation			
• Entertainment	45		
• Books, Music, Movies	20		
• School Expense			
• Clothes & Accessories	55		
• Toiletries & Haircuts	30		
• Gifts Given	25		
• Rainy-Day Fund	30		
• Other			
Total Expenses	**255**		
Total Income Minus Total Expenses	**0**		

A blank copy of this worksheet is provided for your use in the appendix on page 305.

Now we'll do the same thing for expenses.

Expense Worksheet

1. At month's end, track expenses by summarizing actual amounts paid and record these totals on the Expense Worksheet provided in the appendix on page 301.

2. Transfer each category of expense from the Expense Worksheet to the Playing Board-Spending Plan, provided on page 305, under the column two heading, "What it actually costs."

3. Record any money set aside for a Rainy-Day Fund in the space provided in column two.

4. Add up column-two expense categories and put the total in the space provided for Total Expenses. Subtract Total Expenses from Total Income and put the result in the box for "Total Income Minus Total Expenses."

During the month, your son or daughter will pay expenses that vary from what they projected. Just now, don't worry about that difference. Simply record actual money spent on an Expense Worksheet labeled for the current month.

If your son or daughter uses cash pockets to pay expenses, they will need to record how much cash they have removed from each pocket during the month. To do this, they simply subtract what's left in each pocket from the amount set aside for that expense item at the beginning of the month. The difference will then be recorded on the Expense Worksheet.

If your teen pays expenses using a savings account with an ATM card, fill out the Expense Worksheet with figures based on the receipts kept throughout the month. If your teen loses receipts, estimate the expense and include any unaccounted-for amounts under "Other."

If your son or daughter pays expenses by writing checks or using a debit card, they will receive a bank statement. At month's end your teen needs to reconcile his or her check register with the bank statement using *The Real-Life Money Game Bank Reconciliation Worksheet* from chapter six. Itemized debits on the statement will reflect actual expenses for that month. Use the figures on the statement to fill in the Expense Worksheet.

Expense Worksheet

Family Member Player _Karen Wilson_ **Month:** _October_

Date	Food & Eating Out	Car Expense	Trans-portation	Enter-tainment	Books, Music, Movies	School Expense	Clothes & Accessories	Toiletries & Haircuts	Gifts Given to Family or Friends	Estimated Projected Expenses	Other Expenses	Week's Expenses
Week 1		Gas 10			CD 20		Earrings 25					55
Week 2		Gas 10			Book 17							27
Week 3		Gas 10		Movie 15								25
Week 4		Gas 10		Movie 15				Haircut 40				65
Total Expense		40		30	37		25	40				172
Total Expense Teen Pays												

A blank copy of this worksheet is provided for your use in the appendix on page 301.

Paying expenses with an investment account works the same as a checking and debit card account. The expense information comes directly off the reconciled investment statement and should be transferred to the Expense Worksheet.

Karen Wilson summarized the expenses she actually paid during October on her Expense Worksheet shown on the previous page. In her case, the information came from a reconciled checking-account statement. That done, it was time for Karen to transfer her October information to her Playing Board-Spending Plan under column two.

The expenses Karen paid in October came to $172. On Karen's Playing Board-Spending Plan, shown on the following page, the Wilsons helped her record $40 for Car Expense, $30 for Entertainment, $37 for Books, Music & Movies, $25 for Clothes & Accessories, $40 for Toiletries & Haircuts, and no expense amount for Gifts in column two under the heading, "What it actually costs."

Having completed her Playing Board-Spending Plan for actual income and expenses, it was time for Karen to compare her actual amounts with her projected amounts.

Projected Versus Actual (Column 3)

1. Compute the difference between column one and column two and record the amounts, including the totals, in column three.

As you'll see, the income Karen actually received during the month of October was not the same as the income she'd projected on her Playing Board-Spending Plan at the beginning of the month. Karen had projected a total income in column one of $255. Though she didn't receive a gift in October, she did earn more money babysitting than she guessed she would. Karen generated $45 more income than she projected.

Next, Karen compared her expenses. She actually paid out $172 plus the Rainy-Day Fund of $30, for a total of $202. Those were her actual expenses and set-aside for October. As you'll see, they were not the same as the $225 in expenses she'd projected. Though she spent more for Books, Music, & Movies, and Haircuts & Toiletries in October, she spent less on Car, Entertainment, and Gifts than anticipated. She spent $53 less than she'd projected. When Karen subtracts her *actual* expenses, which include the Rainy-Day Fund, from her

The Real-Life Money Game Playing Board-Spending Plan
Family Member Player _____ *Karen Wilson* _____ **Month:** _October_

Income	Income amounts I have projected at the beginning of the month	What I actually received during the month	Difference between income I project in column one with the actual amount received in column two
• Coins			
• Gifts	20		(20)
• Earnings	80	145	65
• Allowance	40	40	0
• Family Fund Contribution	85	85	0
• Savings & Investment Income			
• Investments: Matched Funds			
• Borrowed Funds			
• Rainy-Day Fund	30	30	0
• Other			
Total Income	**255**	**300**	**45**

Expenses	What I expect it to cost	What it actually costs	Difference between expected cost in column one with the actual cost in column two
• Food & Eating Out			
• Car Expense	50	40	10
• Transportation			
• Entertainment	45	30	15
• Books, Music, Movies	20	37	(17)
• School Expense			
• Clothes & Accessories	55	25	30
• Toiletries & Haircuts	30	40	(10)
• Gifts Given	25		25
• Rainy-Day Fund	30	30	0
• Other			
Total Expenses	**255**	**202**	**53**
Total Income Minus Total Expenses	**0**	**98**	**98**

A blank copy of this worksheet is provided for your use in the appendix on page 305.

actual income, the difference is $98. What this boils down to is that she had $98 more at the end of October than she'd projected at the beginning of the month.

Phew! We're done! At least with the number-crunching. Does completing the Playing Board-Spending Plan seem daunting? If it seems so, remember: This is a learning process. If my experience with my son is a fair measure, with a few months of practice, the process will become second nature.

In these beginning months, your son or daughter may make mistakes filling out the worksheet. Numbers may get erased or scratched out or written over. Columns may not be totaled accurately, figures may get transposed. The worksheet may not *balance* as it's designed to. Okay. This is how your teen learns. But I cannot emphasize this point enough—teaching your son or daughter to come up with a visual summary of their monthly financial activity is key. This is the single tool, bar none, most guaranteed to teach them the financial management skills they'll need to not only survive, but to become independent explorers in the money wilderness beyond the family home. Remember that alarming statistic from chapter one? Eighty-five percent of the teen population graduates into adulthood minus even basic resource management skills from high school.

So, we have the numbers. Now what? How exactly does your teen use the information on the Playing Board-Spending Plan to make financial decisions?

They have options. These options include reducing expenses, setting aside money for long-term savings' goals, giving to charity, paying off loans or lending out money, increasing investments, or even paying estimated taxes due. These additional options are explained in complete detail, next, in part two.

My son, who is seventeen at the time of this writing, has been playing *The Real-Life* Money Game since he was twelve. He set aside on his Playing Board-Spending Plan $15 each month for charitable giving and $150 in savings for a car. Any excess funds over and above his projected amounts were transferred to his investment account, for which I provided matching funds. Here is what his filled-in Playing Board-Spending Plan looked like for January.

In column one under "Income amounts I have projected at the beginning of the month," Michael received a $15-weekly allowance which I paid him in cash every Thursday. In *The Real-Life* Money Game, this represents a minimum amount of cash I wanted him to have on hand. At month-end, column two summarizes his actual results.

The Real-Life Money Game Playing Board-Spending Plan
Family Member Player **_Michael Williamson_** **Month:** **_January_**

Income	Income amounts I have projected at the beginning of the month	What I actually received during the month	Difference between income I project in column one with the actual amount received in column two
• Coins			
• Gifts		From grandparents 100	100
• Earnings	Office party cleanup 100	Office party cleanup 125	25
• Allowance	$15/week 60	$15/week 60	0
• Family Fund Contribution	475	475	0
• Savings & Investment Income			
• Investments: Matched Funds			
• Borrowed Funds			
• Rainy-Day Fund			
• Other			
Total Income	**635**	**760**	**125**

Expenses	What I expect it to cost	What it actually costs	Difference between expected cost in column one with the actual cost in column two
• Food & Eating Out	210	95	115
• Car Expense	Car downpayment 150	Car downpayment 150	0
• Transportation	15	0	15
• Entertainment	40	129	(89)
• Books, Music, Movies	25	0	25
• School Expense	15	0	15
• Clothes & Accessories	150	187	(37)
• Toiletries & Haircuts	15	20	(5)
• Gifts Given			
• Rainy-Day Fund			
• Other	Charity 15	Charity 15	0
Total Expenses	**635**	**596**	**39**
Total Income Minus Total Expenses	**0**	**164**	**164**

A blank copy of this worksheet is provided for your use in the appendix on page 305.

After reviewing Michael's Playing Board-Spending Plan results for the month of January, we talked about why he had more in "Entertainment" expense than he projected. Michael realized that he had gone to a movie almost every weekend with his friends that month. We were both comfortable with his explanation and the amount he spent, however, he and I agreed to leave his following month's "Entertainment" expense at $40. It's important to discuss with your teen any major variation in the Playing Board-Spending Plan projected numbers over the actual numbers.

Michael's *actual* total income minus his total expenses exceeded his *projected* total income minus his total expenses by $164 as computed in column three. He and I discussed how he might want to use his excess funds of $164. Michael knew he had some discretionary money. The question was simply whether to spend it, to let it accumulate in order to pay later month's expenses, or to set the excess aside for his next month's Rainy-Day Fund. The key was for him to make the choice, without my looking over his shoulder. He decided to let the money accumulate to pay for a more expensive pair of shoes than he'd originally projected on his Playing Board-Spending Plan.

• • •

Let's sum up where we are. You have introduced your teen to the first two tangible skills, generating income and managing spending. These two skills provide the foundation for your son or daughter's scalable plan. They now have a tool in the form of the Playing Board-Spending Plan that will help them practice these skills until they become second nature. In part two, we'll go into detail to develop additional tangible skills such as saving, giving, borrowing and lending, investing and taxes.

Scorekeeping Box

After helping your teen transfer his or her *actual* Income and Expense Worksheet information to the Playing Board-Spending Plan in column two, and after computing the difference in column three, give your teen point credit using the scorekeeping box on the following page. Add the full score if your teen has successfully completed the activity. Add no score if your teen hasn't. Write down the date of the activity, make note of any discussions, problems or successes, and tally your teen's score. This score will be added to the final score at the end.

Key Concepts	Activity Point Value	Date Activity Completed/Discussion Notes	Point Value Earned
Assist your teen with the following to help him or her earn points:			
• Transfer the information from the Income Worksheet onto the Playing Board-Spending Plan in column two under the heading "What I actually received during the month."	5		
• Transfer the information from the Expense Worksheet onto the Playing Board-Spending Plan column two under the heading "What it actually costs."	5		
• Record any Rainy-Day Fund amount in column two on the Playing Board-Spending Plan.	10		
• Add up column two income and fill in the total. Add up column two expenses and fill in the total. Calculate Total Income minus Total Expenses and fill in the amount on the Playing Board-Spending Plan in column two.	10		
• Compute the difference between column one and column two and record the amounts including the totals in column three.	20		
Total Score	**50**		

Part Two

Resource Management—From Home to the Bank and the IRS

· ·

Part two covers the more complex money-management concepts you may want to use, once you and your teen have established a fund to practice managing the mechanics of spending. The Real-Life Money Game explains the value of tangible money-management skills, such as saving, giving, borrowing or lending, investing, and taxes, as well as offering skill-building tools your teen can use to practice. Again, you'll be encouraged to continue gauging your teen's progress by using the scorekeeping boxes.

Chapter Eleven
Saving: Playing It Safe

The Wilsons long had a rule about savings: Once the money goes in, it never comes out. Karen, their oldest daughter, practiced this rule to perfection. From the time she could baby-sit, most of what she earned she put into her savings. Connie Wilson reported that her daughter had saved a lot of money, close to $1,000. When Karen's parents told her she would need to start using some of these savings to pay for car expenses, Karen complained resentfully. She was reluctant to spend her hard-earned savings.

Casey, their middle daughter, knows this rule as well as her older sister. Casey never saves a penny. She knows, once the money goes in, she'll never get it back. That's her perception anyway. Casey spends all the money she gets.

Nothing illustrates this age-old savings dilemma better than the Wilsons' experience. As parents, we know that the notion of savings means you don't spend all the money you get, all at one time. We know the money is set aside for a reason, that it's still intact, and that it will be available when it's needed. But teaching our teens that savings come back and are *set aside* for a *specific purpose* is harder to do than it seems.

So how do we teach our teens to both save and use their money at the same time?

> ### Why Teach Teens About Savings?
>
> - Because we were told to save growing up.
> - So they won't spend everything they get.
> - So they can earn interest on their money.
> - To help them distinguish simple from compound interest.
> - To pay for anticipated expenses.
> - To pay for unplanned expenditures and emergencies.
> - For "big-ticket" items such as clothes, summer camp, a cell phone, computer, or a car, they'd be hard-pressed to pay for all at once.
> - For college.
> - For investing.
> - To fund a home, business, or retirement.

Before I answer this question, I've learned that it's important for parents, myself included, to think about why we want our teens to save. Do we want our teens to save because we were told to save while we were growing up? Do we want our teens to save so they won't spend everything they get? Do we want our sons and daughters to save to pay for anticipated future expenses? Or for unplanned expenditures and emergencies?

Do we want our teens to save for "big-ticket" items such as clothes, summer camp, a cell phone, computer, or a car; items they'd be hard-pressed to pay for all at once? Or maybe the bottom line for you is simply this: because it seems virtuous to save, you want them to do it as an end in itself.

These are all legitimate motivations to prompt our teens to save. But before we can teach them the tangible skill, we need to communicate clearly why it matters. If we explore our reasoning and discuss it with our sons and daughters, we have a better chance of promoting effective savings habits in our teens.

Right now, take a minute to answer the following savings questionnaire.

Savings Questionnaire
Family Member Player _____

1. Why do you want your son or daughter to save?

2. How much, on average each month, would you like your teen to save?

3. How would you like your son or daughter to use his or her savings and when?

4. Choose one thing you would like your teen to be responsible to save for that might require up to six months? One to five years? More than five years?

A blank copy of this worksheet is provided for your use in the appendix on page 308.

The Real-Life Money Game
Three-Part Savings Plan: Now, Later, Never

Saving For Now:

- Encourages your teen to put aside a fixed amount of money.
- To be used for something that really matters to him or her.
- Rewards the effort by gratifying your teen's shorter-term, more immediate want or need.

Saving For Later:

- Encourages your teen to put aside a fixed amount of money.
- To be used for a longer-term "big-ticket" need.
- Delays gratification until later, while teaching the principles of compounding interest.
- Gets your teen in the regular "habit" of saving a predetermined amount of money.
- Rewards the effort with parent contributions.
- Ultimately, gratifies the longer-term need or want, and builds confidence by achieving the goal.

Saving For (What Seems Like) Never:

- Encourages your teen to regularly put aside money at a young age that will provide a fund he or she can grow over time.
- Teaches the principles of compounding.
- Gets your teen in the regular "habit" of saving a certain percentage of all money they receive.
- Promotes college financing.
- Provides a resource to help teach the basics of investing.
- Funds the purchase of a home, a business, or provides for retirement.
- Rewards the effort by ensuring a substantial sum of money by a certain age.

Having completed the questionnaire, now you have an idea of what's important to convey to your teen about saving money. Additionally, the questionnaire gathers information you can use to help your teen complete a savings-tool worksheet called *"The Real-Life* Money Game Three-Part Savings Plan: Now, Later, Never" shown on the following page.

The worksheet is designed to help your son or daughter learn how much savings to put aside, for what, and when to use it. By combining three savings targets for now, for later, and for (what seems like) never, your teen can learn to save for a specific purpose while at the same time feeling confident that the money will come back!

Playing the Game: *The Real-Life* Money Game Three-Part Savings Plan: Now, Later, Never

Let's see how the three-part savings plan works.

The Real-Life Money Game Three-Part Savings Plan: Now, Later, Never Family Member Player _____				
For When	**For What**	**Total Cost**	**Fixed Monthly Amount**	**Where: At What Rate**
Now				
Later				
Never				
Total Monthly Savings				

A blank copy of this worksheet is provided for your use in the appendix on page 309.

Saving For Now

"Saving For Now" encourages your teen to put aside a fixed amount of money for something that really matters to him or her in the next week or month and rewards the effort by gratifying your teen's shorter-term appetite.

Let's go through a step-by step computation of a short-term savings target and fill in the worksheet. Short term means anywhere from one week to six months.

• •

Saving For Now

Saving For Now encourages your teen to put aside a fixed amount of money for something that really matters to him or her, and rewards the effort by gratifying your teen's shorter-term, more immediate want or need.

1. Determine your teen's short-term immediate need or want.

2. Identify how much it will cost, including tax.

3. Decide how much to put aside each month toward the purchase price and fill in the table with the monthly and total amount.

4. Put this amount aside each week/month in a labeled cash pocket, a labeled money jar, savings, checking, money market or investment account.

• •

The Wilsons hoped that by selecting a short-term savings target for Casey—something that really mattered to her—they could encourage her to put aside a small portion of her earnings. The trick was to teach her to understand that she would get her money back.

Casey had been begging her mom for a manicure and a pedicure from a salon for a special upcoming school event. All Casey's friends were getting manicures and pedicures, and she wanted one, too. Connie was reluctant to spend the money. As she put it, "I don't even get manicures and pedicures—they are so expensive—I usually do them myself." She also worried that she would be setting a precedent. Her other two daughters might want the same treatment. Connie suggested to Casey that she put aside $12.50 a week from her babysitting earnings and allowance to save for the treatment.

The upcoming function was four weeks away. Since Connie knew how hard it would be for Casey to resist spending her money, she told her daughter that each time she set-aside the money, her mom would hold on to it. Connie was willing to take on that degree of *hands-on* responsibility if it would promote her daughter's success. She wanted Casey to understand, at a *gut level*, what she could achieve by not spending all her money at one time.

The Real-Life Money Game
Three-Part Savings Plan: Now, Later, Never
Family Member Player _____ *Casey Wilson* _____

For When	For What	Total Cost	Fixed Monthly Amount	Where: At What Rate
Now				
Four Weeks April 1 to April 30	Manicure/Pedicure for upcoming school event	$50	$12.50/per week for four weeks totalling $50.00	Connie to keep until needed
Later				
Never				
Total Monthly Savings			$50	

A blank copy of this worksheet is provided for your use in the appendix on page 309.

Saving For Later

"Saving For Later" encourages your teen to put aside money for a "big-ticket" need or want. If you'll recall, in chapter one we talked about the fact that learning to delay gratification was uppermost in parents' minds. Recent surveys done by the American Savings Education Council indicate that only about half of teens interviewed save regularly. Once they receive money—whether from allowances, jobs, or gifts—they spend it immediately.

So why is it so important to teach our teens to delay gratification?

They can learn the principles of compounding interest. Small amounts may be insignificant so look at this as a chance to teach them a valuable skill. By accumulating some money, they have an opportunity to see how compound interest grows money. Compounding money makes their resource more renewable.

Below is the visual chart I use in my course to help explain the concept of simple versus compounding interest. Simple interest is interest earned only on the amount of money your teen saves or invests. Compound interest is interest earned on the amount of money your teen saves or invests plus the interest earned. When your money compounds and works for your teen, it has the potential to grow over time.

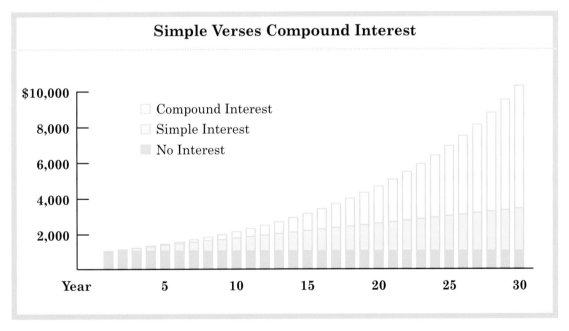

A $1,000 investment with an 8% average annual rate of return grows $80 earning simple interest. With compound interest the $1,000 grows to $1,080 at the end of the first year; $86 to $1,166 by the end of the second year; $93 to

$1,259 by the end of the third year; and so on. Each year it grows by a larger margin. After 30 years, assuming an average annual rate of return of 8%, your $1,000 would have grown to $10,063 before taxes.

Saving For Later

Saving For Later encourages your teen to put aside money for a "big-ticket" need or want.

1. Determine your teen's longer-term "big-ticket" need or want.
2. Identify how much it will cost, including sales tax.
3. Decide how much of the total cost your teen will be responsible to save.
4. Decide how much of the total cost you will be responsible to save.
5. Determine by what future date you will need or want the money.
6. Determine what average annual interest rate your monthly funds can be saved or invested at.
7. Put this amount aside each month in the savings or investment account earning the average annual interest rate.

Let's work through step-by-step instructions on how to fill in the worksheet for Saving For Later. By age fourteen, my son had shown much proficiency with handling money. His dad and I agreed that Michael was ready to start saving money for a car to purchase when he turned sixteen. This would be a long-term savings target for a "big-ticket" item.

We established a base price for the car of $5,500 including tax. We wanted our son to be responsible for $500 of the total amount and we would

The Rule of 72

The rule of 72 states that dividing 72 by the interest rate you're earning tells you roughly how long it will take your money to double (and dividing 72 by the number of years in which you want to double your money will tell you how much interest you need to earn). If you're earning, for example, 8%, your money will double in about nine years.

pay for the remaining $5,000. We would need to save the money over the next two years. We would invest the money at a 5% rate of interest. Following the steps for "What to Save Now For Some Total Future Amount" on page 145, we computed that our son would need to save $20 each month, and we would save $200 per month, to achieve our long-term savings target. We all agreed to the savings goal, and deposited our monthly amounts in our investment account at a compounded annual rate of 5%. Michael's worksheet is shown below.

The Real-Life Money Game **Michael's Three-Part Savings Plan: Now, Later, Never** **Family Member Player** *Michael Williamson*				
For When	**For What**	**Total Cost**	**Fixed Monthly Amount**	**Where: At What Rate**
Now				
Later	Car	$5,500 $5,000 from us $500 from Michael	$20	Investment Account at 5% compounded annually
Never				
Total Monthly Savings			$20	

A blank copy of this worksheet is provided for your use in the appendix on page 309.

You can use the chart on the following page to compute how much your teen should set aside each month to achieve his or her savings goal by some desired future date. You will need to select the average annual rate of return you think your teen can achieve on his or her investment of funds. For example, if the money is invested in a money market account, you might select an average annual rate of 3% to 4%. The chart doesn't represent real-world numbers. It provides only for a calculation of you and your teen's monthly set-aside amount.

What to Save Now For Some Total Future Amount

1. Identify the total amount you wish to save.

2. Determine by what future date you will need the money.

3. Approximate the average annual interest rate you can earn.

4. Using the number of years to your future date shown in the table on the following page, and the average annual interest rate, find the number where these two intersect.

5. Take the total amount you wish to save and divide it by the number from the table.

6. Multiply your result by a factor of 10 to determine the dollar amount to set aside each month.

Many families I've worked with understand the concept of matched funds. For every dollar their teen saves or invests, they contribute an equal amount. Parents can generate income for their teens when they contribute to the total cost as we did with our son. Your son or daughter will see a double reward for their efforts. This is especially important, because teens easily get discouraged or distracted by immediate concerns. Matching funds promotes savings habits by making goals seem more approachable.

Saving For Later – College

One of the primary goals of this book is to help you teach your teen how to strategize and plan ahead. From my experience working with families, there is no financial planning goal more discussed than saving for college. Perhaps there is no other financial planning goal more in need of a strategy than sav-

What to Save Now for Some Total Future Amount

Average Annual Return Rates

Year	3%	4%	5%	6%	7%	8%	9%	10%
1	122	123	123	124	125	125	126	127
2	248	250	253	256	258	261	264	267
3	377	383	389	395	402	408	415	421
4	511	521	532	544	555	567	580	592
5	648	665	683	701	720	740	760	781
6	790	815	841	868	897	926	957	989
7	936	971	1,008	1,046	1,086	1,129	1,173	1,220
8	1,086	1,133	1,182	1,234	1,289	1,348	1,409	1,474
9	1,241	1,302	1,366	1,435	1,507	1,585	1,667	1,755
10	1,401	1,477	1,559	1,647	1,741	1,842	1,950	2,066
15	2,275	2,469	2,684	2,923	3,188	3,483	3,812	4,179
20	3,291	3,680	4,128	4,644	5,240	5,929	6,729	7,657
25	4,471	5,158	5,980	6,965	8,148	9,574	11,295	13,379
30	5,842	6,964	8,357	10,095	12,271	15,003	18,445	22,793

ing for college. Why? It's expensive, and getting more so. The cost of college is spread out over several years, from two to six or more, if graduate school is considered. And if your income falls in the upper-middle to upper category, financial aid will likely not be available except in the form of loans.

Let's look at how Sam Sanchez's daughter was able to save for college and still qualify for financial aid. Sam Sanchez has limited resources. He matched his daughter's college savings goal. However, he included the amount in "Teen's Income" when computing the Family Fund Contribution. Sam could either match his daughter's college savings target, or contribute to her ongoing spending, but not both. Therefore, he encouraged Maria to spend within her resources, so he could put more towards her fast-approaching first year of college.

Because of limited income, Sam found to his relief that various forms of financial aid covered most of Maria's tuition and fees. Still, federal grant money was limited, and

> ### College Financial Planning Important Note
>
> If you or your teen will be applying for financial aid, the calculation will be affected differently depending on who's name college savings and investment accounts are set up in.
>
> To be certain of how the college financial-aid formula will effect you and your teen, here is a list of websites to learn more about college financial planning:
>
> - www.collegesavings.org
> - www.collegeboard.com
> - www.finaid.org
> - www.savingforcollege.com
> - www.ed.gov
> - www.fafsa.ed.gov

between living expenses and unmet college expenses, Maria spent in one year virtually everything she and Sam had managed to save in her college account. Sam wished he'd increased his matching funds long ago. For the next few years he had to go onto an austerity program and save the equivalent of her rent and grocery expenses each month, while encouraging her to increase the amount of her deferred payment loans. Without their savings, however, the first year wouldn't have been possible.

Saving For (What Seems Like) Never

"Saving For (What Seems Like) Never" encourages your teen to put aside money at a young age that will provide a fund he or she can grow over time. It teaches the value of compounding interest, and gets your teen in the regular *habit* of saving a certain percentage of all money they receive. It also can be a means of teaching the basics of investing.

Parents in my course often ask how much our teens should be Saving For (What Seems Like) Never. For adults, the standard savings rule-of-thumb is 10% of their annual salary. Our teens should be encouraged to save anywhere between 10% and 25% of all the money they receive.

Let's look at an example, in step-by-step computation.

• •

Saving For (What Seems Like) Never

Saving For (What Seems Like) Never encourages your teen to regularly put aside money at a young age that will provide a fund he or she can grow over time.

1. Determine your teen's average monthly income over a given period.
2. Determine what "fixed percent" (10% to 25%) of monthly income (over and above "Now" and "Later" amounts) can be set aside.
3. Explore where you wish to save or how you wish to invest the funds and at what rate.
4. Put this amount aside each month in the chosen savings or investment account.

• •

The MacLean's daughter Linda taught sailing during the summer. Since her parents had invested in a mutual fund to finance her college, she decided to put aside 25% percent of all her summer earnings. She expected to receive an average of $1,000 per month for three months. She told her dad she wanted to use a portion of her earnings to learn about investing. She saved $250 over each of the next three months in order to pursue her long-term savings goal. With the assistance of her family's investment broker, she invested the amount in a mutual fund.

The MacLean family helped Linda fill out the worksheet shown on the following page.

The Real-Life **Money Game**
Three-Part Savings Plan: Now, Later, Never
Family Member Player _____*Linda MacLean*_____

For When	For What	Total Cost	Fixed Monthly Amount	Where: At What Rate
Now				
Later				
Never	To invest.	$750	$1,000 x 25% for three months	In a mutual fund with the family's broker at the going rate of return.
Total Monthly Savings			$250	

A blank copy of this worksheet is provided for your use in the appendix on page 309.

• • •

Teaching your teens to save can be very simple. For beginners, you start Saving For Now. For intermediate-level players, move up to Saving For Later. Advanced-level players have an opportunity to set aside money that will grow over time with Saving For (What Seems Like) Never. You can choose a different savings target for your teen, based on his or her level of maturity, proficiency in handling money, and demonstrated follow-through. The ultimate goal, with your guidance, is to establish a savings habit that will make room for all three.

The Real-Life Money Game offers the following summary along with the step-by-step instructions to follow for completing the savings worksheet.

The Real-Life Money Game
Three-Part Savings Plan: Now, Later, Never Instructions

Saving For Now:

1. Determine your teen's short-term immediate need or want.
2. Identify how much it will cost, including sales tax.
3. Decide how much to put aside each month toward the purchase price and fill in the table with the monthly and total amount.
4. Put this amount aside each week/month in a labeled cash pocket, a labeled money jar, savings, checking, money market or investment account.

Saving For Later:

1. Determine your teen's longer-term "big-ticket" need or want.
2. Identify how much it will cost, including sales tax.
3. Decide how much of the total cost your teen will be responsible to save.
4. Decide how much of the total cost you will be responsible to save.
5. Determine by what future date you will need or want the money.
6. Determine what average annual interest rate your monthly funds can be saved or invested at.
7. Using the table on page 145, calculate how much you and your teen will need to put aside each month to achieve the total cost.
8. Put this amount aside each month in the savings or investment account earning the average annual interest rate.

Saving For (What Seems Like) Never:

1. Determine your teen's average monthly income over a given period.
2. Determine what "fixed percent" (10% to 25%) of monthly income over and above "now" and "later" amounts can be set aside.
3. Explore where you wish to save or how you wish to invest the funds and at what rate.
4. Put this amount aside each month in the chosen savings or investment account.

149

Scorekeeping Box

After discussing *The Real-Life* Money Game Three-Part Savings Plan: Now, Later, Never, give your teen point credit using the scorekeeping box below. Add the full score if your teen has successfully completed the activity. Add no score if your teen hasn't. Write down the date of the activity, make note of any discussions, problems or successes, and tally your teen's score. This score will be added to the final score at the end.

Key Concepts	Activity Point Value	Date Activity Completed/Discussion Notes	Point Value Earned
Assist your teen with the following to help him or her earn points:			
• Establish one short-term savings target for Saving For Now and set the money aside.	5		
• Follow the Saving For Later instructions to calculate a long-term savings target, and set the money aside monthly.	10		
• Commit a fixed percent of monthly income for Saving For (What Seems Like) Never, and set the amount aside.	10		
• Fill in *The Real-Life* Money Game Three-Part Savings Plan: Now, Later, Never worksheet with three savings' targets and put aside money for all three.	20		
Total Score	**45**		

Chapter Twelve
Giving: Is It Worse Than a Shot?

Only about half of all Americans invest, but nearly nine out of ten families contribute to a charity. This is according to a survey by the Independent Sector, a coalition of seven hundred nonprofit organizations. In my course, parents are usually surprised at this statistic. In spite of the enormous resource dedicated to charitable giving, there is little guidance on how to give. For our teens' purposes, the process can be simplified. There are three important questions to help them consider: Why give? What to give? Where to give?

So how do parents nurture their teen's philanthropy when often their teen's limited resources make every dollar he or she gives feel like a shot? Or contrarily, what if your teen has a bent for giving but tends to give everything to church, charity, or friends? *The Real-Life* Money Game offers a "Who or What Matters Most to You?" exercise designed to help teens internalize their feelings about money they give away. The exercise will help them answer three key questions. The ultimate goal is for your son or daughter to have enough resource to give spontaneously, but within an identified Playing Board-Spending Plan amount. Learning the tangible skill to give can instill in our teens the intangible skill of generosity.

Playing the Game: "Who or What Matters Most to You?"

Let's see how the "Who or What Matters Most to You?" exercise, shown on the following page, works.

Why Give?

The first section in the exercise is designed to help your son or daughter answer why he or she would want to give money away. Sometimes we impose our own beliefs and causes without really hearing what our teens have to say. When we encourage our teens to say what's on their minds, the responses can be real eye-openers.

"Who or What Matters Most to You?"
Family Member Player _____

If you had some money to give, how would you most like to use it?

Why?

Determine How to Give: Money, Goods, A Gesture, or Volunteer Time	Decide How Often to Give: Per Week, Month, Quarter, Six-Months, or Year	Where to Give: List the Top Five Causes You Care About In Order of Priority	Name Specifically the Local or National Organization or the Cause

A blank copy of this worksheet is provided for your use in the appendix on page 310.

The Wilson family's youngest daughter, Julie, for example, noticed that one of the students at her school never seemed to have a lunch. She told her parents she wanted to buy the student a school lunch once in a while. The Wilsons were thrilled at the generosity of such an impulse and encouraged their daughter to incorporate this expense into her Playing Board-Spending Plan. When teens participate in the charitable-giving decision, they are more likely to commit to the cause.

What to Give?

The second section of the exercise helps your teen decide in what way to give and how often. Let's consider the choices. Giving money is generally the most convenient. Teens can easily specify an amount on their Playing Board-Spending Plan to give once or on a regular basis. My son, for example, started with a weekly $5 donation to a charity of his choice. The money can be set aside in a cash pocket until it is needed. Or the amount can be kept in a checking or debit card account and distributed in the same way as an expense your teen is responsible for paying. Money given can be easily tracked on the monthly Playing Board-Spending Plan as an "Other" distribution to a specified charity or cause.

The idea is to not wait to see how much money your teen has left over on his or her spending plan, but rather to assign an amount to the spending plan up front. This is a much more proactive approach. Parents attending my course report that when they help their sons or daughters establish spending-plan parameters, their teens tend to regulate how much to give on their own. Whatever you and your teen decide, encourage giving on a regular basis. The time intervals for giving can be weekly, monthly, quarterly, every six months, or annually. This tends to reinforce charitable giving and allows your teen time to practice.

If your son or daughter has a hard time identifying where to give the money, it can accumulate in savings until something truly motivates them. There is nothing more exciting for parents to observe than when something triggers their son or daughter's heart-felt empathy. That, and knowing they have money set aside for the cause that won't come from you as a giveaway.

The first time my son gave spontaneously to a cause was when he watched the World Trade Center 9/11 attacks on TV. The news broadcast a relief fund set up to help the victims with an address prominently displayed for where to send the money. My son left the room. I thought he was disturbed by the broadcast. Ten minutes later, he returned with a tiny-relief package, an envelope addressed to the relief fund that held a $20 bill inside. He told me to mail the package and leave the cash intact. It mattered to him that this particular $20 bill that he'd saved be sent to help. The concrete nature of the giving reinforced the impulse. He saw, in a tangible way, what this impulse cost him. This allowed him to attach emotionally to the act of giving. It was a good precedent to set.

The Real-Life Money Game encourages parents to assess when their teen's philanthropic notions should keep within the Playing Board-Spending Plan or when special circumstances such as a family disaster, dictate stepping outside of the plan. There are times when it's appropriate for a parent to offer a little financial relief and play "God." Parents should be ready to bail their teens out when there is a higher value than money.

Sam Sanchez's daughter, Maria, demonstrated this point to her dad when she wanted to buy an electric blanket for her grandmother. Her grandmother was recovering from hip surgery in the hospital. Maria knew how much comfort a blanket, the actual *object*, would provide, even though the purchase price of $50 would tear a huge hole in her spending plan. Sam agreed to pay for the gift, if Maria would contribute $10 toward the cost. She agreed.

Another way to give is to make donations in the form of goods. Consider prompting your son or daughter to round up used books from the neighborhood and donate them to a retirement home. Schools encourage such activities as canned-food drives to stamp out hunger. Teens learn much about giving when they organize fund-raising efforts among their friends. Encourage your teen, for example, to solicit donations for a cause in lieu of giving birthday gifts at a party.

Or, it could be goods donated to organizations in need. Every year around the holidays, my son and I would sort through his toys for the year. He loved his toys, but had outgrown them. Many were like new, so he wanted them to go to a good cause. We boxed them up and took them to the local Children's Hospital. Our annual trips to donate these toys left my son with a keen giving-spirit each holiday.

Giving doesn't have to mean money or goods. Sometimes it can be a gesture, such as a hand-written note with flowers. I discovered how rewarding a heartfelt gesture can be when my son left a note for our housekeeper, Anida. I'm convinced that because Michael had a resource to give, he learned how to be grateful. Here is what the note said with her corresponding response:

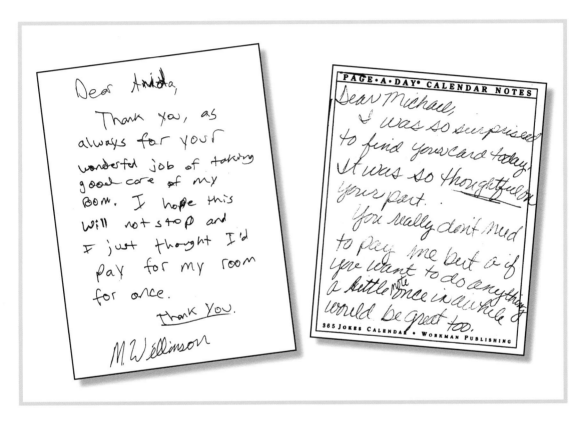

Keep in mind that time is a valuable resource to give. The innovative Wilsons paid their daughter, Karen, to volunteer her time at a hospital thrift store. This was a wonderful way for her to earn money, while at the same time learning about compassion. Some parents resist this idea. Paying for volunteer time seems to contradict the idea of giving charitably to an organization. Each family must decide what makes sense for their own priorities. For some families, paying for time might be a legitimate way to accomplish twin goals: to get a resource into their teen's hands, while at the same time, encouraging them to give. No matter what the decision, the charity wins. The best way to encourage teens to volunteer is to help them find an organization that works in areas of interest to them. The table on the following page lists common "Volunteer Resources" for many teens. Review the list with your teen and watch what peaks his or her curiosity. Then help your son or daughter explore specific organizations within the community.

Encourage your teen to jot down a brief description of the organization and the contact information if it's a volunteer position they're interested in. They will then need to call the organization to find out what positions are available and the requirements of the volunteer job.

Where to Give?

The second section of the exercise also helps your teen identify where he or she might wish to give. The exercise asks your teen to list five causes he or she cares about. Sit down with your son or daughter and show them your checkbook register, so they can see your family's choices for giving. Show your teen catalogs and brochures, so he or she will understand that requests come from everywhere. Your son or daughter will need to figure out what is legitimate and what isn't when identifying where to give money, goods, or time. When picking charities, help your teen identify them first, *generally*, in the third column of the exercise, and *specifically*, in the fourth column. For example, if your teen gives to his or her church, synagogue, temple, or mosque, in column three write religious institutions, in column four record the exact place. When helping your teen make a selection, make it relevant to his or her life. As I mentioned, my son contributed to the World Trade Center Relief Fund and to our housekeeper. These were causes near-and-dear to his heart.

The Wise Giving Alliance, an arm of the Better Business Bureau, evaluates nonprofit groups and lists organizations that meet their standards. The American Institute of Philanthropy publishes a guide that shows what portion of giving dollars goes to the charitable cause versus to administration and fund-raising expenses.

The Internet can also be a valuable resource to help you and your teen plan for giving. The following website, www.guidestar.org, lists approximately 850,000 nonprofit organizations. Another great website resource that helps match donors and volunteers with nonprofits is www.networkforgood.org. This website also lets you donate money online.

Volunteer Resources	
General Area of Interest	**Specific Places**
Animals	• Zoo, animal shelter, farm or ranch
The Arts and Museums	• Museum, historical or heritage society, community center art program, theater, festival
Children and Families	• Boys and Girls Club, Girl Scouts, Friends of Youth, Campfire, YMCA or YWCA, Parks and Recreation, Youth Center, Department of Social and Health Services
Civic	• Service Clubs: Kiwanis, Lions, Rotary, Chamber of Commerce, Youth Council, library, city and town hall
Disabilities	• Buddy program, therapeutic or rehabilitation center, Special Olympics, foundations
The Elderly	• Adult-day center, Parks and Community Services, senior center, retirement home
Environment	• Parks Department, Conservation District, Water and Land Resources, Trail Association or Organization, Nature Conservancy, Audubon Society
Health	• Health Society, Association or Foundation Hospital and Medical Center, cooperative, Public Health Center, Blood Center
Poverty and Homelessness	• Emergency Feeding Program, Multi-Service Center, Habitat for Humanity, Share House, HopeLink
Violence Prevention	• Neighborhood Mediation Program, Students Against Violence Everywhere (S.A.V.E.), Domestic Violence Program

Consider investigating a Youth Volunteer Corps in your area. They recruit teens ages eleven to eighteen to volunteer on team-based projects in the community. The projects are led by trained adult team leaders, and are hosted by community agencies. For example, during the summer, AmeriCorps, a large nonprofit organization, coordinates community projects for teens.

Once you have helped your teen narrow the choices, let him or her make the final pick. Allowing teens to pick their own places to give eliminates that "worse-than-a-shot" feeling. If you want them to really feel good about their personal efforts, have them choose at least one of the five organizations on their list to give to at regular intervals.

One parent who attended my course reported that as part of a school project her daughter's class volunteered to sleep overnight at a shelter for the homeless. Each student was allowed only a quarter with which to buy food in a 24-hour period. The goal of this chaperoned shelter-visit was to encourage empathy in hopes that teens would embrace volunteerism and giving in a personal way. This particular mother, when she first learned of the project, was frantic, concerned with how hungry her daughter would be, not to mention her worry about danger. But because most students attended, her daughter insisted she wanted to go. Her mother felt compelled to agree. The daughter immediately spent the quarter on candy; she and her friends then found the shelter unimaginably awful and so they chose instead to wander the streets (supervised by teachers) through the entire course of one night. Exhausted and famished, the next morning they gratefully stood in line at a Pioneer Square mission for breakfast, not caring particularly who was in line with them.

The next day was spent entirely in bed, catching up on sleep. Her daughter learned a lesson that night about how hard life can be when middle-class comforts and securities are removed. As the mother recounted the story, it was clear that her daughter took away a life-long experience that taught her compassion at a *gut level*.

The habits we form young are the habits that stay with us for a lifetime. I've found that money and time donated in the form of philanthropic giving and volunteering, far from depleting available resources, only broadens your teen's base of friends and allies—never, in my book, a resource you want to undervalue.

Scorekeeping Box

After explaining the "Who or What Matters Most to You? exercise, give your teen point credit using the scorekeeping box below. Add the full score if your teen has successfully completed the activity. Add no score if your teen hasn't. Write down the date of the activity, make note of any discussions, problems or successes, and tally your teen's score. This score will be added to the final score at the end.

Key Concepts	**Activity Point Value**	**Date Activity Completed/Discussion Notes**	**Point Value Earned**
Assist your teen with the following to help him or her earn points:			
• Complete the "Who or What Matters Most to You?" exercise.	5		
• Choose one cause or organization to contribute to on a regular basis.	10		
• Choose one cause or organization to volunteer for on a regular basis.	10		
• Choose one or more causes or organizations to both contribute to and volunteer for on a regular basis.	20		
Total Score	**45**		

Chapter Thirteen

Borrowing and Lending: A Spendthrift's Nightmare or a Wise Money Manager's Hedge Against the Future?

In my course, I spread a dozen or more articles on a table with current headlines from the "Wall Street Journal," "New York Times," "Washington Post" and other urban papers. A sample selection would read—*Debt Mountain Grows: Consumer debt more than doubles in decade as saving rate slides*; *Payday-loan customers risk big debt for fast cash*; *Once Ignored Debts Are Focus of Booming Industry*; *Monthly bills reach for the sky*; *Careful about counseling: Finding right agency can be invaluable for families in debt.* Not a week goes by without some headline warning about the millions of Americans with mounting consumer debt. Overall, we're spending increasing portions of our disposable personal income while saving less, and many of us are slipping perilously close to or into bankruptcy.

Parents attending my course usually raise their heads after perusing the articles and ask if I would advise that their sons or daughters forget about borrowing money or using a credit card until they're at least thirty. My first instinct is to warn of the hazards of debt. Surveys indicate that the average adult holds over $5,000 in credit card debt. This doesn't include loans for cars, consumer purchases, colleges, or mortgages for homes. Worse yet, surveys also report that credit card companies target college-entry-age teens, causing them to fall prey to credit card debt, knowing these students have increased pressure to spend while attending school.

So, yes, there is reason for concern. However, there may be another way to look at this.

In *The Real-Life* Money Game debt is defined as spending expanded beyond cash on hand. Since debt is a reality in most families' households, teaching teens awareness is the first line of attack against a crippling use of credit. Some teens don't even know that they have to pay for their purchases when the credit-card bill comes in! The key is to expose them to the proper use of credit so, they can dodge the credit crisis that hits most students upon graduation from college.

We can start by teaching our teens the difference between a debit card and a credit card. In chapter six you were introduced to debit cards as one spending option available to your teen. Sixteen year-olds can have a debit card cosigned with a parent. A debit card looks to our teens exactly like a credit card. The first thing they need to realize is that debit payments are deducted directly from their bank account. If you don't have the money in the account, then you can't make your purchase. Debit cards, therefore, offer a gateway to make purchases without running up debt. However, one caveat. If your teen has written checks that have not yet been cashed and cleared the account, overdraft charges can occur before teens even see their debit-card statements. They can avoid this problem in two ways: They can look at their ongoing statement online, to identify checks they've written that haven't yet cleared the bank. Or, they can keep a minimum amount of money, $100 for example, in the account.

When the Wilson's oldest daughter got her first debit card, her parents were legitimately concerned. One swipe of the plastic card could pay for anything, or so it seemed to their daughter. Then came the bank statement when Karen had to face the reality of an emptied account with overdraft charges. She looked over her debit card purchases and said, "I can't believe I spent this much!" Many items, she admitted to her mom, she didn't really need or want. Within three months of using her debit card, Karen put it away and decided to pay for items with cash. She told her mother that swiping plastic made spending too easy. Connie was thrilled that her daughter, who would be attending college the next year, was catching on. However, she also realized that somehow Karen would have to learn this means of accessing her resources; in the *real* world, cash isn't always readily at hand or practical.

A credit card is a contract your teen signs with a bank or a credit-card company to borrow money up to a certain amount with an interest charge tacked on to any balance not paid in full each month. Teens can have a credit card in their own name at age eighteen. Many credit card companies and banks offer joint family credit cards. Parents co-sign and each person is given a credit limit—$1,000 for example—the maximum amount available for purchases. Interest rate charges vary by company or bank and investment institutions. Credit card interest is usually the highest priced debt. If a person pays off the entire balance each month, no interest is charged. If only the minimum is paid, interest accumulates. Interest accumulates on top of unpaid interest each month when the small minimum payment is made. This is the credit card trap many people fall into. Teens are especially vulnerable as they tend to want big-ticket items but lack the resources to make large payments.

A credit card properly used, however, offers a credit record—a key advantage over a debit card. Just one major credit card is all it takes to establish a credit history. A good credit record can assist your son or daughter to borrow money to start a business or to one day buy a house.

One situation came up recently for a real-estate broker who wanted to help her son buy a house. Her son thought that he would be a worthy candidate, because he had never used a credit card, borrowed money, or gotten into debt. The lending institution saw it otherwise. When the time came for him to sign the mortgage papers, his mother had to step in to co-sign on the loan. The mortgage company had a policy that they would not make a loan without seeing a history of timely debt payments.

Encourage your teen to use a debit card over a credit card as often as possible. If your son or daughter decides to use a credit card for emergencies or unanticipated expenses or for establishing a credit history, share with them the importance of paying the balance off monthly. Our teens need to learn how much debt costs, that the cost is compounded when debt is accumulated, and how to pay debt off in a timely manner. Both debit cards and credit cards, when used properly, can be valuable tools to teach your son or daughter the wise use of debt.

Remember in chapter four I mentioned loaning my son $300 to buy a new computer. Most parents can probably predict what happened when he got the computer. For the first couple months, Michael followed-through by working the agreed upon number of hours. But it annoyed him that his working hours paid money to me rather than to him. When I dinged him for the agreed-upon interest out of his Family Fund Contribution, he changed his mind about the whole plan. He took the last $150 out of his savings account and paid me off early. He was thrilled to have his obligation behind him. This process was invaluable, because he discovered the challenge of paying off debt that lingered long after the gratification received from the purchase. In our society and culture, there is too often a direct correlation between the need for gratification and debt. My son got off easy with his first borrowing experience at home where it was safe. He didn't borrow money from a bank, or use a credit card. When the time arrived for Michael to purchase his car, he was quick to pay his portion. He'd learned his lesson. Better to pay up front, even if it means giving up savings, than to wait for the bill later. Through Michael's experience I helped him intuitively become aware of what it feels like to borrow money and pay it back.

Credit comes in many different forms tailored for many different uses. Legitimate reasons *do* exist for using debt as a money-management tool. The following table lists some key reasons.

Teen Borrowing Uses and Consequences

Legitimate Uses of Debt	Consequences of Borrowing
• Backup funds for an emergency.	• Provides some security.
• Purchase a car to get to a job.	• Earnings can be used to cover the monthly car payment.
• Fund a "Teen Business."	• Potential to make money on the venture.
• Buy a computer to earn or invest money.	• Information access advantages. Provides a way to search for a job or learn about investing.
• Pay for a college education.	• Potential for increased earning power. Studies reveal that people with college degrees on average earn more money than those without a degree.
• Purchase an asset that will increase in value.	• Assets that increase in value such as a business or real estate cover the cost of borrowing.
• To establish a credit rating or history.	• Opportunity to buy a house or start a business.

Two worksheets, *The Real-Life* Money Game Borrowing Chart and *The Real-Life* Money Game Lending Chart, are designed to help parents teach their teens how to use debt responsibly.

Playing the Game: *The Real-Life* Money Game Borrowing Chart

Help your teen answer the questions when your son or daughter borrows money. Put the chart in his or her personal financial binder for future reference under the index tab marked "Borrowed Funds."

The Real-Life Money Game Borrowing Chart
Family Member Player _____

What are you borrowing funds for?	
Is it a legitimate use of debt?	
Is there any other way you could come up with the money or only borrow some portion of the amount?	
How much are you borrowing and from what source?	
How will the debt be paid off—where will the money come from?	
When will the debt be paid off?	
What is the interest rate you will be paying and what will be the total cost of borrowing to you?	

A blank copy of this worksheet is provided for your use in the appendix on page 311.

Playing the Game: *The Real-Life* Money Game Lending Chart

Help your teen answer the questions when your son or daughter lends money. Put the chart in his or her personal financial binder for future reference under the index tab marked "Lent Funds."

The Real-Life Money Game Lending Chart Family Member Player _____	
What are you lending funds for? Is it a legitimate use for lending? Is there any other way to come up with the money besides a loan from you?	
How much are you lending and to whom?	
How will the loan to you be paid off— where will the money come from?	
When will the loan be paid off?	
What is the interest rate you will be paid and what will be the total income to you for the loan?	

A blank copy of this worksheet is provided for your use in the appendix on page 312.

Maria Sanchez, who'd been learning thrift and good saving habits, found herself in the constant position of making small loans to her high-school friends who were not good at managing their cash and would otherwise have to forego their lunch or gas money.

The amounts were typically $10—very occasionally, $20, and they were usually not to close friends, though they were to students she crossed paths with in school on a regular basis. Sam asked Maria to make sure the students had the means to pay her back before she loaned the money. Sam also asked that she insist on a time for repayment. Of course, the problem was, she couldn't enforce her terms. It required voluntary cooperation on her friends' part and they didn't always cooperate. Whenever Sam insisted Maria ask for repayment within the week, she would know all the excuses why they couldn't. He finally laid down the law and said he refused to give her any more draws from the Family Fund Contribution, and if she ran out of her spending money for the sake of lending to her friends, she would have to tap into her savings.

She of course earned no interest. Most of the kids did eventually pay her back. The main problem was that out of misguided sympathy for her schoolmates, she was creating cash flow problems for herself. Maria would beg Sam to reimburse her Family Fund Contribution. He'd refuse point blank—she had to learn by feeling the consequences.

A day or so later invariably she'd come to him with an alternate plan. "Dad" she'd say, "You know I always get $50 for my birthday or for the holidays, and often it's $100 or more. So if you lend me the $40 now, I promise I'll pay you back with interest in December." And sure enough, not only would she be good for the principle plus interest, she'd also have calculated for that shortfall and have adjusted her holiday spending plans accordingly.

Parents who encourage their teens to follow *The Real-Life* Money Game Debt Rules can teach them how to use debt wisely. The table shown on the follwing page lists the rules.

As the scalable plan changes with any borrowed or lent funds, help your teen include the amounts paid or received on his or her monthly Playing Board-Spending Plan.

The Real-Life Money Game Debt Rules

- When money is borrowed from parents, the interest owing or the full amount comes out of the following month's Family Fund Contribution first.
- Complete *The Real-Life* Money Game Borrowing Chart and put a copy in your personal financial binder. Follow your loan terms to pay down your note in a timely manner.
- Complete *The Real-Life* Money Game Lending Chart and put a copy in your personal financial binder. Follow your loan terms to receive timely payments.
- Use your debit card.
- When transitioning from a debit card to a credit card at age eighteen, use only *one* major credit card to establish a credit history and rating.
- Try to use your credit card only for emergencies or unanticipated financial circumstances.
- Pay the credit card balance off each month.
- Know the rate of interest and the amount you will be charged on any unpaid balance.
- Learn how to get and read a credit report. To request a copy of your credit report you can go online to:

  Equifax: www.econsumer.equifax.com

  Experian: www.experian.com

  Trans Union: www.transunion.com

Scorekeeping Box

After reviewing the difference between a debit card and a credit card, discussing legitimate uses and the conseqences for borrowing, and going over *The Real-Life* Money Game Debt Rules, give your teen point credit using the scorekeeping box below. Add the full score if your teen has successfully completed the activity. Add no score if your teen hasn't. Write down the date of the activity, make note of any discussions, problems or successes, and tally your teen's score. This score will be added to the final score at the end.

Key Concepts	Activity Point Value	Date Activity Completed/Discussion Notes	Point Value Earned
Assist your teen with the following to help him or her earn points:			
• Complete *The Real-Life* Money Game Borrowing Chart and follow the terms of the loan to pay it back in a timely manner.	5		
• Complete *The Real-Life* Money Game Lending Chart and follow the terms of the loan to receive payments in a timely manner.	5		
• Use a debit card, in lieu of a credit card, on a regular basis.	10		
• Apply for one major credit card (available at age eighteen) and use only for emergencies.	10		
• Pay credit-card debt off monthly.	20		
• Request a credit report and understand the importance of having a credit history and rating.	20		
Total Score	**70**		

Chapter Fourteen
Investing: Creating More Resource

How many times have you heard your teen say ,"Oh, if only I were rich...?"

A common misconception among teens holds that they can only buy what they want by begging their parents for the money or by saving up for it. What they usually don't understand is that they can better realize their dreams by renewing their resource through investing. Understanding investing also means learning how to take financial responsibility, to think independently, and to manage a resource to plan for the future; these are three intangible behaviors parents attending my course agree are worth instilling in our teens. The key is to teach investing at home while the consequences of mistakes aren't so severe. *The Real-Life* Money Game offers tools designed to take the mystery out of investing.

Perhaps the most important reason for teaching our teens about investing is to accustom them to the notion of growth. The stock market's rate of return has averaged approximately 10%, historically. Contrast that with savings and money market rates of return—around 1 to 3% —and you will show your teens a way to grow their resource that doesn't tie them down to that weekend job. Generally, our teens have fewer spending commitments, so they're free to earmark more of their resource for investing. Parents who encourage their teens to invest at an early age also give them the opportunity to watch their money compound. In my course, parents report that nothing seems to excite their sons and daughters more than watching their money grow.

At your next monthly meeting with your teen, ask him or her to write down one financial dream. Help your teen estimate how much he or she thinks it might cost to fund that dream. Jot the dream and the amount down on *The Real-Life* Money Game Plan worksheet. Then talk about when your teen might like to realize that dream. Set a date. Studies show that people are five times more likely to take action on things they have written down. Teens willing to take calculated investment risk can turn their financial dreams into realities.

Develop a Resource

Before we can teach our teens about investing, we first need to help them come up with a resource. We start by differentiating money set aside for investing from money used to pay expenses, back debt, contributions, or taxes. Any money set aside for mid or long-term savings goals such as for a car or for college—and especially set aside for a home or for retirement—are good resources to invest. By reviewing your teen's monthly Playing Board-Spending Plan, together you can determine how much might be available for investing over and above these other financial commitments. If your son or daughter maxes out his or her Playing Board-Spending Plan and has nothing left over, encourage your teen to forego an expense the next month and to use those funds for investing, instead. Or, prompt your son or daughter to earn a little extra from their existing income sources. In my course, I encourage parents to match any money their teens earmark for investing. This added incentive seems to work remarkably well because teens see that they have immediately doubled their money! One of the best investments they could ever make is receiving matched funds. And all it takes is a little commitment of resource on their part, and their parents' willingness, of course.

Once you have developed your teen's resource base, you are ready to move through each investment step. The following sidebar identifies each step explained in further detail throughout this chapter.

Five Steps to Investing

1. Learn Investment Basics
2. Understand the Market
3. Identify a Strategy
4. Evaluate Investment Alternatives
5. Track and Manage Investments

Step One: Learn Investment Basics

Your teen needs to start with the simple basics of investing, from learning a glossary of investment terms to reading the financial pages. When the "vocabulary" of investing feels familiar, it's time to introduce more complex investment concepts, such as: diversification through asset allocation, identifying and managing risk, and measuring results through rate of return. While this may sound like Greek, remember, it's just terminology. The concepts are purely commonsense, and easy to master. Think of it as traveling to a foreign country.

You'd want to at least manage a *hello* and *goodbye*, maybe *how are you*, maybe *where is the toilet*, and *what kind of food is that*. That's where we're at here. Basic hello's. The following table lists and defines those key investment "hello's" your teen should become familiar with.

Glossary of Investment Terms	
Key Investment Term	**Definition**
Stock	A share in a corporation entitling the shareholder to dividends and to other rights of ownership.
Bond	An interest bearing security issued by corporations, governments, or other institutions, guaranteeing payment of the original investment plus interest by a specified future date.
Securities	Multiple shares of stocks or bonds.
Mutual Fund	An investment company that takes the cash of many shareholders and invests it in securities of other companies.
Portfolio	A group of investment securities held by an individual, an institution, or a mutual fund.
Stock Market	A place where stocks, bonds, or other securities are bought and sold on an *exchange* such as the New York Stock Exchange (NYSE) and the NASDAQ-AMEX Market Group.
Index	A selection of securities such as the Dow Jones Industrial Average (DJIA), the Standard & Poors 500 (The S&P 500), and the NASDAQ Composite Index whose collective performance is used as a benchmark to measure the stock market.
Market Capitalization	A company's total stock market value, calculated by multiplying the current price of a single share of stock by the total number of shares outstanding, to categorize each according to size in dollars.
Return	Return on investment (rate of return) measures how much profit an investor has gained or lost (in percentage terms) on any financial investment.
Risk	Risk measures the potential loss an investor is willing to accept in exchange for the gains he or she seeks on any financial investment.
Asset	Items such as cash, securities, bank and investment accounts, real estate, jewelry, art, and cars that have monetary value and can be sold or converted into money.
Company Asset Classifications	Asset classifications such as *income, value,* or *growth* used by investors to identify certain qualities or characteristics with the intention of combining or differentiating companies.
Volatility	The degree of movement in the price of a single security often measured in both short-term and long-term investment time frames.
Diversification	Investing in a balance of varying size companies with different asset classifications to minimize volatility and stabilize investment returns.

Review the list with your teen; don't worry about memorization. The language will sound more friendly after it's explained. You can always refer back to this list, as you would a travel dictionary. Later, after each term is discussed in more detail throughout the chapter, you can refer back to the definitions as needed.

In addition to the investment terms, teens need to learn how to read the stock and mutual fund listings in the financial pages. It sounds like a daunting task, but really it's no more difficult than comparing receipts to see if your grocery spending has gone up or down. The table on the following page illustrates how to read stock and mutual fund listings. Looking at these terms in the pages of a book, such as this one, is far less satisfying than looking at the real thing. So grab a copy of the Wall Street Journal, crack it open to the financial page, show your teen the symbols and watch how quickly he or she catches on. Once your teen becomes familiar with the listings, peruse the Internet to see if you can find the same stock and mutual fund information. Search for stock, bond, or mutual fund quotes using one of the many financial resource websites available online.

Step Two: Understand the Market

For our teens to truly understand what it means to invest in a company, we need to explain, in simplified terms, the fundamental philosophy of our capitalistic economy. Why? Because it helps to have an understanding of how businesses work if you want a sense of how the stock market works.

Companies produce products and services for people to buy. Consumers are free to spend their money on whatever products or services they wish. Companies receive money—*revenue*—for the prices they charge consumers, and this is how they make their money. Because consumers are free to buy, businesses attempt to grow or improve their products or services, so consumers will not buy similar items from businesses that produce the same products or services. Companies who produce the same products or services are called competitors. As companies compete with each other for consumers' spending, products and services tend to improve while prices tend to stay affordable to buyers.

When you and your teen buy stock in a business, you are actually *buying an ownership "share"* of that company's revenues. To truly understand the market, just remember that you and your teen *invest* in a business as both consumers and as owners.

Stock and Mutual Fund Abbreviations

Stock Listings

Stock	Listed company name.
Sym	An abbreviation for the company's name that is used as shorthand by stock-quote reporting services and brokerages.
Div	The latest annual dividend paid by the stock.
Yld	The yield is the stock's latest annual dividend expressed as a percentage of that day's price.
PE	The price/earnings ratio is the price of the stock divided by the earnings reported by the company for the latest four quarters.
Vol 100s	The number of company shares actively traded in the day.
Prices	Reported in 1/8-point increments. One-eighth of a dollar is .125 cents.
Hi	Highest stock price traded that day.
Lo	Lowest stock price traded that day.
Close	Final stock price when the stock market closed.
Net Chg	How much the stock changed up or down from the previous day's closing price.
52 Weeks Hi Lo	The highest and lowest stock prices over the last 52-week period for the listed company.

Mutual Fund Listings

Name	Mutual fund name.
NAV	Net asset value, what a share of the fund is worth.
Buy price	Price paid per share of mutual fund.
YTD % ret	Year-to-date return in percentage terms.
Net Chg	Change in the funds net asset value from the previous day.
NL	No load – no sales commission paid on purchase.
p	Annual fee covering marketing costs.
r	Back-end load – fee charged on redemption of fund.
t	Both annual fee and back-end load charged.
x and/or e	Ex-cash dividend and ex-capital gains distribution. Fund distributes income to current shareholder. The NAV will be reduced by the amount of the distribution per share.

Companies sell "shares" of their business to improve, to grow, or to simply continue to operate their businesses. In exchange for the use of your money, you hope the company you invest in receives more revenues from consumers than they pay out in expenses. Excess revenues over expenses are called company profits. When companies are profitable, you have the potential to receive more money back than you originally paid for your stock. That's because if your company is profitable, other people want to buy the stock. If you were to sell the stock and receive more money than you originally paid, you have a gain. In simple economic terms, the gain on your stock investment is based on the supply and demand for that company's stock in the stock market. This gain is called a return on your investment. You might also receive a return on your investment in the form of a dividend. A dividend is money a company pays its shareholders from the money it makes on its business operations.

The most fundamental principle of any *market* is this: sellers ask a high price, buyers offer a low price, and in the *exchange* they agree on a price somewhere in between. This exchange, what a willing buyer would pay and what a willing seller would sell, is called an arm's-length transaction. And this is how the stock market works. Stocks are bought and sold on an exchange to determine a company's stock price. It's the most basic level of supply-and-demand economics.

A closing price is the last price during the day at which a stock is bought or sold on an exchange. A company's stock price can go up simply because many more people wish to buy the stock than there are shares available. Or conversely, a stock price might go down simply because there are few people who wish to buy the stock of a particular company. The key investment objective for any investor is to buy low and sell high.

Key Investment Objective

- Buy low and sell high.

Okay. You've heard all this before. You know it's not that simple. Other forces are at work. Forces beyond your control. Later we'll talk about how to diversify to protect your investment from unpredictable fluctuations. For now, let's continue working with basic principles.

Bonds, also called fixed-income securities, work the same way as stocks, except that bonds represent money your teen lends to a company. In exchange, bondholders generally receive fixed interest payments at specified rates of return. Bonds are more stable than stocks, because company's that fail must pay bondholders back before stockholders. Investors who want to receive cash on a regular basis, might, for example, prefer to buy bonds rather than stocks.

Market Capitalization

In addition to single stock or bond prices, investors also evaluate an entire company's value. They do this by calculating a "market capitalization." This term refers generally to the company's net worth or total stock market value. This value is calculated by multiplying the current price of a single share of stock by the total number of shares outstanding. Current market price and shares outstanding can be found on most companies' Internet websites. Based on the result, investors categorize companies according to their market capitalization size as follows:

- Large capitalization: $5 billion or more
- Mid capitalization: $1 billion to $5 billion
- Small capitalization: $250 million to $1 billion
- Micro capitalization: Less than $250 million

These capitalization categories are important to recognize. Smart investors purchase a mix of stocks from different size companies. For example, small-cap companies tend to be riskier than large-cap companies. Stock market performance can vary significantly between sizes, and by investing in a mix, ideally you achieve a greater average rate of return than you could by investing in a single company. Investing in a mix of varying-sized companies with the intent of balancing your investment portfolio is a concept called diversification. And diversification is ultimately what your teen's strategy should be. But more later on how to do that.

Try This Exercise

Calculate the "Market Capitalization" of a chosen company using the formula below. Determine whether the company represents large, mid, small, or micro capitalization.

Current Market Price x Shares Outstanding = Market Capitalization

Asset Allocation

Another way to achieve diversification, in addition to monitoring company size, is to invest in companies that have different asset classifications. Companies are often classified by certain qualities or characteristics. Investors use these classifications in an effort to combine or differentiate companies. Many classifications exist. However, the three most important for you and your teen to understand the market are: *income*, *value,* and *growth*.

Companies classified as *income* stocks tend to pay dividends regularly and to have minor changes in their stock prices. These stocks tend to be very low risk. Utility stocks are a good example.

Value companies, or "out-of-favor" companies, generally have current stock prices that are relatively cheap compared to their prior prices. This can be due to a downturn in their business operations, less demand for their products or services, an ineffective change in management, or it can be a great company trapped in a poor economy.

Growth companies are characterized as having increasing profits in the range of 10% to 25%. Generally, investors want to buy stocks in profitable companies. As you and your teen learned, when the stock is in demand, the price tends to go up. This is great if you own the stock. But if you are a buyer, you may be paying too high a price. Increasing profits are difficult for businesses to maintain over a long period of time, so growth stocks tend to be higher risk; the stock price can drop as quickly as it shoots up.

Investors combine company size (market capitalization) with company classifications (*income, growth,* and *value*) to come up with a balance of non-correlating securities in their portfolios. There's a word to practice until it rolls off your tongue: non-correlating. Non-correlating securities are those companies whose share prices move in opposite directions in the stock market. That's all. Easy. Again, your goal is to ensure that your investment performance (return on investment) is not tied to any one company's size or business characteristics.

Investing in a balance of companies by both size and character classification is called asset allocation. Diversification through asset allocation lowers stock-price volatility and produces greater rate-of-return predictability. There. That's a mouthful of foreign speak, but now it's no longer gibberish. You understand that diversifying through asset allocation is a key investment objective.

Asset allocation not only means dividing up your teen's investment resource between companies, it also means dividing up an investment resource between stocks, bonds, and cash to achieve the highest return at the lowest risk. How much resource your teen puts into stocks, bonds,

or cash depends on his or her age and how long he or she has before the money is needed. Teens generally have long time frames—three to ten years—to invest in stocks which are riskier than bonds or cash, but over a longer period of time, can produce a higher rate of return. They can also produce greater loss. That's the risk. We will go into more detail about risk and rate of return in step three.

The following pie-chart shows how a typical teen might allocate his or her investment resource between stocks, bonds, and cash, and the stocks between company size and characteristics.

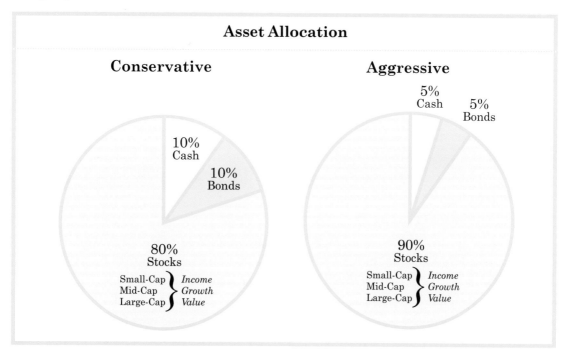

Asset Allocation

As mentioned, teens, having a longer timeline to invest, might allocate the majority of their assets—anywhere from 80% to 100%—in stocks, which are riskier than bonds or cash in the short run but produce better rates of return in the long run. In addition, the stock-resource allocation can then be reallocated between company size and character-type. The goal is this: to maintain the asset-allocation mix that achieves your teen's identified risk tolerance and desired rate of return, concepts discussed next in step three.

Step Three: Identify a Strategy

So how does your teen choose the best investment strategy? Your son or daughter basically has two things to consider: the amount of risk he or she is comfortable with, and the rate of return your teen requires.

Risk measures the potential loss an investor is willing to accept in exchange for the gains he or she seeks on any financial investment. Remember that when your teen buys an ownership share in a company, he or she is taking a risk that the company will do well and that your teen will not only receive the original cost of the stock back, but will also receive some kind of a return—that is, receive more money back than originally paid for the stock. A company does not "guarantee" a return. If a company operates poorly, your teen might receive less than what he or she originally paid, or possibly receive nothing back at all. The risk of losing money in the stock market is called *stock-market risk*.

Your key investment objective, therefore, is to identify your teen's risk tolerance. Ask your son or daughter this question: how much are you willing to risk losing of your original investment resource in the short run, in hopes that you will achieve your financial dream in the long run?

> ### Key Investment Objective
>
> • Identify your teen's risk tolerance—the potential loss he or she is willing to accept in exchange for the gains your teen seeks.

At seventeen, my son answered the question this way. His financial dream is to buy a small house that he can fix up and rent when he graduates from college. He decided that the house he wants will cost approximately $250,000 and he would need a down payment of 10% or $25,000. The rest he will borrow. He has researched how much he could get in rent in the residential area he is looking to buy, and he is sure that the rent will cover the monthly mortgage payments.

He has saved $10,500. He'd like to invest the entire amount over five years. He will add money when he can until he graduates. His hope is to come up with the $25,000 down payment in five years. Of his original investment, he is willing to lose $500 over the next five years or 4.75% of his original $10,500 to achieve his financial dream of $25,000. This means that if and when his losses exceed $500, he'll pull out and re-examine his options.

Return on investment—rate of return—measures how much profit an investor has gained or lost (in percentage terms) on any financial investment. This could be an investment in stocks, mutual funds, bonds, a business venture, or any other type of financial product. Return is calculated using the formula shown below.

Try This Exercise

Calculate the "Rate of Return" of a chosen company.

Sales Price of Investment (What you received on the sale) – Purchase Price (What you originally paid) / Purchase Price x 100 = Annual Percent Rate of Return

For example, if your teen bought a share of stock for $50 and sold it one year later for $60, the return would be as follows: ($60-$50)/$50 x 100 = 20% per year.

Once your teen understands how to measure investment return, the next question is, what is your teen's desired rate of return? The desired rate of return is a measure of what your son or daughter needs to achieve (in percentage terms) on his or her investment in order to realize that financial dream you've written down on *The Real-Life* Money Game Plan worksheet.

To continue my son's example, to achieve his financial dream, the return he needs is 18.8% on his original investment of $10,500. This takes into consideration his risk tolerance of $500, the amount he is willing to lose.

There is a trade-off between risk and reward. Generally, the higher the desired rate of return, the higher the risk of loss. The key investment objective is to expect the highest rate of return at your teen's identified level of risk.

Key Investment Objective

- Expect the highest rate of return at your teen's identified level of risk.

How do we know what is a desirable rate of return?

We can consider how the market has performed historically, though that is no guarantee of future performance. Historically, the stock market has achieved an average rate of return of approximately 10%. This is the amount that over the long run, your son or daughter could expect to achieve. But what do we mean by "long run"? Five years? Twenty years? A hundred years? My son could not look beyond five years, not exactly "long run" as the market goes. In his case, it behooves him to consider market performance.

We do this by looking at what are called stock-market indicators or indexes. Indexes are a grouping of several selected companies' stock prices adjusted for things such as stock splits. The three most commonly referenced stock market indicators are the Dow Jones Industrial Average (DJIA), The Standard & Poor's 500 (The S&P 500), and the NASDAQ Composite Index (The NASDAQ Composite). These indexes, and many others, are used as benchmarks or standards to measure stock-market performance. And in turn, investors, such as my son, can use these indexes to measure their own investment performance.

Try This Exercise

Choose one "Stock-Market Index" from the business section of your paper, identify what companies it includes, and determine if it is going up or down.

In the short run, the stock-market indexes can be used to compare your teen's investment strategy to determine whether he or she will achieve the desired rate of return within the time period chosen.

Try This Exercise

To achieve my financial dream in the amount of $_____, I need a return on my investment of _____%, for which I would accept a loss of $_____, over the period of time I wish to realize my dream _____# of months.

Investment Alternatives

Investment Alternative	Definition	Advantages	Disadvantages	Average Rates of Return
Cash	Money you keep on hand.	Convenient; no tax consequences; no investment risk.	Doesn't earn money for you; doesn't outpace inflation; can be lost or stolen.	0%
Checking or Debit Card Account	Money you keep in a bank checking account.	Convenient; no tax consequences; no investment risk.	Minimal earnings; doesn't outpace inflation; can be lost or stolen.	0%-2%
Savings Account	Money you keep in a savings account.	Convenient; insured by the FDIC if bank fails, so no risk.	Low interest rate; doesn't outpace inflation.	1%-2%
Certificate of Deposit (CD)	Money you keep in a certificate for a specified period of time: 6 months, 1 year, 2-1/2 years, etc.	Higher interest rate than savings; minimal investment risk.	Money tied up for period CD must be held; doesn't outpace inflation; penalty for early withdrawal.	3%-5%
Money Market Fund	A mutual fund that invests in very short-term, high liquidity investments such as CDs and bonds.	Works like a savings account; safe; generally no minimums; no fees.	Moderate returns.	3%-4%
Single Company Stock	Money you invest to buy stock in a single company.	Can diversify some, if able to purchase several single company's stock.	Not highly diversified; high risk; can pay large commissions for small amounts of stock on both purchase and sale; requires independent research from yourself or broker.	Difficult to determine. Can look at stock price history for clues, but no guarantee of future returns.
Stock or Equity Fund	A mutual fund that invests in stocks which can be of certain types such as *income, growth,* or *value* funds or micro-cap, small-cap, mid-cap, or large-cap funds.	Actively managed. Opportunity for greater returns at certain times in the market; easy to get into; diversified.	Actively managed so fees are significant and larger than index funds; requires minimum amounts to invest; can require a front or back load—money you pay to get into or out of a fund; SEC limits funds to no more than 5% in each company; can be too diversified; actively traded, so often results have a tax consequence.	May look to past performance, but no future guarantee; tend to under-perform market-index averages.

DRIP	Direct Investment Plan	Can purchase small numbers of shares directly from the company; bypass broker's commissions; dividends are automatically reinvested; no minimums. Can invest small amounts of funds.	Not highly diversified; requires independent research.	Difficult to determine. Can look at stock price history for clues but no guarantee of future returns.
Index Fund	A passively managed mutual fund that seeks essentially to duplicate the performance of a particular market index. It typically charges lower fees compared to actively managed mutual funds.	Passively managed so fees are less than stock funds. Usually doesn't require a front or back load to get into or out of the fund; simple; minimal trading so less tax consequence.	Requires minimum fund amount to invest.	Can follow index to determine performance Produces average market rate of return.
U.S. Treasury Securities or Government Bonds	Debt issued by the government.	Receive a fixed amount of interest; can invest small or large amounts; issued by the government so debt repayment is secured and safe; can purchase varying length maturities: intermediate or long-term; not as volatile as equities.	Lower earnings than equities over the long-term.	Treasury 1%-3%; Government 1%-6%
Single Company Bonds	Debt issued by corporations or institutions.	Receive a fixed amount of interest. Not as volatile as equities.	Not highly diversified so increased risk; can pay large commissions on purchase and sale for a small denomination; requires independent research; a company may "call" (take the bond back) prior to the maturity date; generally requires a minimum investment of $1,000.	5%-7%
Fixed Income Fund	A mutual fund that invests in bonds.	Actively managed. Opportunity for greater returns at certain times in the market; easy to get into; diversified.	Actively managed so requires fees; requires minimum amounts to invest; can require a front or back load— money you pay to get into or out of a fund; can be too diversified; active trading, so often results in a tax consequence.	2%-6%

Step Four: Evaluate Investment Alternatives

In order to achieve your teen's investment strategy identified in step three, your son or daughter needs to know what investment options are available. The table shown on pages 183-184 identifies common investment alternatives.

Note that each investment alternative is general, not specific. So how does your teen choose a specific investment alternative? Here's where it gets simple. You only have three options. You can invest using an active manager. You can invest using a passive manager. Or you can invest independently using no manager at all. The following table indicates important considerations to keep in mind when selecting an active or passive manager.

Active and Passive Investment Managers	
Investing with an Active Manager	**Investing with a Passive Manager**
When selecting an active manager consider the following: • Will you use an online or local office broker? • Do you need a minimum amount to open an account? • What are the fees and commissions you will be charged to invest? • Can you invest in mutual funds?	When selecting a passive manager consider the following: • Will the referral come from an online directory of Registered Investment Advisors, a Certified Financial Planner, an accountant or CPA, your family's banker, or from a friend who uses one? • Do you need a minimum amount to use the manager? • What is the fee you will be charged for the investment advice?

Let's say that your teen decides that he or she wants more help in the beginning. Your son or daughter can seek an active manager, such as an investment broker. Brokers offer investment products for which they receive commissions and fees. They do the investment research and make specific recommendations. The advantage of using an active manager is that your teen doesn't have to get too involved in learning about investing. The disadvantage is that fees and commissions lower his or her returns.

Let's say that instead your teen wants to get more involved. Your son or daughter has already identified his or her investment strategy in step three:

they've determined the required rate of return to achieve their financial dream. A passive manager, also referred to as an independent investment advisor, doesn't sell investment products. Instead, the manager helps select specific investments that achieve identified objectives. The immediate advantage is that your teen saves fees, and, therefore, stands to earn a higher return. The disadvantage might be finding the right passive manager.

Now, let's suppose that after your teen becomes familiar with reading the financial pages, you encourage your son or daughter to investigate investment alternatives on his or her own. The sidebar lists recommended books for further independent exploration with your teen.

The first two authors offer fundamental information on investing based on their own experience. The last two authors are academics who offer investment theories based on verifiable and provable, empirical data; their theories on investments predict *probable* outcomes; that is, an outcome that is likely to happen but not guaranteed.

Investing On Your Own Recommended Readings

- *The Warren Buffett Way* by Warren Buffett
- *One Up On Wall Street* and *Learn to Earn: The Beginners Guide to Investing* by Peter Lynch
- *Security and Portfolio Analysis: Concepts and Management* by Dan W. French
- *Foundation of Finance: Portfolio Decisions and Securities Prices* by Eugene F. Fama

Encourage your teen to peruse these at the book store. If one seems too advanced, consider reading portions of the book with your son or daughter. Make investing a family affair. You can also help your teen explore this book's website www.reallifemoneygame.com for links to other online investment resources.

Try This Exercise

Choose a fund and a single-company stock. Make a hypothetical investment in each, calculate the rates-of-return, and compare the two results.

When my son first started learning how to invest, he got a major dose of *real-life* experience. A well-intentioned, family friend who had some experience investing told Michael about a cellular phone company stock that was sure to go up. He was so sure, that he invested money in the stock himself. Michael was excited and called our family broker and said he wanted to invest $500 in the stock also. At the time, this high-growth area of stocks was generally doing well. As it turned out, Michael's stock value plummeted within a week. The company's stock price had been inflated by rumors that it might be bought out by another company, which often causes the price to go up. However, the rumor became mere speculation. The stock dropped and Michael lost most of his money. Losing money on the stock market from a hot tip is like losing money from a dice throw.

Tips are random possibilities, *not* probabilities based on verifiable information or data. Those odds are against you. A smarter approach is to make investment decisions based on an identified strategy. Still, no guarantees, but at least this way your teen can turn his or her dice throw into a viable investment probability. It took Michael a long time to get over how sour he felt about losing his investment. We agreed that any future investment decision Michael made would be based on an agreed-upon strategy.

> **Key Investment Objective**
>
> • Choose investments that offer the broadest range of access to asset classes to minimize risk and increase return.

Step Five: Track and Manage Investments

Now that your teen understands the market and has an investment strategy, it's time for the fun: tracking and managing those investments.

The following is probably the question most frequently asked by investors young and old: when do you buy and when do you sell an investment? In other words, how do investors manage their investments?

The easiest strategy is called *buy-and-hold*. This means that when your teen makes an investment, no matter how the stock market is performing, your son or daughter keeps the investment until the time he or she needs it. That means holding the investment through all the stock-market ups and downs. In this scenario, you and your teen never try to forecast or "predict" how the stock market will perform. It doesn't matter. Except on the day you take the money out.

The second strategy is called *timing*. Investors who *time* the market attempt to predict whether the market will go up or down. They buy when the market is low, and try to sell when the market is high. These investors, in the long run, typically don't beat the average returns on investments that buy-and-hold strategists do. And they spend more time and stress in the process.

But there's a third option, and this is probably the one I'd most recommend, most of the time: *dollar-cost averaging*. This means that your teen invests the same amount of money over regular intervals and buys into an investment at the current market price. This is a great option, because you can encourage your son or daughter to earmark a monthly amount for investment on his or her Playing Board-Spending Plan. And as an added incentive, you can offer to match the agreed upon amount.

• • •

If your teen uses either an active or passive investment manager, the investment portfolio or fund information is usually summarized on a monthly statement. The statement generally reports what investments your teen is holding, any dividends and interest your teen received throughout the month, and any securities sold for a gain or loss. One concept your teen needs to understand is the difference between realized and unrealized gains and losses. Investment statements generally report both.

Unrealized gains and losses occur on investments you own, but have not actually been sold. The price you paid for your investment plus or minus the unrealized gain or loss is referred to as the *market value* of your investments. These gains and losses are computed by taking the difference between what you paid for an investment and the closing price on the investment-statement date.

Realized gains and losses only apply to investments actually sold. These are gains and losses that you must report for tax purposes. These gains and losses are computed by taking the difference between what you paid for an investment, also called *cost basis,* and the amount you received on the sale.

Unrealized and realized gains and losses will be discussed in greater detail in chapter fifteen. You can help your teen compute his or her unrealized and realized gains and losses using the formulas in the following exercise.

Try This Exercise

Calculate the *unrealized* investment gain or loss using the formula below.

Market value – original price paid (cost basis) = unrealized gain/loss

Calculate the *realized* investment gain or loss using the formula below.

Amount received – original price paid (cost basis) = realized gain/loss

If your teen received any interest or dividends, or realized gains on investments, help your son or daughter record this on his or her Income Worksheet for the month. Only do this if the income is used to pay your teen's Playing Board-Spending Plan expenses. If your teen does not need investment income to pay expenses, but leaves the funds in his or her investment account to be reinvested, you need only record the income at year-end. If your teen has a loss, discuss with your son or daughter how he or she will make up the shortfall.

Refer to chapter fifteen to determine how much money to set aside for taxes that will be owed at year-end on any investment income or realized gains.

Let's consider how the Wilsons encouraged their daughter to invest. Karen invested $1,000 of her own money that her parents matched. The Wilsons wanted their daughter to have enough resource to diversify her investment. With the help of her parent's broker, Karen invested in a mutual fund. She had two years to invest until she needed the funds for college.

In the first year, Karen made money on the mutual fund, and decided she wanted to use the gain she made as a down payment on a sound system for her car. She was happy to be making a contribution to her own wants and needs. Her parents, however, were concerned that she might not have enough resource for college. They asked her to rethink her plan. They also reminded Karen that at the end of the year, she would owe tax on any gain. She would need to set that money aside. Her parents helped her compute how much tax she would owe, and how much she should set aside each month on her Playing Board-Spending Plan.

Karen decided to go forward with her plan. She would take her chances that her investment in the mutual fund would continue to go up. She knew she was taking a risk. But she also understood that her risk was a calculated one, and that was the nature of investing. She also knew, of course, that her parents would help pay for her college. Because of that, she could accept a higher level of risk. Teens are in a prime spot to learn about the world of investing precisely for this reason. They're not yet on their own. It's not yet a matter of survival. They can make mistakes and it's okay.

Investing with a Traditional IRA or a Roth IRA

For the teen thinking long-term a traditional Individual Retirement Account (IRA) or a Roth Individual Retirement Account (Roth IRA), either one are worth considering.

A traditional IRA is a tax-deferred retirement account set up with a financial institution such as a bank or investment firm in which annual contributions are tax-deductible and may be invested in many types of securities. Tax is paid on the investment at the time the funds are withdrawn during retirement.

A Roth IRA is a retirement account in which annual contributions to the account are *not* tax deductible, but withdrawals are tax-free at the time of retirement.

The Real-Life Money Game encourages parents to offer their teens the option of a traditional IRA or Roth IRA. This may seem counter-intuitive given the long road to retirement, but the benefit is twofold. First, a traditional IRA or Roth IRA account teaches the concepts of compounding. Remember that compounding refers to the rate at which money grows if your teen leaves all the profits he or she makes in his or her investments. Secondly, either one offers teens the opportunity to watch their money grow over time. Because withdrawals of the fund are restricted, teens will not be tempted to take the money out. Please keep in mind, and counsel your teen accordingly, that retirement accounts, like any other investment, may go through prolonged down periods. Be willing to ignore these vagaries. Historically, these return well above savings interest, and are a good idea no matter how they perform in the short run.

The following box summarizes the criteria for both an IRA and a Roth IRA.

Investing With a Traditional IRA or a Roth IRA

Traditional IRA Requirements:

- Maximum contribution of $4,000* or 100% of *pre-tax* annual earnings whichever is less.
- Tax-deferred growth until the money is withdrawn at retirement age.
- Withdrawals may begin at age 59-1/2, but must begin at age 70-1/2.
- Can withdraw contributions *before* retirement to pay for certain expenses such as college or expenses to buy a "first" home without paying penalty, but *must pay* the tax.

Roth IRA Requirements:

- Maximum contribution of $4,000* or 100% of *taxed* annual earnings whichever is less.
- Withdrawals may begin at age 59-1/2. Contributions can continue after age 70 if still working.
- Can withdraw contributions after a five-year holding period *before* retirement for certain expenses such as college or expenses to buy a "first" home, *without paying* tax or penalty.

So how do you and your teen know which one to invest in? Here are the criteria to consider. If your teen is intending to use the investment to fund college before the Roth IRA five-year holding period, consider using a traditional IRA. If your teen can make the maximum contribution plus what he or she needs to pay the tax on the earnings, the Roth IRA results in a non-taxable retirement fund at age 59-1/2, whereas, the majority of the IRA is taxed.

Playing the Game: Putting the Five Steps to Investing Together

The following table puts the Five Steps to Investing together. Help your teen through each investment step after determining his or her key objectives. Let your teen dream about what those investment earnings might bring. But remind your son or daughter, there is risk. Your teen may may have to learn to watch his or her resource shrink before it grows. It's probably a good thing if this does occur. It will teach your son or daughter to not venture what he or she can't afford to lose.

Five Steps to Investing

Step One: Learn Investment Basics	Identify a resource—figure out how much your teen is willing to set aside for investing and note on the Playing Board-Spending Plan where that will come from. Review the glossary of investment terms with your teen.
Step Two: Understand the Market	Read through the financial pages or online with your son or daughter and practice identifying company abbreviations. Help your teen determine a company's size based on market capitalization and a company's characteristics: *income, value, or growth*. Talk with your teen about what it means to allocate his or her investment resource between a mix of cash, bonds, and stocks to diversify assets.
Step Three: Identify A Strategy	Identify your teen's risk tolerance and desired rate of return. Assist your teen with filling in his or her financial dream and what rate of return he or she will need to achieve it.
Step Four: Evaluate Investment Alternatives	Choose a portfolio of investments that will include a diverse range of non-correlating companies based on size and characteristics to achieve your teen's highest rate of return at his or her identified level of risk.
Step Five: Track and Manage Investments	Decide how involved your teen wants to be in the management and tracking of his or her investments; for a beginner player, you may wish to pay the extra fees and commissions and use an active investment manager to get started; once your teen becomes familiar with the process, as an intermediate player, he or she can choose a passive manager and get more involved in the decision making. Finally, as an advanced player, your son or daughter can do more investigation, research and analysis and invest independent of a manager.

Okay, just so you see it's not so strange and difficult, here's what I did with my son. In the beginning, I showed Michael the financial section of the Wall Street Journal. We looked at the New York Stock Exchange (NYSE) and the NASDAQ-AMEX Market Group to see what companies were listed under each. Michael wanted to use Microsoft's information to learn how to read stock prices, since he had two cousins who worked for the company. While watching MSNBC at dinner, I pointed out to Michael that he could follow stock prices and listen to ongoing company news and updates on this channel, 24 hours each day. He pointed out Microsoft's company ticker symbol MSFT that ran along the bottom of the screen. We searched the Internet using the key words "Microsoft Stock Price" and found an easy-to-navigate site called "Microsoft Investor Relations" that offered company and stock price information. Michael clicked on links such as *Stock Information and Analysis*, *Financial History*, and *Corporate Information*, just to mention a few.

He found out that Microsoft trades on the NASDAQ-AMEX Market Group exchange, and he found the company's *outstanding shares*. We then computed Microsoft's company size using the *market capitalization* formula. Microsoft is a large-cap company, we determined.

Historically, the company's earnings have been increasing, and Microsoft rarely pays dividends. The company's profits have generally been reinvested in the organization to further its growth. At the time Michael and I reviewed Microsoft, it was characterized as a *growth* stock.

Michael had approximately $500 available resource. Microsoft stock was selling for approximately $27 per share on the day he looked at the price. He was eager to buy.

I cautioned Michael that sometimes investing in a single company stock is risky, and at that point we talked about the concept of diversification. I asked him how much gain he hoped to receive on the future sale of his stock. He said he wanted to double his money! How much would he be willing to lose? "Nothing!" This, of course, was an introductory lesson in risk and rate of return.

Finally, we discussed that investing in a diverse group of non-correlating companies would be less risky, considering his risk tolerance was zero! We talked about why waiting to accumulate more resource might work to his advantage. With more resource, he could invest in several companies.

Over the next six months, my son set aside more funds for investing. With the help of the family broker, Michael negotiated a discounted commission rate to purchase Microsoft stock. While his investment was not ideally diversified, given Michael's risk tolerance and 100% rate of return target, he never lost his desire to invest in Microsoft. To counterbalance the investment, Michael has added more stocks to his portfolio. To this day, he still owns his original Microsoft stock. Though he hasn't achieved his strategy of doubling his money, he hasn't lost money on the investment, either.

Michael has now earned enough from his car detailing business to set up a Roth IRA. Together we've agreed that the funds will be invested in a highly diversified, passively-managed index fund, which he can let grow for his future.

Scorekeeping Box

After explaining the Five Steps to Investing give your teen point credit using the scorekeeping box below. Add the full score if your teen has successfully completed the activity. Add no score if your teen hasn't. Write down the date of the activity, make note of any discussions, problems or successes, and tally your teen's score. This score will be added to the final score at the end.

Key Concepts	Activity Point Value	Date Activity Completed/Discussion Notes	Point Value Earned
Assist your teen with the following to help him or her earn points:			
• Set aside a resource for investing and note the amount on the Playing Board-Spending Plan.	5		
• Review the key investment terms.	5		
• Compare the financial pages and the Internet to the stock listings and mutual listings symbols.	5		
• Talk about how businesses operate in the economy.	5		
• Discuss the fundamental principle of the stock market and key investment objective: Buy low and sell high.	10		
• Calculate a company's market capitalization and classify it by size.	10		

- Identify a company's characteristics as *income*, *value*, or *growth*.   10

- Discuss the key investment objective that non-correlating assets—companies whose share prices move in opposite directions in the stock market—reduce volatility by investing in a balance of asset classes called diversification.   10

- Talk about asset allocation, which means choosing where to put a resource whether in cash, stocks or bonds, and between a balance of companies by size and classification to diversify investments.   10

- Identify risk tolerance—the potential loss to accept in exchange for the gains sought.   10

- Calculate a desired rate of return and expect the highest rate of return at the identified level of risk.   10

- Choose a stock-market index as a standard for measuring the potential return on an investment.   10

- Review *general* investment alternatives available.   10

- Select *specific* investment alternatives using an active manager.   10

- Select *specific* investment alternatives using a passive manager.   20

- Select *specific* investment alternatives independent of a manager.   20

- Choose investments that offer the broadest range of access to asset classes to minimize risk and increase return.   20

- Track investment income on the Income Worksheet if used to pay Playing Board-Spending Plan expenses.   20

- Track investment income, gains, and losses, annually.   20

- Calculate realized and unrealized gains and losses on investments.   20

- Discuss the necessity to buy-and-hold investments rather than timing the market.   20

- Invest using Dollar-Cost Averaging.   20

- Invest using either a traditional IRA or a Roth IRA.   20

Total Score   **300**

Chapter Fifteen
Taxes: An Invisible Resource Depletion

••

I am a CPA. As you can imagine, from January through April, the subject of taxes demands a lot of my family's attention. Even so, my son is still somewhat confused. One day he came home from school and asked me, "Is there a reason you would send your tax return in before it was due?" Michael mentioned that his math teacher was happy because when he filed his return *early*, he got money from the government. My son's question was if you file *early* would you get a *monetary reward* or *payment* for doing so? I explained to him that his math teacher received an *income tax refund* for a portion of money that was *withheld* from his paycheck to pay for federal taxes. The incentive is that if you are due a refund of your withheld taxes, the earlier you file, the earlier the government sends your money back.

He asked a number of other questions, including, "How do you know how much tax you're supposed to pay?" I explained that job earnings, net profits from a business, *unearned* interest and dividends on investments, as well as gains and losses from investment sales, just to name a few, are all considered when computing taxes. It was not until he said, "I heard employers *match* the same amount of taxes that an employee pays to the government," that I realized just how deep the lack of understanding went. I began to explain the difference between Social Security tax and income tax when I realized there was too much information to cover.

And who could blame Michael for being confused? Was he supposed to learn about taxes through osmosis?

What Teens Need to Know

Many legitimate reasons exist for parents to clear up the confusion about taxes now, rather than later. Our ultimate goal should be to teach our teens the *real* tax cost to them, and how to set aside an appropriate amount on a monthly, quarterly, or annual basis to include in their Playing Board-Spending Plan. Many people focus on whether they are getting a refund of tax or have to pay a balance due. Neither reflects the true tax cost. The easiest way to clear up this confusion is to show your teen on his or her tax return the exact amount of total tax expense, not just what he or she pays or receives the day the return is filed. That's the *real* tax bottom line.

The sidebar identifies important information teens need to know about taxes.

I understood from my son's sour expression after our initial discussion that he wanted to learn about taxes, but not *all at once*. And, not *at that exact moment*. Right then, I filled out *The Real-Life* Money Game Plan worksheet. The discussion could wait for the right timing, but my memory wouldn't. I jotted down a few notes on the points I wanted to explain more completely to him. With Michael's tax return due in another month, and myself knee-deep in clients', family's and friends' taxes, I decided this would be an excellent time to broach the subject fully at our next regularly scheduled meeting.

What Teens Need to Know About Taxes

- Both federal and state taxes are paid.
- The difference between Social Security Tax (FICA) and income tax, and that employers match only the FICA.
- If you are self-employed, you pay the FICA and the match.
- How to compute withholding tax using federal Form W-4, and how to make estimated tax payments using federal Form 1040-ES.
- A tax refund means you have *over-paid* your tax and you get some back, whereas a *balance due* means you have *underpaid* your tax and you need to pay the shortfall.
- To distinguish between balance due and total tax expense.
- To prepare a tax return and compute taxes—both federal From 1040 and state, if applicable.
- How much to set aside for taxes on the Playing Board-Spending Plan.

When the time came, Michael and I spent a half-hour talking about what income he is taxed on, where the numbers come from, and how to record the amounts on his tax return. We then compared his current year's information with his prior year's return, to see how his taxes had changed.

If your explanations appear to overwhelm your teen, as was my case, divide the discussion into several meetings. Remember, the key to developing any new skill is to begin with an awareness. Practice can then follow. One great way to start is to show your son or daughter the following pie-chart to demonstrate that the tax slice is large and is a cost that cannot be ignored.

The pie-chart represents 100% of a family's income. For a family with income between $50,000 and $75,000, the average tax expenditure (as a percentage of income) ranged between 16% to 19% over the last 22 years. This federal tax rate includes income tax, Social Security tax, other payroll taxes and excise tax. This tax rate does not consider state, county, city or local tax.

Estimate your own tax slice and demonstrate to your son or daughter how much your family pays in taxes.

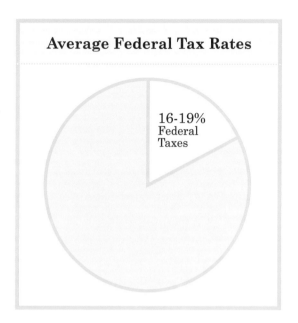

Average Federal Tax Rates

16-19%
Federal
Taxes

What Parents Need to Know

This is a good point in *The Real-Life* Money Game to introduce your teen to basic tax concepts. The information provided here primarily includes those tax concepts that affect teens as soon as they start to generate income.

Federal Income Tax

Taxes On Job Earnings

If your son or daughter has a job, the earnings they receive are included as income for purposes of the federal income tax calculation. When they are first hired, they are asked to fill out federal Form W-4. Explain to them that this is used to help estimate how much income tax they need to pay out of their earnings for each pay period—*in advance* of filing their tax return. This is called federal withholding tax. Also, let them know they will receive a federal Form W-2 at the end of the year that summarizes how much they earned and how much they paid in withholding tax. Show your teen how to include these amounts on his or her federal Form 1040 tax return.

Teens can earn up to $5,150* from a job before having to pay tax. If your teen has had a portion of his or her earnings withheld from a paycheck, but is within this limit, he or she will receive a tax refund on filing a federal Form 1040.

* 2006 Limits and Rates

If you claim your son or daughter as a dependent on your return, he or she will not be allowed a personal exemption on his or her return. However, your teen will get a standard deduction of his or her *earned* income plus $250* of *unearned* income (such as investment interest and dividends) not to exceed $5,150.* Put another way, if your son or daughter has $250* in *unearned* income, he or she can offset up to $4,900* of *earned* income against the allowable standard deduction of $5,150.* Any *unearned* income greater than $250,* and any *earned* income that exceeds $4,900* will be taxed.

Taxes On a "Teen Business"

If your son or daughter has a "Teen Business," the net profits they earn are included as income for purposes of the federal income tax calculation. The income and expenses are reported on Schedule C (Form 1040). Although a teen claimed as a dependent on his or her parents' tax return can't claim a personal exemption, he or she does get a standard deduction. The same rule applies as above. For purposes of the rule, *earned* income includes net profits from self-employment. That means there may be no income tax due on up to $5,150* of earnings from the business.

Michael earned $3,500 from his "Teen Business." This included his car-detailing enterprise that he shared with a friend, along with getting paid for all his services in the neighborhood. He and his friend were each responsible for reporting his share of the car-detailing profits on his individual tax return, and paying the resulting tax.

Taxes On Investment Income

Teens can make up to $850* in investment income—primarily in interest and dividends—without having to pay any taxes. Income between $850* and $1,700* will be taxed at your teen's individual rate. If your teen is under age eighteen, income above $1,700* will be taxed to him or her at *your* rate, even though your teen is the principal owner of the account. That's the "kiddie tax," intended to prevent shifting your income to your teen's lower tax rate. At age eighteen, however, your teen's income is taxable at his or her individual rates.

If you legitimately choose to shift income, make sure your teen's Social Security number is used as the tax identification number on any account on which your name also appears as a co-signer.

* 2006 Limits and Rates

Investment gains and losses are also included in the federal income tax calculation, but they fall under different tax rules. Here is where the concept of *unrealized* versus *realized* gains and losses, discussed in the last chapter, come into play. Remember only *realized* gains and losses from investments actually sold are considered for tax purposes. Using the formula in chapter fourteen, help your son or daughter compute his or her realized gains and losses to be included in the computation of your teen's taxes.

Gain or loss from the sale or exchange of an investment asset is character-ized as either short-term or long-term, depending on how long your teen has held it. Long-term means investments held for "more than twelve months." If your teen has both long and short term investment transactions during the year, each type is reported separately, and gains and losses from each type are first netted separately. The net long-term gain or loss for the year is then com-bined with the net short-term capital gain or loss for the year to arrive at an overall net capital gain or loss.

When capital gains exceed capital losses, the overall gain is included in your teen's other income. Net long-term capital gain for taxpayers in the 10% to 15% tax bracket is taxed at 5%. For taxpayers in higher brackets, the maximum tax rate is generally 15%. When capital losses exceed capital gains, the amount of deductible loss may be limited. Both net long-term capital losses and net short-term capital losses may be used to offset up to $3,000 of your teen's other income included in their tax computation. Your teen can carry over any unused capital loss to future tax years until it is used.

Throughout the year, Michael sold stock from his personal investment ac-count as well as his college fund. These stocks were sold and reinvested on the advice of his broker. Michael ended the year selling $4,000 of securities for a net long-term capital gain of $535. He reinvested the proceeds of the securities as well as the gain, less the taxes owed of $27, in another company's stock.

Federal Social Security Tax (FICA)

Explain to your teen that every United States citizen is required by a law called the Federal Insurance Contibutions Act, or FICA, to apply for a Social Security number to pay into our country's retirement and Medicare systems. The Social Security Administration is the agency that collects and administers the tax. This mandatory long-term retirement savings is collected by the federal government. The government then redistributes the money to retired individuals who have paid FICA tax throughout their working years. Encourage your teen to put a copy of his or her Social Security number in the personal financial binder and emphasize the importance of safeguarding this information.

Taxes On Job Earnings

Your teen will pay a Social Security and Medicare tax on up to $94,200* of job earnings at 7.65%,* which employers match. This is called a "payroll" tax because it is collected from your teen's paycheck. The reason for this, as I'm sure your teen will appreciate, is that this insures the tax is collected. At the point your teen begins to work and to pay into Social Security, explain to your son or daughter that he or she will receive a report summarizing his or her potential retirement benefits.

Taxes On a "Teen Business"

Your son or daughter will also pay Social Security and Medicare tax on any self-employment income he or she earns (newspaper carriers under age eighteen excepted). That 15.3%* levy starts with the first dollar of *net* self-employment income. Net self-employment income is revenue received less expenses.

My son, for example, will pay self-employment tax of $535.50 on his $3,500 of self-employment net income. He will, however, get a deduction on his tax return for half the amount he pays, which is standard for all businesses.

State Income Tax and County, City and Local Tax

Every state has a different taxing system. Some collect a state income tax. Some states charge a sales tax on purchases. Others charge a tax on business revenues or services. The best place to get information on your state, county, city or local taxes is to call the local Chamber of Commerce. The Internet can be an invaluable research tool, as well. If your teen is working, or is starting a new "Teen Business," help him or her research state tax requirements online at www.irs.gov. Search the keywords "state taxes."

Federal Gift and Estate Tax

You can gift up to $12,000* annually to as many individuals as you wish without paying a gift tax, an attractive estate-planning tool for many people. If your son or daughter is a minor, custodial accounts are designed to allow money to go directly to your teen when he or she reaches legal age, and the funds are taxed at his or her individual rates. Each state law specifies the legal age requirements. Consider carefully, when gifting to your teen, whether he or she has enough skills to manage the resource wisely. Use your teen's Playing Board-Spending Plan to help guide your son or daughter.

Tax Computation Web Sites

The sidebar below lists several Internet sites with programs designed to help you teach your teen how to prepare a return, both federal and state, compute his or her current year's tax, and estimate the upcoming year's amount. Your teen's job can be greatly simplified by using one of these programs.

Tax Computation Web Sites

- Internal Revenue Service: www.irs.gov
- Quicken: www.quicken.com
- SmartMoney: www.smartmoney.com
- TD AMERITRADE: www.tdameritrade.com
- TurboTax: www.turbotax.com
- Yahoo!Finance: www.finance.yahoo.com

Assist your teen in computing his or her current tax. Put a copy of any estimated tax payment vouchers for the upcoming year in the month they are due: April, June, September, and January. Federal Form 1040-ES is available at your local library, or you can order the form from the IRS website. Divide the annual tax estimate by twelve to set aside monthly amounts, or by four to set aside quarterly amounts. Include these on the Playing Board-Spending Plan in column one in the month they come due, and in column two when they are paid. Help your teen fill out his or her tax return, until he or she has had enough practice to complete it on his or her own. Encourage your son or daughter to put a copy of the tax return in his or her personal financial binder.

Scorekeeping Box

After reviewing what your son or daughter needs to know about taxes, give your teen point credit using the scorekeeping box on the following page. Add the full score if your teen has successfully completed the activity. Add no score if your teen hasn't. Write down the date of the activity, make note of any discussions, problems or successes, and tally your teen's score. This score will be added to the final score at the end.

Key Concepts	Activity Point Value	Date Activity Completed/Discussion Notes	Point Value Earned
Assist your teen with the following to help him or her earn points:			
• Discuss what a Social Security number is and why one is needed.	5		
• Put a copy of the Social Security number in the personal financial binder and talk about the importance of safeguarding the information.	5		
• Discuss how job earnings are reported and taxed. Look at a paycheck stub and understand how to complete federal Form W-4.	10		
• Review how net profits from a "Teen Business" are taxed and how to report them to federal and to state governments.	10		
• Show how *unearned* interest and dividend income and investment gains and losses are computed to determine federal and state taxes.	10		
• Complete federal Form 1040-ES to pay quarterly estimated taxes.	20		
• Prepare federal Form 1040 and any state tax forms to compute, report, and pay taxes owed.	20		
Total Score	**80**		

Part Three

Playing the Game and Keeping Score

Part three explains in five, detailed steps how families play *The Real-Life Money Game*. Both you and your teen will learn winning strategies—techniques to ensure successful results—as well as discover a four-step method to help resolve money conflicts. Part three additionally offers guidance for dealing with the disruptive circumstances of divorce, disability, and death. *The Real-Life Money Game's Word on Worth* provides a simple tool to calculate your son or daughter's financial worth. Finally, what you've been waiting for: you'll arrive at the last scorecard, a means of identifying your teen's player level.

Chapter Sixteen
The Real-Life Money Game Five-Step Instructions

In this chapter we'll get busy playing *The Real-Life* Money Game. To make the game as user-friendly as possible, I've developed what I call *The Real-Life* Money Game Five-Step Instructions. Along with the instructions, I'll summarize the information we've covered and highlight key points.

Let's consider what we've learned so far. In part one you were given tools to help your teen practice generating income and earning money, and you were shown how to compute a monthly Family Fund Contribution based on your family's resources. Then we talked about how to help your teen manage the mechanics of spending, which included advice on how to create a Playing Board-Spending Plan, pay expenses, and earmark a Rainy-Day Fund for unanticipated costs. With these fundamentals in place, we moved on in part two to further tangible financial skill-building. These included: the concept of savings; instilling a mind-set for giving; understanding borrowing and lending and learning how to use debt wisely; learning how to invest; and understanding taxes.

That's a mouthful to swallow all at once. That's why I'm providing here step-by-step instructions to help you proceed. But before we begin, I'd like to remind you of why all this matters. Recall that *The Real-Life* Money Game defines money as a renewable resource. If we teach our teens to manage their financial resources well, they will develop strategies, as well as assets, to help prepare them for the years to come. Toward this end, *The Real-Life* Money Game employs a scalable plan flexible enough to expand as your teen's financial needs and proficiencies change. In addition, a scalable financial plan is designed to help you safely transfer control of money to your teen so he or she can take more personal responsibility for his or her finances. And that finally is the bottom-line object of the game.

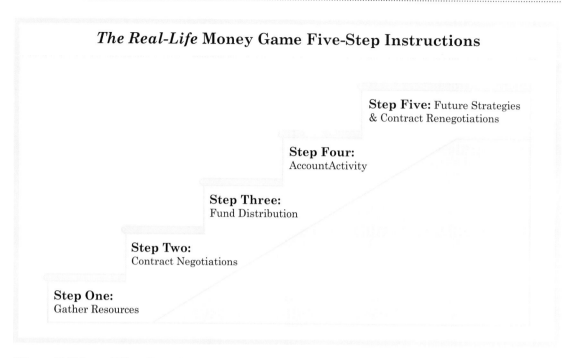

The *Real-Life* Money Game Five-Step Instructions

Step Five: Future Strategies & Contract Renegotiations

Step Four: AccountActivity

Step Three: Fund Distribution

Step Two: Contract Negotiations

Step One: Gather Resources

How I Play *The Real-Life* Money Game With My Son

Following the *The Real-Life* Money Game Five-Step Instructions, here is how I go through the process with my son:

Step One: Gather Resources

At the beginning of the month, I compute the Family Fund Contribution (FFC) amount taking into consideration Michael's earnings for caddying, umpiring, and paid jobs, and estimate upcoming month's expenses such as a ski-trip vacation, clothes, extracurricular school activities, sports, holidays, and gifts.

Michael fills out his upcoming month's Playing Board-Spending Plan column one with all projected income and expense amounts, including money earmarked for giving and savings goals.

I write a check for the upcoming month's Family Fund Contribution amount, and Michael prepares a deposit slip that includes both his earnings and the FFC check. He makes a deposit to Bank of America, where he holds a checking account with a debit card. Michael records the deposit in his check register.

Michael prepares a check from his Bank of America account to Merrill Lynch for $150 to be deposited into his investment account. This represents his monthly savings amount for his car down payment. At age thirteen, he computed the monthly amount using the compounding table to determine how much he would need by the time he turns sixteen. He prepares a Merrill Lynch deposit slip, takes a copy for his records, and mails the check to his broker.

I pay Michael a $15 weekly allowance (included in the Family Fund Contribution formula) each Thursday in cash.

Step Two: Contract Negotiations

On the Sunday closest to the first day of the month, we talk over any open items I have written down on *The Real-Life* Money Game Plan worksheet, and I answer any questions Michael may have. For example, we need to decide how he will invest his Roth IRA funds, discuss how well his investments are performing, and how his car-purchase research is going.

Step Three: Fund Distribution

During the month, Michael pays for the expenses included on his Playing Board-Spending Plan by writing checks, using his debit card, or paying cash from an ATM.

Michael keeps his receipts in his wallet or check register, and updates his check register balance throughout the month to keep an ongoing total of his cash.

Step Four: Account Activity

At the end of the month, Michael reconciles his current month's Bank of America statement with his check register using *The Real-Life* Money Game Bank Reconciliation Worksheet.

Michael fills out both an Income and Expense Worksheet for the transactions recorded on the bank statement. With this information, Michael fills in his Playing Board-Spending Plan, column two, to reflect how he actually used his money. He then calculates the difference between column one and column two and fills in the totals in column three.

<hr />

Step Five: Future Strategies and Contract Renegotiation

<hr />

On the Sunday closest to the first day of the month, Michael and I review the Playing Board-Spending Plan to see if he has run short of funds or has any money left over. If he's short, we talk about why and whether to modify the Family Fund Contribution for next month. If he has an excess of funds, we agree on whether the money should be left to cover next month's expenses, used for discretionary spending, earmarked for a savings goal other than his car, "matched" for investing, used to pay borrowed funds, or set aside in his savings account for estimated taxes.

If the amount is used for investing, Michael prepares a check and mails it along with my "matching funds" check to his Merrill Lynch investment account.

Michael keeps *The Real-Life* Money Game Five-Step Instructions in his personal financial binder. At first, each month he would refer to the steps. After about six months of practice, the monthly steps became for him second-nature. Now he rarely glances at them anymore.

● ● ●

Over the years playing the game with Michael, I remember a few things vividly. He struggled most learning how to reconcile his cash balance to the bank balance each month. The hardest concept for Michael to grasp was the need to pay back interest on any money he borrowed. As a result, he rarely borrows anymore. If he does, he pays the funds back promptly. He's discovered he doesn't like the high cost of debt.

After the third year managing his own resource, he paid close attention to his spending. His $150 monthly car savings had grown. Watching with excitement, he sent every dollar unspent or every extra dollar earned into his car account. A satisfying result for both of us.

We stay organized. We engage in positive, problem-solving money discussions. Since we began playing *The Real-Life* Money Game, arguments have become rare. Michael understands clearly what tangible skills to hone.

We use the flexibility of the Family Fund Contribution formula to expand with his ever-increasing personal responsibility as he pays for more and more of his expenses. Now, he is highly motivated to earn money. Not so much because money has become his goal in life, but rather because he has grasped the idea that in order to get what he wants, he has to manage his resources. At first he resisted. He didn't want to spend his time earning money just to pay expenses. But he learned quickly the advantages of pooling his earnings with the Family Fund Contribution. Once he realized this would afford him an even greater resource to manage, he enthusiastically added his own contributions. Before, he was suspicious that I was trying to take away *his* money by making him spend it on things not necessarily of his choosing.

Perhaps the most exciting result is that he handles finances intuitively. He understands at a *gut level* the consequence of each financial decision he makes. Managing his money has become automatic. Enjoying the benefits of a well-managed resource has clearly made it worthwhile.

Finally, the day arrived, a week before his sixteenth birthday, for him to purchase his bright-red BMW. He rejoices now at having his own transportation. He has expanded his car-detailing business to include a partner and assistants. And he sends every spare dollar to his investment account for matching funds, with an eye looking ahead to college. Rewards abound for us both! I watch his financial evolution, while he revels in his financial freedom.

The Real-Life Money Game Five-Step Instructions

Now let's look at *The Real-Life* Money Game Five-Step Instructions in detail. Each step is broken into tasks that you can go through one at a time with your teen. Each task relates to a key concept and to scorekeeping activities learned in prior chapters. Refer back to the related chapters for the specific details.

Step One: Gather Resources

The goal of step one is to gather resources, including information and accessories, and to put together a fund of money (currency) for your teen to practice with. The list below will help you find the information you need in the first five chapters.

Chapter One

- Sit down with your teen and explain the concept and the object of *The Real-Life* Money Game.

Chapter Two

- Complete the Parent Player Profile Questionnaire and the Teen Player Profile Questionnaire for each family member.

Chapter Three

- Gather the accessories, organize your teen's personal financial binder, and open bank and/or investment accounts.

Chapter Four

- Determine teen-generated income sources which include coins, birthday or holiday gifts, earnings, savings or investment income, and borrowed funds. Once this information has been gathered, it will be used in the computation of the Family Fund Contribution formula.

- Use the Activities Pie-Chart to identify your teen's available time, if any, to earn money. Then select at least one way your teen can earn money: from paid household tasks and chores, from a job, or from a "Teen Business."

- If earning money from household tasks and chores, complete *The Real-Life* Money Game Household Tasks and Chores worksheet to identify each task or chore, when it will be accomplished, and how much each task will earn.

- If earning money from a job, discuss the tangible and intangible job skills, know the labor laws, use the Teen Jobs: Select, Land, and Keep checklist as a guide, and review Job Areas For Teens to prompt ideas.

- If earning money from a "Teen Business," review "Teen Business" Ideas, and complete the "Teen Business" Plan to gather all information needed.

Chapter Five

- Determine parent-generated teen-income sources which include allowance and the Family Fund Contribution.

- Complete the Income Worksheet using current month's information as an estimate of your teen's income to use in the computation of the Family

Fund Contribution formula. Complete an Expense Worksheet for the current month showing all the expenses you are paying on your teen's behalf and what your teen is paying.

- Using the Estimated Projected Expenses worksheet and the Estimated Projected Clothes Expense worksheet, project estimated expenses needed later, and a clothing expense amount.

- Highlight expenses you would like your teen to be responsible for paying using the established guidelines. As your teen develops skills in paying expenses, additional expense items can be added. Each time new expenses are added, highlight the original worksheet to remind yourself that your teen is now responsible for paying them.

- Determine a Rainy-Day Fund, the amount set aside for unanticipated costs or emergencies.

- Using the formula, compute your teen's monthly Family Fund Contribution.

Step Two: Contract Negotiations

Step two requires that you and your teen sign a contract agreeing to the terms of how resources will be used. An important next step. All family members need to understand from the outset what is expected of them. For help with this, refer to the information indicated in the two chapters below.

Chapter Eight

- Go over *The Real-Life* Money Game Rules, including the Golden Rule For Parents.

- Talk about what sanctions (consequences for noncompliance) might occur if *The Real-Life* Money Game is not played according to the instructions and the rules. Write these down. Sign the contract agreeing to follow the instructions and abide by the rules.

Chapter Nine

- Identify at least one goal at the start of the game that you hope to achieve by teaching your teen tangible money-management skills and write it down on *The Real-Life* Money Game Plan worksheet.

• Use the tangible and intangible skills list as a guide. Come up with a detailed list of tasks to accomplish the goal. Review *The Real-Life* Money Game Plan worksheet with your teen to discuss the result you wish to achieve. You can do this monthly, quarterly, or as the need arises.

· ·

Step Three: Fund Distribution

· ·

In step three you will decide how the funds are distributed throughout the month and begin keeping track of the activity. For help with step three, consult the chapters in the list below.

Chapter Six

• Discuss how the money will be distributed using one of the four spending options and review the instructions with your teen. The four spending options include Cash Pockets, Savings Account and ATM Card, Checking and Debit Card Account, and an Investment Account.

Chapter Seven

• At the beginning of the month, fill in the Playing Board-Spending Plan column one with the Family Fund Contribution amount, your teen's projected income, and the expenses you highlighted that your teen will be responsible for paying. Explain to your teen that the Playing Board-Spending Plan identifies how much money he or she has available and how the money will be used.

Chapter Eleven

• Help your teen identify savings targets using *The Real-Life* Money Game Three-Part Savings Plan: Now, Later, Never.

Chapter Twelve

• Plan how your teen might give and in what way using the "Who or What Matters Most to You?" exercise.

Chapter Thirteen

• Encourage your teen to follow *The Real-Life* Money Game Debt Rules, and decide whether debt repayment will require additional monthly funds.

Chapter Fourteen

- Explain each Step to Investing and use the Key Investment Objectives to establish your teen's investment guidelines.

Chapter Fifteen

- Help your teen review tax consequences associated with his or her financial activities, project any tax expense to set aside, and determine where the estimated amounts will be held until they are needed.

Step Four: Account Activity

Step four asks you to summarize account activity at the end of the month. The chapter listed below will guide you in this.

Chapter Ten

- During the month, review with your teen how to record money received on the Income Worksheet. At month's end, show your teen how to record his or her spending on the Expense Worksheet using collected receipts, a check register, or the monthly bank or investment statement.

- Using the completed Income and Expense Worksheets, show your teen how to fill in the amounts in column two of the Playing Board-Spending Plan. Total up the information using a calculator. Compute the difference between the projected amounts in column one and the actual amounts in column two and fill in column three.

Step Five: Future Strategizing or Contract Renegotiation

In step five, the final step, you will be asked to discuss future strategies and re-negotiate contracts as needed to take into account both you and your teen's changing financial situation. For help, see the chapters listed below.

Chapter Nine

- Address any notes written during the month on *The Real-Life* Money Game Plan worksheet. Revise the plan as your teen's skills develop and as your goal's change. Continue using *The Real-Life* Money Game Plan Overview as your guide.

Chapter Ten

• Each month, preferably at the same day and time, discuss the monthly Playing Board-Spending Plan results. Review with your teen whether they have a shortfall or excess of funds and how to handle either result. Revise the Family Fund Contribution formula amount as your teen's needs change. Update the following month's Playing Board-Spending Plan to reflect these changes.

• • •

To help you achieve the success that I've experienced playing *The Real-Life* Money Game with my son, part three offers winning strategies for both you and your teen. In addition, *The Real-Life* Money Game provides a tool to promote problem solving, as well as solutions for financially disruptive circumstances. You can also assist your teen in making long-term financial goals by teaching him or her the concept of net worth. And to assure yourself that your teen is making progress, you can summarize all the previous chapters' scores in the last chapter's cumulative scorekeeping box.

Chapter Seventeen
Winning Strategies For Parents

At this point you have learned how to play *The Real-Life* Money Game. You have been introduced to the tools you can teach your teen to help him or her develop money-management skills. Now it's time to implement some winning strategies.

Winning. In my workshops, the word alone makes parents' eyes role and heads shake. Most confess they barely negotiate stalemates, let alone achieve victories. This chapter offers strategies designed to help both you and your teen win *The Real-Life* Money Game.

Winning strategies start with teaching financial skills in a time-tested order of priority while avoiding the "Seven Deadly Sins," the seven most common financial mistakes parents tend to make with their teens. We'll also talk about the need to open lines of communication with your teen about your family's finances. Ultimately these winning strategies are designed to help your son or daughter manage that resource that will be theirs to nurture and cultivate.

Teaching Skills In Order of Priority

In my course, parents often ask questions such as these: Should my teen get a job? Should my teen use his or her own money to pay for clothes? How can I get my son to stop spending his money and save for a car? When should I introduce my daughter to debit and credit cards? Should I encourage my teen to invest?

What parents are really asking is how to prioritize their teen's needs and what skills to foster first. I tell them that their teens need to learn a *bundle* of money-management skills, not just one or two skills in isolation.

Tangible Money-Management Skills Order of Priority

- Generating Income—Earning Money
- Practicing Spending Mechanics
- Applying Savings Concepts
- Encouraging Giving
- Understanding Borrowing and Lending
- Investing Wisely
- Considering Taxes

To teach these skills effectively, *The Real-Life* Money Game recommends introducing them in an order of priority. We start by teaching tangible skills first. The sequence that works best, based on my experience working with families, follows the sidebar's list on the previous page, in order from top to bottom.

The order begins with the most basic *tangible* skills: understanding where money comes from which includes earning money, and learning how to spend within some pre-established parameters. These are the top two money concerns parents express most often to me. Either their teens don't know how or are not motivated to earn money. Or if they do earn money, they tend to spend it as fast as they receive it! Sound familiar?

Teens need to learn how to generate income so they have a resource to manage. Once teens have a resource, they need to learn to prioritize their spending and to work within the boundaries of their monthly Playing Board-Spending Plan. Your teen's monthly plan, of course, will be scalable; that is, it can grow and change as your son or daughter's needs change.

Next comes the tough task: convincing your teen to set aside earnings to save. At first, mistakes will happen. The resource will be depleted. But once teens learn that they have control over spending, as well as responsibility for certain costs, they will come to understand the need to move carefully and husband that precious resource.

To prevent them from becoming over-cautious, you can encourage them to use the resource for giving. Investing may be accompanied by borrowing as a means of expanding the resource base. But I recommend to parents that they hold off on these concepts until their teens have had, at minimum, six months of success with basic earning and spending and saving. Let your teen feel confident with a fixed resource base first. Then seek to expand it. Finally, introduce your teen to the concept of taxes. Help your son or daughter evaluate the tax effect of every financial decision he or she makes.

As you guide your teen through this recommended tangible skills list in order of priorities, consider, also, the winning strategies in the table shown on the following page. Each strategy relates to *The Real-Life* Money Game tool offered in previous chapters covering each tangible skill.

218

The Real-Life Money Game Winning Strategies

Earning	Help your teen fill out the Activities Pie-Chart to identify his or her available time. Choose one way your teen can earn money so he or she will have time to practice. Talk with your son or daughter about the three ways he or she can earn money: doing household tasks and chores; landing a job; starting a "Teen Business."
Spending	Establish a Playing Board-Spending Plan to: • Identify clearly who will be responsible for paying what expenses. • Open discussions about what spending habits are or are not working. • Strategize and plan spending goals. When your teen becomes proficient using one spending-mechanic option, move on to the next.
Saving	Set up a three-part savings plan that satisfies your teen's short-term and "big-ticket" longer-term needs, so he or she will be less inclined to balk at savings that will seem earmarked for *never*. Once your teen sees his or her money grow in a fund, he or she will more cooperatively put away a portion of earnings.
Giving	Encourage your teen to complete the "Who or What Matters Most to You?" exercise. Choose at least one cause or organization your son or daughter cares about to contribute to or volunteer for on a regular basis.
Borrowing/ Lending	Follow *The Real-Life* Money Game Debt Rules so your teen will understand how to borrow and lend and use debt wisely.
Investing	Promote your teen's interest in investing by matching his or her funds. Follow the Steps For Investing and review the Key Investment Objectives to establish your teen's investment guidelines. Find one simple investment vehicle that will teach your teen the basic principles, such as investing with a traditional IRA or a Roth IRA.
Taxes	Whenever your teen makes a financial decision, encourage him or her to consider the tax ramifications.

By practicing the tangible-skills strategies and the discipline that goes with them, the net side effect, whether you are aware of it or not, is that you will insulate your teen against life's woes with an admirable set of *intangible* skills.

Intangible Money-Management Skills

1. Valuing assets (what they have)
2. Delayed gratification (curbing impulses)
3. Differentiating wants from needs (and understanding the importance of contributing to both)
4. Problem solving
5. Personal responsibility
6. Self-discipline
7. Self-confidence
8. Self-motivation
9. Independent thinking
10. Strong work ethic

Seven Deadly Sins: The Seven Most Common Financial Mistakes Parents Make With Their Teens

As parents play *The Real-Life Money Game* with their teens, sometimes they will encounter traps and pitfalls that curtail their effectiveness. Two conditions in particular exist that can undermine parents' efforts. Either parents intrude too far into the money-management process, or, conversely, they fail to offer enough help. As parents become aware of these *deadly sins*, they can avoid unwanted consequences by asking this question: How can I turn this trap into an opportunity for my teen to make a choice that will promote independent thinking?

Seven Deadly Sins: The Seven Most Common Financial Mistakes Parents Make With Their Teens

1. Overly Excessive: The Free Handouts
2. Overly Strict: Never Enough Money
3. Secrecy: "My teen knows nothing about our finances."
4. The Cyclical Nature of Negative Presumption: Never Good Enough
5. Saying Too Much: The "I told you so!" Syndrome
6. Saying Too Little: The Fallacy of Sink or Swim
7. Money for the "Goods": Pressure to Perform

1. Overly Excessive: The Free Handouts

The Problem

One day I casually mentioned to a parent friend of mine that I was practicing money management with my teenage son. He said, with tongue in cheek, "Yeah, so am I. I just give it to them." As Thomas Greene so aptly put it, he had fallen prey to the temptation to offer free handouts which amounts to giving your teen money without holding him or her accountable.

Loose money arrangements without accountability are missed opportunities to teach teens about spending. The problem is that parents do the thinking and parents make the decisions. They, not the teen, have taken the responsibility for the cost.

As mentioned previously, the MacLean family had first-hand experience falling into this trap. Darcy MacLean was uncomfortable doling money out to her daughter, Linda. Two things troubled her. First, Darcy worried that Linda wasn't learning to appreciate how much money was being spent on her behalf. Secondly, she wanted her daughter to understand how much things cost. This came home to roost when Darcy realized that every time she and her daughter shopped, Linda conveniently left her wallet behind. It became apparent to Darcy that her daughter assumed that her mother would pay for everything. And her daughter was right. Darcy would, simply because it was easier. Yet this meant Linda nagged her mother constantly for every little thing she wanted.

The Remedy

You can do four simple things to start holding your teen accountable:

- Make sure your son or daughter spends his or her own money, as established on the Playing Board-Spending Plan.

- Encourage your teen to keep receipts.

- Get in the regular habit of giving exact cash.

- Ask questions following a purchase that will encourage your teen to see the big picture, such as, "Will the expenses for the month still to be covered?"

Karen Wilson learned to cover her gas expenses by staying within an agreed-upon $50 monthly expense. When she had to ask her father for more gas money because she'd been giving all of her friends rides home, it became apparent to James, her dad, that Karen was not aware of how much her decisions were costing.

To encourage Karen to start thinking about this, James asked his daughter the following questions: Can your friends share in the cost of your gas? Are others driving you home and sharing in the carpooling? Have you looked to see what service station sells the cheapest gas? By asking thought-provoking questions, James encouraged Karen to think about the costs associated with the choice she had made. Karen, in turn, announced to her dad after school one day that she had filled the tank with gas from a discounted station and that her friends volunteered to contribute money toward the cost. Karen was learning to take some personal responsibility for her actions, and soon found that gas expenses weren't taking away from the resource she'd planned to spend on entertainment.

The Skills Developed

Teens who learn how to manage their money using the Playing Board-Spending Plan see a connection between their spending and the consequences associated with that spending. They take responsibility for the cost, and therefore, for their actions.

2. Overly Strict: Never Enough Money

The Problem

Some parents believe that if you give your teen less money than actually needed, he or she will learn frugality. Such parents often end up with a contrary result. Teens who never have enough money often feel frustrated and begin to associate money with negative feelings. These teens may learn to be cheap rather than frugal, may learn stinginess rather than generosity. Sometimes this prompts teens to borrow from their friends. When parents are overly strict with money, teens often don't have enough range to make independent choices. It is very difficult for a teen to develop financial skills if resources are too restricted. Also, teens who have to ask their parents for money all the time tend to feel vulnerable and inferior, not to mention resentful. Often the un-spoken message these parents send their teens is that their sons or daughters can't be trusted and that the parent knows best. This only breeds the desire on the teen's part to prove them right. For families where money is chronically tight, it isn't the amount that matters so much as the opportunity. Even man-aging a small resource will give a teen a feeling of independence coupled with responsibility.

My family fell prey to this pitfall. The entire impetus for teaching my son money-management skills when he was twelve came as a result of his biggest complaint: he never felt he had enough money. Michael had the choice to get the shoes I picked out or none at all. He invariably chose to get the shoes. But a week later we'd go shopping and he'd want money to purchase another pair of athletic shoes. To him, shoes mattered.

I felt the need to hold back, not so much because I had a legitimate reason to have to, but because I wanted to teach my son not to spend frivolously. This was my commission of the deadly sin. The point wasn't to teach him *not* to spend, the point was to teach him *how* to spend, within the means of his re-source base.

The Remedy

The way to avoid this trap, and the most effective way to teach teens how to live within their means, is to do the following:

- Establish a *realistic* Playing Board-Spending Plan using the Family Fund Contribution formula that takes into account your family's resources.

- Give your teens access to a portion of that resource sufficient to cover their *real* costs. This can include discretionary costs—those *wants* such as movie money or music CDs. Or it can also include fixed costs—their *needs* such as clothes and school supplies.

At the outset, I set up a Playing Board-Spending Plan that included only my son's discretionary expenses. Michael had had no previous experience with money aside from spending his allowance, so I left out his fixed costs such as the clothes he needed. We based his discretionary costs on what we had actually spent over the last year on the following expense items for one month: $10 for entertainment, $25 for "extra" clothes, $35 for games, and $20 for books. But what Michael really loved to buy was shoes. Without my nagging, he saved a little of his money each month, usually five to ten dollars, until he had enough to buy that extra pair of athletic shoes.

Michael was thrilled to have enough money to make spending decisions for himself. I discovered that not only was he more satisfied with his purchases, but sometimes he made better choices than I did. I'm convinced that every time I hear him in the garage banging the sod out of his shoes, it's because he is using his own funds. He now takes better care of his shoes than I do mine.

The Skills Developed

Teens who have access to enough money learn to manage their resources within a realistic Playing Board-Spending Plan, and they also learn to live within their means. They learn to distinguish between their wants and their needs and to understand the importance of contributing to both. They are happier with what they have, because they've been able to exercise their own spending choices. Teens who have an adequate fund of money to manage are also less confrontational. And this, dear parents, can be a blessing beyond measure.

• •

3. Secrecy: "My teen knows nothing about our finances."

• •

The Problem

Too often parents say, "We don't want our teen to know anything about our finances." These parents are concerned their teens will "blab" sensitive, personal financial information all over the neighborhood. Or, that their teens will not understand the complexities of what they hear. Very often parents are reluctant to talk about money their teens will one day receive. Parents are concerned, perhaps rightly so, that their teens will not be motivated to earn money if they become aware that large resources are available from family funds. On the flip side of the coin, parents who don't talk with their teens because both might be embarrassed by impoverished circumstances are committing the same error. Without sufficient information, teens can't learn money-management skills. Instead, they learn to be sneaky or bullying or, worse, they learn to ask for handouts from others.

Sam Sanchez describes the generational differences between how his family talked about money when he was growing up versus how he talks to his daughter Maria.

When Sam was fourteen he wanted to attend a private boarding school in Colorado. His parents agreed as long as he paid for the tuition. Sam worked all summer to earn money to make a contribution. But at the end of the summer, his parents told him he would have to work two jobs at the school—serving in the cafeteria breakfast line and delivering students' dry cleaning. Sam was angry. He felt he'd done his part during the summer.

Sam's parents neglected to explain the family's financial circumstances to him. His parents' generation was not inclined to talk about this information. But Sam could have been more accepting of his financial role and the responsibility for earning money if he'd been privy to more of his parents' financial situation. Sam could have learned how to strategize, to develop a mutually agreed-upon plan with his parents, to learn more about what it takes to manage a household, and what it means to borrow. Overall, he could have learned how to make better financial decisions. In this way he would have had an opportunity to understand why certain decisions were made and to start thinking independently. Instead, Sam felt he had been thrown into the world unprepared.

To help avoid Sam's anger and sense of martyrdom, his parents could have pointed out what they could afford, have showed him the household costs, and together, with Sam, have worked out a plan. Their plan could have been something like this: Sam could have earned a portion of his tuition each month working at the school. His parents could have set aside an amount each month along with the savings from groceries they were not buying for Sam, and together they could have agreed on how to make up any tuition shortfall.

With his daughter heading for college, Sam feels he has done a better job of communicating how necessary it is to have foresight. Together, hoping to avoid the resentment he felt toward his parents, he and his daughter are investing a portion of their monthly earnings to prepare for her upcoming college costs.

The Remedy

- Because discussions about family finances can often be sensitive, the best way to avoid this trap of secrecy is to use a model. A pie chart works wonderfully. Parents can show teens their family's financial circumstances without using *real numbers*. *The Real-Life* Money Game provides a Pie-Chart Model For Family Financial Discussions as follows:

Pie-Chart Model For Family Financial Discussions
Family Member Player _____

The pie represents 100% of your family's income. Slice the pie into percents to show how the family income is used for the points bulleted below:

- Costs of a Home

- Food and Entertainment

- Clothes and Education

- Transportation Costs

- Medical

- Vacation

- Emergencies, Savings, Investing

- Debt

- Charity

- Taxes

A blank copy of this worksheet is provided for your use in the appendix on page 313.

First, explain that this pie represents 100% of the family income, and that the pie is sliced into pieces to show how the income is used. Out of the pie, explain to your teen that 33%, for example, is needed to pay for the house (home mortgage), protection for the house (insurance), payment to support our community (taxes), heat, lights, water, yard maintenance, and housekeeping. Show your teen by roughly drawing a one-third slice in the pie. Of course, you determine your own percentages based upon your actual situation. It's okay if the numbers are a rough approximation; teens will still get the point. Often this is a revealing exercise for parents as well.

Continuing the example, let's say that 10% of the income goes toward groceries, going out to eat, movies and fun family activities (entertainment). Draw the same approximate slice in the circle. Then show your teen that another 10% slice pays for the following items: clothes, teen's activities, sports equipment, lessons, education. Another 5% slice covers the costs to get around: car payments, gas, car insurance, repair and maintenance, bus (transportation), and another 5% pays for doctors and health care (medical). Some portion of the pie will be spent on vacation, let's say 7%. That leaves 30% of the pie left to divide up for any unforeseen expenses, to put aside in savings for a large purchase perhaps, or to invest.

Next, compare your amounts to the national average that family-household consumers are spending in your area on the various expense categories. You can do this by accessing the Bureau of Labor Statistics at www.bls.gov. Talk about where your family fits in relation to consumers in your geographic area.

Finally, using a new pie-chart, encourage your teen to identify his or her own spending habits.

The model can springboard into many valuable financial discussions with your teen. For example, as my son learned more about our family finances, he began to pay attention to what jobs and professions people chose. He started asking realistic questions, such as how much certain jobs or careers paid, how much schooling they required, how many hours were involved, how hard you had to work, how secure were the positions, and where the companies were located. Open discussions about our finances not only resulted in my son's greater awareness of how much income we needed to live, but he also started to think about what it might take for him to live on his own.

The Skills Developed

Teens who are privy to financial information have a greater capacity to accept money decisions that affect them, even if parents have the final say. Teens who participate in family financial discussions tend to be more supportive of their family's well-being than those who don't. By communicating family financial information, parents enable their teens to learn what information is needed to make effective money decisions and how to strategize and plan ahead. This in turn helps teens distinguish between fixed needs and discretionary wants, as well as to understand why sometimes they need to curb impulse spending and delay their gratification.

4. The Cyclical Nature of Negative Presumption: Never Good Enough

The Problem

Says one mother of a thirteen-year-old, "My son is your poster child of un-readiness. He can't keep his hands on his bus pass, let alone on cash. He's clueless about spending. Wants nothing to do with it. He'd give his entire sixty-dollar monthly budget to his church and forgo his clothes if he could." Like this mother, many parents struggle to effectively teach money management to their teens for legitimate reasons. Often parents say their teens are too young or not developmentally ready to learn these skills. Or they report that their teens are not interested. Other parents say their teens just don't understand money concepts. These parents commit the sin I call *the negative cycle of presumption.*

Even well-intentioned parents bring presumptions—prior beliefs—to the task of teaching their teens about money. These presumptions color their thinking regarding their teens' abilities. Studies have shown that teens are especially vulnerable to opinions expressed by their parents. Teens tend to act according to what they've been told about themselves, producing a "self-fulfilling prophecy." When parents presume their teens are not capable of handling money, they set up a recurring pattern of failure.

Sam Sanchez got himself into a negative cycle of presumption with Maria without realizing it. As mentioned previously, money was tight in their household. Even though Maria had her own spending money, before she turned sixteen and could drive a car and earn a regular income, it bothered Sam that she wasted her money on CDs, most of which she quickly lost interest in. He couldn't understand why their mutual anger flared over spending choices. Though he disapproved of her choices, he thought he was being liberal-minded by keeping his opinion to himself. Imagine his surprise when he asked her what was on her mind, and she said, "I'm never good enough, never smart enough, you are never satisfied with anything I do."

Stunned, her dad asked, "What could you possibly mean? I've never said anything like that to you." And it was true. He knew better. He was a smart and well-intentioned father who understood how damaging words of this kind could be to his daughter's feelings of self-worth and confidence. Nevertheless, Maria felt she wasn't living up to her dad's expectations, especially when she spent her money on CDs for which she knew he didn't approve.

Sam understood there was a problem. Determined to pay closer attention to his own behavior, he discovered he was sending his daughter nonverbal cues that conveyed his negative attitude. Whenever he felt disappointed about a spending choice his daughter was making, his posture would grow stiff and tense. He would frown. He'd turn silent. Though he didn't say outright that he expected better results or more disciplined spending, his body language was saying to Maria that her behavior was not good enough. The conclusion she drew was that she was stupid and incompetent. In essence, he was telling her that he knew better then she, that he was wiser and that her choices were inferior. This made Maria feel incompetent and inadequate and set up a cycle of negative beliefs and feelings and distrust between father and daughter. This is the common trap that negative presumption sets up.

The Remedy

To overcome this negative presumption parents can:

- Flush presumptions out in the open, recognize them for what they are, and give their teens a chance to prove themselves. Parents can become students of themselves by adopting enough self-awareness to recognize negative messages when they are being sent and to pay attention to any body language and nonverbal cues they send to their teens.

- Focus on a positive cycle of presumption rather than on a negative one. Parents can send their teens the message that they are capable as each tangible skill is introduced in priority order.

- Give credibility to their teens; let their teens feel confident and competent by relaxing a tight grip on their own opinions. Let teens voice their own values first. They need an opportunity to have a say in how their needs are met.

- Trust that their son or daughter, as they take on greater responsibility, will learn to be self-disciplined.

The Skills Developed

When the call for a spending decision comes from teens, they begin to discipline themselves. They grow confident in their decision-making because they feel trusted by their parents. Once trust is established, teens who are allowed to make their own decisions learn how to curb their own impulses and to delay gratification. Parents who send messages to their son or daughter that they are capable instill confidence in them.

5. Saying Too Much: The "I told you so!" Syndrome

The Problem

When parents say "I told you so," the message they're really conveying is that they consider themselves to be the wise authorities on all subjects. Teens stop thinking for themselves when parents fall into the trap of behaving like know-it-alls. As a result, teens do not learn to rely on their own judgment. Instead, they can become resentful and in turn resist any parental influence.

As mentioned previously, Sam Sanchez had this problem with his daughter. During her senior year in high school, she learned how to use a checking account with a debit card. She wrote checks occasionally, but most often she would withdraw cash from an ATM to cover her weekly expenses. Toward the end of the year, she started writing checks and making purchases with her debit card for upcoming college expenses. At the same time, she was phasing out of her job, knowing she was leaving for college, and thus her deposits into her account were smaller. She soon discovered upon receipt of her bank statement that she had made a mistake in her check register and was short by $17. Unfortunately, four checks came in after the shortfall was detected. By the time her deposit was recorded by the bank, she had been charged check fees of $30 for each check that cleared after the shortfall—a total of $120.

When Sam talked with Maria about the problem, his daughter admitted that instead of recording all transactions in her check register, she relied on the balance she got from her last ATM withdrawal. The balance didn't reflect outstanding checks.

Sam wanted to say, I told you that you needed to keep your check register current, but he didn't. He didn't interfere, but let his daughter take responsibility for her own actions. And she did. She called the bank, but they made no exception on the fees.

Upon reflection, Sam realized that what he had wanted really, if he was honest with himself, was to have his daughter conform to his way of doing things because he had the experience and knew how to do it the *right* way. Or so he told himself. The problem was, his daughter wouldn't learn anything if she simply did what he told her to do. Later, as Maria was heading off to college, Sam felt relieved that she had already had her trial by fire and that they had both gotten through it without being burned too badly. In college, of course, the stakes would be higher. But now Sam felt confident that Maria was prepared.

The Remedy

- Consistent with the Golden Rule For Parents discussed in chapter eight, parents need to be sensitive to situations and learn to not say too much or to insist upon the correctness of their own opinion.

- Parents need to be willing to allow their teens to make mistakes. Teens learn at a gut level from having made their own good or bad choices, not from obeying their parents. The choice they make isn't half as important as their need to understand that they are responsible for the consequences of those choices.

The Skills Developed

When parents practice the Golden Rule For Parents, teens are then given the opportunity to think independently, to practice making decisions, and to learn to live with their choices. Over time teens will grow more confident and, in turn, they will develop more reliable judgment.

6. Saying Too Little: The Fallacy of Sink or Swim

The Problem

If silence is the Golden Rule For Parents, then isn't it a contradiction to say that it's a deadly sin to "say too little?"

Many of us are inclined to think, "My daughter will just have to figure things out for herself the hard way, like I did," or, "It's too bad that my son got himself into this mess." Parents are really telling their teens that there is a consequence to their actions. Fine. We've all been there. We've all been submerged at least once in the backwash of our actions and somehow bobbed back to the surface. But sometimes this process is counter-productive. If the consequences pose too great a hardship, teens can become fearful to act.

Recall that Darcy MacLean was at the point of giving up on her daughter Linda's attempts to manage $600 twice a year to cover clothes. Linda was intimidated by the process. Because Linda did not know how much clothes cost, she was fearful of buying anything. Because she was fearful of the consequences of overspending, she would "conveniently" leave her wallet at home whenever she went shopping with her mom. Her mom would end up paying for the clothes purchases to avoid the hassle.

So how do teens learn if not from the consequences of their actions?

The Remedy

Offer teens support rather than the extreme ultimatum of sink or swim. What teens need is a little floating buoy in the vast lake of consequence that they can hang on to. For example, Darcy feels justified in giving Linda the occasional reminder to bring her wallet when they go shopping, but without offering to take away her initiative to pay. Parents can:

- Share input rather than interfering.
- Listen actively instead of commenting judgmentally.
- Exchange experiences in lieu of expecting certain outcomes.
- Offer information instead of imposing opinions.

The MacLeans decided to set up a fund for Linda's discretionary spending only for those smaller items such as makeup and jewelry. She was given $75 each month instead of the original $600 for half the year, a smaller pool of money to spend over a shorter period of time. These terms were far less intimidating. To make poor choices would result in far less harsh consequences. Darcy was thus offering her daughter a safe-harbor alternative. Linda could practice managing her Playing Board-Spending Plan with minimal struggle, thereby developing the skills she would one day need without being fearful to act.

The Skills Developed

When parents provide support, thus saving their teens from the harsh sink-or-swim method of learning, teens find the security they need to diminish their fears. In so doing, teens develop a greater willingness to act, to try again, to not give up. Also, teens who are offered effective support will in turn become confident problem-solvers.

7. Money for the "Goods": Pressure to Perform

The Problem

Considering the law of averages, *all* teens will be good at something, but *no* teen can be good at everything. One consistent trap parents fall into is paying their teens for the "goods": good grades, good behavior, good performance. Using money as a motivator—either as a reward or as a punishment—seems too powerful an incentive for parents to resist. But the approach is rampant with problems. Sometimes what teens may be "good" at might not be the same "good" parents are paying for.

The Delaney family illustrates how tempting it is to use money as a motivator, especially when a non-cooperative teen pays lip service to participation but doesn't follow through. Laura Delaney shared how completely exasperated she was with her seventeen-year-old son, Edward. Edward was an excellent student, achieved high accolades for his volunteerism, played basketball on a championship team, but refused to clean his room.

Laura said, "I was at my wits' end whenever we'd plan a dinner party. So you know what I did? I took Edward's debit card away."

Laura achieved her goal. Edward cleaned his room. But what did Edward learn about money in the process? As parents with grown teens such as the Delaneys can attest, over time, teens learn to resist. They stop taking the payoff at the point where money matters less to them than their freedom to choose. Or, conversely, adolescents and older teens become conditioned to expect payment for everything they do.

The Remedy

- Define success as a process and avoid paying your teen for the "goods."

- Turn goal-oriented solutions—*short-term, nothing learned*—into process-oriented solutions.

- Come up with a workable solution by identifying each individual's needs and negotiate until all needs get met. Chapter nineteen offers a four-step method to help families resolve conflict in this manner.

Laura and Edward came up with a workable solution by identifying each of their needs. Laura's need was to have an entirely clean house for her dinner parties. Edward's need was to have the freedom to make his own choice, in particular about the right to have control over his room.

To find a process-oriented solution, Laura and Edward negotiated who would clean the room, when and who would pay for it. Laura, in return for offering her son the right to have his room messy, took enough money away from her son's Playing Board-Spending Plan to offset the cost of having a housekeeper straighten his room before important events. They agreed on a charge of $25. Edward was encouraged to make up the $25 shortfall in his spending plan by producing income from another source. Instead, he chose to forego a portion of his entertainment expense.

Paradoxically, what parents often discover when they ease up on the pressure is that their teens think "control" isn't as important as the "price they pay." As it turns out, Edward, after a few expense hits, didn't think that the right to have a messy room was worth the $25 it cost him. Instead, Edward chose to clean his room for Laura's dinner parties. But, now the arguing and resentment were gone. He'd participated in the decision.

The Skills Developed

Teens who are free from pressure learn to develop high levels of self-motivation. With this control, teens learn to take personal responsibility for their choices. This, in turn, develops a strong work ethic as well as a clear sense of independence.

• • •

Take time to study the Seven Deadly Sins summarized in the following chart.

Seven Deadly Sins: The Seven Most Common Financial Mistakes Parents Make With Their Teens

The "Sin"	What It Is	Why It's A Problem	The Remedy	Skills Learned
1. Overly Excessive: The Free Handouts	Loose money arrangements with no accountability.	Parents do the thinking and decide on costs.	Hold teens accountable by requesting receipts.	Taking personal responsibility for spending and costs.
2. Overly Strict: Never Enough Money	Minimal money to maintain control or to teach frugality.	No range for independent choice-making.	Establish a realistic spending plan.	Living within their means.
3. Secrecy: "My teen knows nothing about our finances."	Parents don't discuss the family's personal finances with their teens.	Eliminates opportunities for teens to hear and observe how their families handle and value money.	Use a pie-chart model to discuss family financial information without using "real" numbers.	Knowing what information is needed to make effective money decisions and how to strategize and plan.
4. The Cyclical Nature of Negative Presumption: Never Good Enough	Parents presume teens are not capable of handling money before their teens have had a chance to prove themselves.	Sets up a recurring pattern of failure and negativity.	Send positive messages that reinforce teens' capabilities.	Growing confident in decision-making and trusting their own behavior.
5. Saying Too Much: The "I told you so!" Syndrome	Parents act like the all-knowing and wise authorities on all subjects.	Teens do not learn to rely on their own judgment.	Practice the Golden Rule For Parents and resist the urge to blame.	Making decisions and learning to live with their choices.
6. Saying Too Little: The Fallacy of Sink or Swim	Parents expect their teens to learn from the consequence of their actions.	Too harsh a consequence can cause teens to become fearful to act.	Support teens by offering information instead of opinions.	Becoming confident problem-solvers in support of other people, too.
7. Money for the "Goods": Pressure to Perform	Using money as a motivator by paying teens for the "goods": good grades, good behavior, good performance.	Teens stop taking the payoff at the point where money matters less than their freedom to choose.	Use money as a teaching tool by turning goal-oriented solutions—short-term, nothing learned—into process-oriented solutions that allow teens to make independent choices.	Developing high levels of self-motivation and strong work ethics.

235

Seven Deadly Sins: The Seven Most Common Financial Mistakes Parents Make With Their Teens
Family Member Player _____

1. **Overly Excessive: The Free Handouts**
   Action to Take:

2. **Overly Strict: Never Enough Money**
   Action to Take:

3. **Secrecy: "My teen knows nothing about our finances."**
   Action to Take:

4. **The Cyclical Nature of Negative Presumption: Never Good Enough**
   Action to Take:

5. **Saying Too Much: The "I told you so!" Syndrome**
   Action to Take:

6. **Saying Too Little: The Fallacy of Sink or Swim**
   Action to Take:

7. **Money for the "Goods": Pressure to Perform**
   Action to Take:

A blank copy of this worksheet is provided for your use in the appendix on page 314.

To help you identify whether you are making one or more of the seven most common financial mistakes with your teen, make notes about your "sins" on the preceding exercise. Using the remedies as your guide, write down any actions you would like to take to turn traps into choices that will help promote your teen's independent thinking.

● ● ●

Every teen's wants and needs will be different while playing *The Real-Life Money Game*. The challenge facing parents is roughly the same: how can I nudge myself toward hands-off parenting in order to allow my teen to do more hands-on money management? By teaching tangible skills in order of priority, by following the winning-strategy guidelines, and by avoiding the Seven Deadly Sins, you are well on your way to providing opportunities for your son or daughter to think independently.

Chapter Eighteen
Winning Strategies For Teens

• •

The first thing I tell parents on the first day of workshop is to practice, practice, practice. When we look to our own growing up, it's easy to see that if we excelled, it was invariably the result of sheer hard work and endless repetitions. But once we'd achieved mastery, what we were able to do looked like *magic* to others.

A parent attending my course, after a few days of working through the mechanics of money management with her son, admitted that getting cooperation felt a bit like a life lesson in chaos theory. Why? Because suddenly she'd discovered that her teen had a mind of his own.

So the second thing I tell parents is that teaching our teens good money management is also about patience. Patience means being generous with time. Giving them time to practice these skills over and over again. Giving them time to make mistakes and learn from them. Putting in the time with them when they are ready. With practice and patience, skills can become ingrained. Even teens who have no interest in being entrepreneurial can develop a financial instinct.

Let's explore some common mistakes teens make as they practice playing *The Real-Life* Money Game and the ways you might deal with them—whether to intervene, and if so, to what degree.

Common Mistakes To Help Your Teens Avoid

The following sidebar lists the top four most common mistakes teens make while playing *The Real-Life* Money Game.

Mistake 1: Lose things they've paid for.

Let's consider the Wilson family's shoe debacle.

"Athletic shoes. Our great American icon is getting to me!" Connie shakes her head, recounting a recent story. Her

> **Mistakes Teens Make While Playing *The Real-Life* Money Game**
>
> 1. Lose things they've paid for.
> 2. Run out of money.
> 3. Don't keep track of their cash, resulting in overdraft charges.
> 4. Regret what they buy (buyer's remorse).

daughter, Casey, prior to playing *The Real-Life* Money Game, got involved with *indoor* soccer. In order to play, Casey needed a special pair of Adidas soccer shoes, designed for use on gym floors. Connie made a special effort to skip her work-day lunch, and instead, purchase the shoes right away, so Casey would have them for her first practice. The shoes, retailing at $125, were expensive. As it turns out, in spite of Connie's best efforts, her daughter continued to wear an older pair of non-regulation tennis shoes. Casey kept the new Adidas in a plastic bag, and had been taking them to the gym with her each time she had a practice or a game. Just two weeks after Connie had purchased the shoes, they didn't come home with Casey. Casey lost them.

"I was furious!" Connie tells me. "The shoes were brand new and Casey wasn't even wearing them!" Connie was especially upset because her daughter had been in the habit of losing things. She'd lost two brand new Gap sweatshirts over the past year and had left her expensive flute behind in various places. Connie demanded that Casey look for her lost shoes. Connie told her daughter to put notes up all around the school, to which Casey replied, "I'm not putting notes up—no way!" Casey told her mom she had already searched the gym and locker room and as far as her daughter was concerned, the shoes were lost. Connie, at her wits' end, said that this time Casey would have to pay for the shoes. Casey couldn't believe her mom expected her to pay for the shoes and said to her, "As if you've never lost anything."

That's the standard response every time Casey loses something, Connie tells me. What bothers Connie most is her daughter's attitude. Casey doesn't seem inclined to want to take responsibility. She doesn't take ownership of her things. She thinks her mom can just go out and buy another pair of shoes or another of anything for that matter, the moment it's lost or forgotten.

The morning after Connie told Casey she would have to pay for the shoes, Casey asked her mom if she would take her to school early, before other students showed up, so she could take another look around the locker room. Connie thought how interesting it was that once Casey knew she would have to pay for the shoes, her daughter was more committed to finding them.

At school, after a close and careful inspection of the locker room, Casey found the Adidas. A tiny visible portion of the bag was sticking out of a locker. Connie speculated that a janitor probably stuck the bag in a locker and shut the door loosely so it wouldn't lock. Connie was relieved, but still she felt consternation. Had she and Casey not searched before other students had come in, it's very likely the locker would have been closed completely, locking the shoes in until the end of the school year—several months away—when the janitor would use a master key to clean them out. That Casey wouldn't therefore have had the use of the shoes wasn't the main issue. It was her complete indifference to cost and relative value that most troubled Connie. This did not bode well for Casey's financial future.

The story doesn't end here. The same week Casey lost her soccer shoes, Karen, Connie's oldest, lost her $60 track spikes. Having observed how angry and upset her Mom had been with Casey, Karen decided not to say anything to her Mom until the situation cooled down. In desperation to locate the shoes, Karen called her track coach. Together they searched the track field, the locker room, the school yard, the coach's car, Karen's gym bag, even the lunch room and library, retracing Karen's school day.

"You know where they found the shoes?" Connie recounted. "In the garbage can!"

Connie admitted outright that our *throw-away-society* seems to perpetuate this irresponsibility in our teens.

So what do we do as parents? Do we intervene when our sons or daughters make mistakes? Do we break the Golden Rule For Parents?

One or two mistakes are expected and needn't be seen as a reason to break the Golden Rule For Parents or to intervene. However, *patterns* of irresponsible money handling *do* justify an intervention. In the Wilsons' situation, Casey lost things regularly. Karen, her older sister did not. Connie needed to intervene—to insist Casey pay for the shoes out of her monthly Playing Board-Spending Plan. Connie's goal was to connect the problem to the consequence.

By holding Casey responsible, Connie sent her daughter a clear message: If she continued to treat material things that cost money with such disregard, no one would pay for the losses but herself. This can be a hard truth for a teen to swallow. But swallow it they must if they are to understand that the resource being managed is theirs. And that if it is diminished, so their power to control their own lives—a key issue for teens—is diminished.

When we hold our teens accountable, we are telling them that they are capable of handling this responsibility and that we expect this from them. In this way, they have an opportunity to learn from their mistakes, and to develop a successful financial mind-set.

Mistake 2: Run out of money.

One consistent mistake teens make is running out of money. Recall in chapter eight, rule one says that if your teen has a shortfall of funds in a given month, you cannot bail your teen out by adding money that isn't part of the original fund. Your teen either comes up with more funds or forgoes an expenditure, or somehow adds income.

If your son or daughter is in the habit of constantly running out of money, here is an exercise your teen can use to practice *not* running out of money. Parents can intervene without taking the responsibility for the problem out of their teen's hands.

Spending Habits Questionnaire
Family Member Player _____

1. List the five most important things to spend money on between now and the end of the month.

2. How much money do I need to spend on each?

3. How much money do I have left on hand?

4. If I'm short money, how can I adjust the dollar amounts listed for each item to make up the shortfall? What items could I eliminate?

A blank copy of this worksheet is provided for your use in the appendix on page 315.

Mistake 3: Don't keep track of their cash, resulting in overdraft charges.

Sometimes parents and teens find themselves at polar opposites playing *The Real-Life* Money Game. While teens seek shortcuts, easy-outs, and good-enough results, parents, on the other hand, expect a superlative effort. Nowhere is this opposition more prevalent than when teens lose track of their cash, resulting too often in costly overdraft charges. It's a hard mistake for parents to watch silently.

Recall in chapter six, Sam Sanchez's experience with his daughter who guessed at her bank balance. She was charged $120 for her total overdraft checks, and the bank wouldn't waive the fees. Sam wanted to intervene, but he sat back and allowed Maria to take the hit for her own carelessness. A smart move on Sam's part. Maria didn't make the mistake again.

My son was also resistant to the idea of tracking his cash. He didn't want to take the time to record his check and debit card transactions in his check register. He wanted instead to rely on the bank statement balance, no matter how patiently I explained that his check register was used to keep track of his ongoing balance. The bank statement, though used to reconcile his balance, would not be current enough on any given day to be relied upon as accurate. Finally, I stopped trying to convince him to see it my way. I realized the process wasn't perfect. Michael needed to learn the hard way, to experience the mistake first-hand. Like the Sanchez family, all it took was one major overdraft charge before Michael realized the importance of keeping track of his cash.

Once teens make this mistake and experience for themselves what happens when they don't track their ongoing fiscal activity, they are usually more receptive to reconciling their checking and debit card account with the bank and more willing to go through each step on *The Real-Life* Money Game Bank Reconciliation Worksheet. Encourage your teen to keep a minimum balance in his or her checking account as a cushion; $100, for example.

Mistake 4: Regret what they buy (buyer's remorse).

Parents consistently report that their teens often cannot wait to buy something, only to later regret their purchase. Buyer's remorse is a challenging lesson even for parents. But teens who regret what they purchase once or twice can learn an invaluable lesson from their mistake.

Michael, for example, couldn't wait to get his hands on a Microsoft Xbox game player. These machines, hot and new at the time, were in high demand and short supply. In an attempt to be resourceful, Michael called his older cousin, who worked for Microsoft, to see if he could get a newly-released machine. His cousin told Michael he'd reserved two, but the machines hadn't come in yet.

Michael was too eager to wait. He placed bid after bid on an Xbox being sold over the Internet until he finally got the machine—at a premium price of $360. The retail price at the time was $300. He immediately sent in his money order. Two days later, he received his Xbox and was thrilled.

Two weeks later, at a holiday gathering, Michael's cousin gave him an Xbox. Surprise! Michael felt terrible. Not only had he used most of his savings to pay for his premium-priced Xbox, he was overwhelmed by his cousin's generosity, for which he had no gift in return. Michael had no funds left to buy his cousin a gift. Feeling badly, he asked if I would lend him money for a gift for his cousin. His plan was to sell his original Xbox and pay me out of the proceeds. I weighed the pros and cons. Let him flounder and learn that lesson, or let him learn the duty of debt? I agreed to loan him $150. A few days later he purchased a $150 book store gift certificate for his cousin. Before Michael could put his plan to sell his Xbox into action, the bottom dropped out of the Xbox market. The machines were available everywhere. Michael attempted to sell his machine on the Internet without success.

Unable to sell his Xbox, the $150 he'd borrowed from me was accruing interest at an annual rate of ten percent. Month after month, he confessed how much he regretted purchasing the Xbox. But he continued to get the word out among his friends at school that he had an Xbox for sale. Three months later, a student from Michael's high school bought the original Xbox machine for $285.

Michael was relieved to finally have money to pay me back, as well as put some in his checking account. I was proud of him for his resourcefulness. He never gave up. He accepted responsibility for his impulsive purchase, solved the Xbox dilemma, and learned from his mistake. From his experience, he learned not to live beyond his means, not to purchase impulsively, and learned as well, to appreciate the high cost of debt.

As your teen practices playing *The Real-Life* Money Game, keep in mind that there's no way to master money-management skills without making mistakes.

It may be hard to sit back without intervening and observe your son or daughter making poor decisions, but we need to keep in mind that we've had practice. Making mistakes is how they start their practice. With the help of our patience, our teens will learn successful money habits. This, in turn, will promote the kind of savvy financial instincts that will prove invaluable to them later in life.

Developing a Teen's Financial "Instinct"

In chapter two your son or daughter was encouraged to complete the Teen Player Profile Questionnaire. The purpose of the questionnaire was to gather information about your teen's current money habits. Over time, as your teen plays *The Real-Life* Money Game, money habits are bound to change. The goal is to help your teen develop flexible winning strategies that will accommodate their changing needs.

Based on my own experience, and by surveying workshop participants, I've put together a list of financial habits, shown in the sidebar, that hold true for teens who go on to develop, at a young age, financial independence and security.

Starting young means playing *The Real-Life* Money Game with your son or daughter around age twelve. We talked about the necessity to practice regularly, to allow time for your teen to make mistakes, critical to *gut-level* learning.

That's a good starting point, but it's important to have your teen learn to work from an organized *scalable* plan, the foundation of *The Real-Life* Money Game. A flexible plan adapts to you and your teens changing financial needs and resources.

> **The Seven Financial Habits of Successful Teen Financiers**
>
> 1. They start young.
> 2. They practice regularly over time to gain hands-on, *gut-level* experience.
> 3. They work from an organized *scalable* plan.
> 4. They learn at an early age how to balance money distributions.
> 5. They make themselves aware of a variety of financial options.
> 6. They learn to think like risk-taking entrepreneurs.
> 7. They are open to creative thinking about money-making opportunities.

What financiers call "balancing money distributions" is really nothing more than earmarking income for spending, saving, giving, debt repayment, investing, and taxes. Successful teen financiers learn this important habit early.

Perhaps one of the most rewarding habits is to think like a risk-taking entrepreneur. Entrepreneurs are creative visionaries, not afraid to risk failure for potential reward. It's rare in today's world to tap into the "American Dream" merely through frugal spending and careful saving. Allowing your teen to practice the entrepreneurial spirit from the safety of home will help remove those fears for them when they're launched into adulthood. Developing the spirit of entrepreneurship begins with the habit of being open to creative thinking about money-making opportunities.

Here is an exercise that can help promote your teen's financial creativity.

Financial Creativity Questionnaire
Family Member Player _____

1. Look around you for opportunities to make money. Ask yourself what your business community, church, or environment needs to develop a viable money-making idea.

2. Identify and interview local entrepreneurs. What do they do? How did they get started?

3. How might you add or improve on a simple business idea?

4. How might you increase the resource base?

5. How could you create a demand or market for your money-making idea?

A blank copy of this worksheet is provided for your use in the appendix on page 316.

One mother participating in my course, described how her son launched a computer research and repair service in his neighborhood. She thought any services relating to computers would be flooded with competition. Surprisingly, her innovative son found that many neighbors had computer service needs but couldn't afford the going rates charged from more experienced computer service repair businesses.

•   •   •

After six months playing *The Real-Life* Money Game, ask your teen to fill out the Teen Player Profile Questionnaire again. Compare your teen's original questionnaire with the new one, and ask yourself, this question: Is my teen practicing the seven financial habits of successful teen financiers? If so, your son or daughter is well on his or her way to developing a savvy financial instinct. If not, keep practicing the basic tangible skills. If mistakes make your teen wary, go back to a simpler step in the process. Allow your son or duaghter to build confidence through successfully overcoming mistakes. With practice on his or her part, and patience on yours, soon your teen will show the kind of independence and responsibility that will launch him or her successfully into the world of adult financial demands.

Chapter Nineteen
Resolving Conflict That Arises As *The Real-Life* Money Game Is Played

··

Connie Wilson called home from work one afternoon to check on her girls after school. She got the phone answering machine instead. Her oldest daughter's recording came on: *Hi, this is Karen. I'm turning sixteen on Thursday and I need a car. Please leave a message after the beep.*

Connie was appalled at her daughter's presumptuousness. The moment her daughter turned sixteen, Karen thought she had the *right* to have her own car, not the *privilege* to drive the family car. The problem, says Connie, is that her daughter didn't want to get a job to earn money to contribute to the cost of a car. She didn't even know how much insurance and gas cost.

"All the other parents buy their kids cars when they turn sixteen," Karen claimed, whenever she argued this point with her mother. Connie couldn't dispute Karen's remark. Instead, Connie launched into her latest case point. Karen didn't *need* her own car; she just *wanted* one. Hearing that, Karen walked away and wouldn't listen to Connie's reasoning.

Shortly after the conversation, without Connie knowing, Karen called her father, James, at work and asked if she could get a car. James knew this was an issue but was caught off-guard and said the standard, "Well, sure." At home, later, berated by Connie for not being firm, James complained that his daughter was spoiled. She had grown up too used to having her wants met and without having to work for them. Connie and James agreed that this was a problem that came with raising teens in a household privileged with a comfortable income. Connie Wilson, in an attempt to resolve the problem, asked her brother-in-law what he did when his son turned sixteen and wanted a car. He said, "We just bought him one! He's our only child. What's the big deal?"

Connie's brother-in-law was no help. Exasperated, she complained that his approach wouldn't teach her daughter how to contribute a dime toward her own wants.

Common Problems Parents Can Anticipate

The Wilson family's situation illustrates a common dilemma: How do families respond to issues that involve money when every family member has a different point of view and their teens are accustomed to taking for granted that their wants and needs will simply be met? Should parents lay down their law? Should teens have a say? Who is to decide?

And how many times have you confronted that age-old argument from your son or daughter that it's *their money* so they can

> **Common Problems Parents Can Anticipate**
>
> • Differing Points of View Causing Ongoing Arguments
> • Peer Pressure
> • Sibling Rivalry
> • Resistance/Noncompliance
> • My Money/Your Money
> • Entitlement

do with it what they desire? Or maybe you've used the argument with your son or daughter that it's *your money* and you've earned the privilege to be in charge of it! My son felt particularly possessive of his money when he first started playing *The Real-Life* Money Game. He'd earned $20 washing a neighbor's cars, the first *real* money that hadn't come from his parents. When I suggested that he pool his earnings with his Family Fund Contribution, he was adamant. It was his money! He'd earned it! And he wasn't going to let me take it away! This is a common problem you can anticipate as you play *The Real-Life* Money Game with your own teen.

The Four-Step Method For Problem Solving

Parents playing *The Real-Life* Money Game can learn how to respond to their individual family dynamics using a tool called the Four-Step Method For Problem Solving. The Four-Step Method is a refreshingly realistic and simple approach to solving problems such as that faced by the Wilsons. The four steps are summarized in the sidebar.

> **Four-Step Method For Problem Solving**
>
> *Identify:*
>   1. The Problem
>   2. The Tangible Skill Required
>   3. The Intangible Result
>   4. The Workable Solution

Four-Step Method For Problem Solving
Family Member Player _____

1. **The Problem:** Come up with a statement of the problem that both you and your teen agree on.

2. **The Tangible Skill Required:** Choose one tangible money-management skill required to address the problem.

3. **The Intangible Result:** Choose one intangible money-management skill you wish to achieve with your teen.

4. **The Workable Solution:** Identify and write down both parents' and teen's needs. Make a list of possible solutions. Choose solutions that get both parents and teen's needs met and eliminate the rest.

Parents' Needs	Teen's Needs

List of Possible Solutions:

Ultimate Solution:

A blank copy of this worksheet is provided for your use in the appendix on page 317.

The Real-Life Money Game offers families the worksheet on the preceding page to assist in applying the four steps. What it amounts to is this: identify the problem; the *tangible* money skill required to solve the problem; the *intangible* skill parents wish to achieve; and the workable solution that gets both parents' and teens' needs met. A "Detailed Action Plan" worksheet is also provided, on page 258, to help families implement their solutions.

Consistent with the scalable-plan concept, the Four-Step Method provides enough flexibility to resolve each family's problems without compromising individual money values.

Step 1: Identify the Problem

The purpose of step one is to come up with a statement of the problem that is agreed upon by both you and your teen. To formulate a problem that is agreeable to both parents and teens, you begin by sitting down and explaining the Four-Step Method to your family. Use your regularly-scheduled monthly meeting to engage your teen by letting him or her know you think there is a problem. Explain that you would like to get his or her perspective on the problem so together you can formulate it in a way that is mutually agreeable.

Let's consider how the Wilson Family resolved their current car dilemma by applying the four steps. Connie started the conversation and asked Karen to sit down for a moment to talk. Even though they'd already discussed the car issue, she told Karen that she and her Dad were very uncomfortable with the message she'd left on the answering machine. They needed to get to the bottom of this problem so it could be resolved.

Connie described her meeting with Karen as follows: Karen wriggled in her chair, looked down at the floor. Connie continued in an even-toned, matter-of-fact voice in spite of her daughter's deflecting body language. Connie didn't want to come across as accusing or blaming. She told Karen that she thought there was a way to resolve the problem that would meet everyone's needs. But in order to go forward, they all had to agree on what the problem was. Connie asked Karen to tell her how she saw the problem.

Karen pushed her hair definitively behind her ears. She'd be able to drive soon, and she'd like a car. "A bunch of my friends drive to school. I'd like to be on my own and drive myself to school. Our car is always loaded with my sisters and their friends. I want to be with my own friends." Connie looked over at James. Connie wasn't surprised by the response. At least her daughter was willing to say how she felt.

"Speaking for myself," Connie told Karen, "I'd like you to drive also. It would take a load off my carpooling responsibilities." But here is the problem for Connie. A car is a big responsibility. It costs a lot of money. There is gas and insurance. Not to mention maintenance. Connie is also concerned about safety, especially with other kids in the car. She needs some proof her daughter can handle the responsibility.

James chimed in, stating that the problem for him is that he'd be paying for everything: the car, the gas, the insurance, the whole bit. When he was young, he'd had to get a job.

Karen blurted out that her friends didn't pay for their cars. Connie called for calm. They agreed to take a break and continue the discussion when less upset.

What became clear to Connie was that Karen saw the problem differently. In Karen's eyes, her parents were stubborn and unwilling to get her a car. Karen knew her parents could afford to buy her a car, but believed they wouldn't because they were too conservative when it came to spending their money. Connie and James, on the other hand, were fearful that Karen was not ready to take on the financial responsibility that comes with owning a car. The car itself wasn't the issue. They felt they needed to help their daughter acquire some resource-management skills, and the independence would follow.

When they came back to the table, Connie wrote down all the input on the worksheet, and read her notes back to James and Karen. She read: *Karen wants a car so she can drive to school on her own. Connie wants proof Karen can handle the responsibility of a car. James wants Karen to share in the costs of owning and operating a car.*

Connie asked if they all agreed on the problem. James and Karen nodded.

Connie suggested they end the discussion on that point. They agreed to each think about possible solutions and then talk again. Connie was relieved they had agreed on the problem without an argument.

Identifying the problem is the critical first step to resolution. As you practice sharing points of view the first step can become less confrontational.

Step 2: The Tangible Skill Required

Once the problem has been identified, the next step is to determine what *tangible* skill might address the problem. Refer back to the tangible skills lists provided in chapters one and nine. Generally, it's easier to hone one skill at a time rather than overwhelm your son or daughter with several new and unfamiliar concepts. The point is this: Teens are especially receptive to developing new skills when there is much at stake of immediate importance. If it matters enough, they will usually engage.

The Wilsons decided that the one tangible money-management skill they hoped to teach Karen was how to earn money to pay for some of her own expenses. They were concerned that Karen didn't understand the need to generate income for herself. They wanted her to take more personal initiative.

To support the effort, Connie encouraged her daughter to get a lifeguard job at the local pool. Karen resisted. Connie knew Karen was a capable swimmer, but she also knew that her daughter lacked the confidence to work in an unfamiliar setting. Karen claimed that none of her friends were working at the pool. This fear of the unfamiliar was foreign to Connie, but out of respect to her daughter, she gave Karen a chance to choose her own solution.

Karen suggested getting paid for jobs at home such as cleaning out the garage, a task her mother had been wanting done for months.

The Wilsons had never paid their daughter for household jobs. They were concerned that by making this offer, Karen might not follow through with the housework that was expected of her. But Connie realized she might miss an opportunity to boost Karen's confidence if she didn't give her a chance.

Step 3: The Intangible Result

Once you've isolated the tangible skill, the next step is to determine what *intangible* skill you wish your teen to learn while addressing the problem. Again, refer back to chapters one and nine for a list of the intangible skills parents most often connect to resource management.

I like to ask myself, "What will make all this haggling with my teen worth the trouble?" Often conflict between parents and teens results from a parent's commitment to instilling value their teen may not appreciate. This, coupled with the teen's strong commitment to having a say, adds up to conflict. If parents can pinpoint clearly what moral, attitude, or belief they hope to share with their teen, and be honest about it, and realize that their teen may have a different opinion, they are far more likely to achieve some measure of their desired result. Teens will at least appreciate the honesty. It keeps families focused on the outcome, rather than getting bogged down with personality conflicts. And, it helps parents avoid sending mixed messages—their teen's invitation to rebel.

The Wilsons wanted Karen to understand why earning money to make a contribution to her wants was necessary and important. Connie Wilson said to me that she and James wanted to understand how to respond to Karen. To be less reactive. To send her fewer mixed messages. James and Connie agreed to focus their efforts on teaching her one important intangible skill: personal responsibility. Working on this skill, they decided, was worth the haggling.

Step 4: The Workable Solution

The workable solution consists of three parts: identifying and writing down you and your teen's needs; listing possible solutions; and choosing the *ultimate* solution. It's important for parents to answer this question honestly: Am I interested in teaching my teen how to develop money-management skills and to make decisions on his or her own, or am I only interested in reinforcing my demands?

For Connie Wilson, keeping an open mind was difficult. "Whenever I try to explain to Karen why she can't have a car, she doesn't listen to my reasons." Connie admitted that she should have been expecting this conflict; Karen had been talking about wanting a car for two years. But Connie said all she could think about during that time was her own experiences—she made due with the family car when growing up. Connie had come to realize that her own past experience might not be as relevant to her daughter as she had first thought.

A workable solution begins by taking a family "emotional accounting." To help with this, the Four-Step Method For Problem Solving provides space to write down your family's needs. On the right side, write down your teen's needs. On the left side, write down your needs. If one parent has a different need than the other, this gets written down as well. Then parents and teens start listing ideas that might solve the problem. The ultimate solution is arrived at when ideas are chosen that meet both the parents' and teen's needs.

Four-Step Method For Problem Solving
Family Member Player _____ *Wilson Family* _____

1. The Problem:

Karen wants a car so she can drive to school on her own. Connie wants proof Karen can handle the responsibility of a car. James wants Karen to share in the costs of owning and operating a car.

2. The Tangible Skill Required:

Teach Karen how to earn money to share in the costs of owning and operating a car.

3. The Intangible Result:

For Karen to understand the necessity for taking some personal responsibility.

4. The Workable Solution:

Parents' Needs	Teen's Needs
• Understand what costs are associated with owning a car: insurance, gas, repairs and maintenance. • Earn money to make a contribution towards gas and insurance—the costs associated with owning and operating a car. • Understand what causes insurance rates to go up, and be aware of the statistics on accident rates among young drivers.	• Own a car at age 16. • Want parents to pay for a car. • Want parents to pay for car maintenance and insurance.

List of Possible Solutions:

- Wilson parents buy Karen a car for her 16th birthday.
- James buys a new car and gives Karen his old car that is still in good condition.
- Karen gets a job as a lifeguard at the local city pool.
- Karen gets paid for "jobs" around the house.
- Parents explore insurance costs and accident statistics with Karen.
- Karen explores the costs of gas, repairs and maintenance at the local gas station.
- Karen forgoes a car and any kind of job to earn money.

Ultimate Solution:

- Connie and James agree to pay Karen for babysitting her younger sisters and for washing both cars. Karen, in turn, will contribute $50 each month toward gas to drive James' existing car. James will commit to a date to buy a new car for himself. Karen will have a car to drive, albeit, her dad's old one.

A blank copy of this worksheet is provided for your use in the appendix on page 317.

Referring to the completed worksheet, the Wilsons agreed to eliminate the first and last ideas since they clearly did not meet either Karen's or her parents' needs. Karen rejected the idea of the lifeguard job at the local pool. However, Karen was agreeable to the idea of earning money for "jobs" at home. All three agreed to explore insurance information and the costs associated with owning a car. A real snag came, though, when James wasn't ready to make the decision to buy a new car for himself, and Karen didn't want to drive her parents' old car.

This was the critical point, the potential flash point. The Wilsons could either leave the whole affair unresolved, or they could make a commitment to finding a solution. They chose to find a solution. Perhaps the most effective part of the process, Connie reported later, was how she and James were finally able to get Karen to agree to driving her Dad's old car. She simply told Karen that this solution wasn't cast in stone. If it didn't work, they'd go through the steps again. To Connie, the mere fact that her daughter was willing to participate in finding a workable solution was a delightful surprise.

Detailed Action Plan

Once families have come up with a workable solution, they need to decide how to implement their decisions. I've found that it's vital to set a timeline and to decide who will do what and when. Families can write down the agreement on the Detailed Action Plan worksheet, as the Wilsons did on the following page.

The Wilsons agreed to try their plan. Connie believed six months would give her daughter the needed "job" experience. By June, it would be summer and the lifeguard opportunity would be available again. If Karen felt more confident and chose to take the position, she would need a car to get there. James agreed six months would give him ample time to select a new car. In the meantime, Karen would contribute $50 each month toward gas to drive James' car, even though it was not hers to drive until June. Connie agreed to make the call to arrange for Karen to be included on the insurance policy as a third driver on James' car. At the same time, Connie would find out the cost for additional insurance if Karen were to drive James' old car exclusively. Karen agreed to investigate average gas prices at the local stations.

At the end of the agreed on timeline, families should revisit their situation by answering the checklist of questions to monitor the results of their solutions.

Detailed Action Plan
Family Member Player _____*Wilson Family*_____

Solution Start Date: January 1

Solution End Date: June 30

Detailed Action Plan:

- Karen will earn money babysitting and washing cars and pay $50 every month for gas to drive James' car. She will investigate gas prices at local stations by January 31.
- Connie will pay Karen $10 per hour for babysitting and washing cars. She will add Karen to the existing auto insurance policy and find out how much additional cost would be included if Karen drove her own car. She will get the information by January 31.
- James will pay for any gas over Karen's $50 monthly allotment and for car repairs, maintenance, and insurance. He will agree to let Karen drive his car by June 30, at which time he will buy a new car and make his old car available to her.

Was your son or daughter happy with the results?

Did the commitment prove too difficult to carry out for either parent or teen?

Is the tangible skill being learned?

Is the problem being resolved? If not, why not? What changes can you make to the original solution to promote success?

Has the problem changed such that you need to go through the Four-Step Method For Problem Solving again?

A blank copy of this worksheet is provided for your use in the appendix on page 318.

"Just going through the four steps helped relax the tension in our family," reported Connie. Instead of replaying the same argument, she said they each knew exactly what their commitment was to solving the problem. So far the solution has worked.

The Sanchez Family Four-Step Method For Problem Solving

Sam Sanchez faced a somewhat different problem when his daughter wanted a car. He was able to buy a used car to make available to her, but he couldn't afford the additional insurance. On his tight budget, neither could he pay her for extra "jobs" at home. He and his daughter came up with the following solution: The car would be available for Maria to drive if she would earn enough money to pay for the insurance. The choice was to forgo the car or get a job. He established his parameters. The job couldn't be more than twelve hours per week (except in summer); otherwise, it would interfere with Maria's school work.

Also, she'd have to get to her job by bus until she could pay for the insurance. Maria agreed to take responsibility for her part. Maria was resourceful. She found a part-time job at a second-hand thrift store in the neighborhood close to her school. She used public transportation to get to work and home, with only minor inconvenience. In six months time, Maria had earned enough money to pay for the insurance at which point Sam relinquished the car.

The MacLean Family Four-Step Method For Problem Solving

Darcy MacLean elaborates on her concerns, teaching her daughter Linda about spending. "I'm paying all Linda's expenses now, and every day she asks for money. Linda's needs are usually legitimate—dinner out, movie with friends, a school sweatshirt—but the most recent request was for money to buy five of her school friends holiday gifts." Darcy thinks this should come from Linda since it is a personal gesture on her daughter's part, but Linda thinks this is an expense that isn't for her personally, so it should be paid for by her parents.

"I don't want Linda to think I'm just a money machine with an endless supply," says Darcy. "I want my daughter to see some meaning behind all the handouts." The problem, Darcy admits, is that the decision on how to spend money on gifts for friends is appropriate for her daughter to make. But Linda's babysitting earnings have come to a halt. She is too busy with school, homework, and crew-practice two hours in the afternoon to have any free time left for earning money.

In an effort to resolve the problem, the MacLean family applied the Four-Step Method For Problem Solving. Darcy determined that there was a group of money-management skills she wanted her daughter to learn. First, she wanted Linda to have some funds to manage so she could make her own spending decisions. That way Darcy wouldn't have to make choices that should more appropriately be made by her daughter, such as buying gifts for Linda's friends. Also, she wanted her daughter to develop a realistic understanding of how much things cost.

Ultimately, Darcy hoped to achieve this result: for Linda to appreciate that spending means making tradeoffs and sacrifices.

The MacLeans ended up with the following workable solution. The family made a list of Linda's fixed expenses and her discretionary expenses. Her fixed expenses included clothes, school supplies, and toiletries. Movies, CDs, gifts, small clothing accessories, and makeup were listed as discretionary expenses. In this process, Linda's needs were differentiated from her wants. They agreed that Linda would receive only $75 for her discretionary spending each month.

• • •

At first, going through the Four-Step Method For Problem Solving might seem like a lot of work. But experience has shown that as families work through the toughest, most emotionally-charged arguments and see that they are able to work through to a solution, the process quickly becomes second nature. With practice and patience, families working through this process can find creative, satisfying, and long-lasting solutions to their problems.

Chapter Twenty

Special Circumstances: How *The Real-Life* Money Game Deals With the Three Disruptive "D's"

Nothing traumatizes a family quite like the three "D's"—divorce, disability or death. While adult lives are turned upside down, a teen's world becomes even more unstable. The teen years are a time of experimentation and risk-taking. At this time, more than ever, they need support and stability from their parents. When the family core is cracked, the obstacles confronted by teens can seem almost insurmountable.

One big worry teens face in such special circumstances is what will happen to the money. To make matters worse, teens often feel powerless to affect their circumstances. They cope better when they believe they have some degree of control over their lives. What teens seem to need most are a sense of security and a feeling of empowerment. *The Real-Life* Money Game offers solutions to help with both.

Divorce

Divorce presents teens with a myriad of potential family configurations: single-parenting, shared-parenting, step-parenting, dual-step parenting. Your teen, who might have felt challenged managing a savings account before, now may have to face as many as four adults with conflicting financial goals. Your son or daughter may feel overwhelmed.

Problem

A common factor in divorce is the parents' struggle with money. Both parents may want to teach their son or daughter reasonable spending habits, but one often sees the choices of the other as too hard or too soft. For example, one parent may want their teen to work, the other would prefer they don't. One wants their teen to save for a car, the other to save for college.

Here is one family's experience.

A month before this couple's son turned sixteen, the husband moved out. Before that, the family had been faithfully playing *The Real-Life* Money

Game. The wife, who once had a career, worked part-time, so that she could spend time with their son who had medical issues. As the divorce process proceeded the family's finances changed. As a result, the son's Family Fund Contribution was cut in half. The mother helped her son go through his monthly Playing Board-Spending Plan to cut his expenditures.

Her son, in turn, took the initiative to increase his resources by expanding his teen business: car-detailing work. He dipped into his savings to pay for supplies. Appreciative of his willingness to participate, his mother agreed to match the funds he put into the business, once the family's finances stabilized. In this way, he could replenish the savings he'd earmarked for other goals.

Okay, if you haven't guessed, this is the author's personal experience!

Here is another family's story.

David Horowitz' son, Kyle, was ten when David and his wife divorced. David's ex-wife immediately remarried and had a second child. Kyle lived with his mom and spent more time with her new family when he was young. But as he got older, in his teens, he didn't get along with his stepsister or his step-dad. Kyle decided to move back in with David.

David wanted to teach Kyle some responsibility, so he set up a monthly Playing Board-Spending Plan with a Family Fund Contribution. Kyle agreed that he would contribute money into savings to pay for the insurance on a used car his father was willing to buy for him. The step-household's dad said that *The Real-Life* Money Game was too much trouble and refused to cooperate.

David maintained his commitment to teaching his son financial responsibility, so at his household Kyle played the game. Kyle understood that there were different rules for different houses. But when Kyle turned sixteen, his step-dad bought him a car outright without any contribution on Kyle's part. David had been willing to buy the car, but, for one, he didn't have the resources yet; and, for another, he wanted Kyle to save for his part first. Of course, Kyle jumped at his step-dad's offer. Kyle abandoned the long-term savings goal he'd set up for the payment of car insurance. This caused a rift between David and Kyle that wasn't resolved until college.

When college came up, Kyle's step-dad was unwilling to make any financial contribution to his step-son's financial needs. David was willing, but only under the condition that Kyle reinstate *The Real-Life* Money Game and contribute by getting a job. Kyle, shaken by what he saw as abandonment by his step-dad, agreed to the terms. Kyle, admitted that he should have stuck to the original agreement. The short-term gratification did not turn out to be a good long-range plan. Kyle moved back in with David the summer before college, and the Horowitz family began to rebuild both their personal and financial relationship.

Solution

The Real-Life Money Game suggests first, that you explain to your teen how the overall resource will change with the ultimate divorce. Will you need to adjust expenses on the Playing Board-Spending Plan? If so, which ones and how much? Or will you need to increase resources instead? If so, where will the money come from? How much?

To promote security and to empower your teen under transitional circumstances, maintain your family's commitment to *The Real-Life* Money Game. Incorporate into the Playing Board-Spending Plan how the overall financial picture changes. Adjust expenses or expand resources. Don't undermine efforts with give-aways—money for which your teen is not held accountable. Encourage your teen to stay committed to *The Real-Life* Money Game. Maintain the money-management foundation established before the divorce. Respond to the financial decisions that are within your control. Your teen, once the storm has passed, will learn from your consistency.

Disability

When a family is faced with disability, the overall financial resource will inevitably change. It's likely that the family's income will be reduced. Even if one parent goes back to work or increases working time to compensate, increased medical expenses often change a parent's ability to provide the Family Fund Contribution.

Problem

How do you effectively communicate the family's changed financial status to your teen? Is it reasonable to expect your teen to contribute to the family's support? If so, how does this change your son or daughter's monthly Playing Board-Spending Plan?

A parent who contacted me to inquire about my course, confided that she'd been diagnosed with MS a few years before. Within the past year, she'd divorced and been forced to cut back at her family law practice to part-time, accepting partial disability payments along with child support to help make up some of the lost income.

Her son, at this point, a sophomore in high school, was aware that child support payments were being made on his behalf. He felt entitled to his direct share. Secretly, she admitted, her son was looking for an easy way to put aside money for a car without having to work. She was in a quandary. What to do? I suggested she offer him an exchange. If he would do extra jobs around the house, she would earmark a portion of the child support for him as a Family Fund Contribution. Then she could establish a savings' goal for a car that he could contribute to as part of a monthly Playing Board-Spending Plan.

Solution

Recall from chapter seventeen, *The Real-Life* Money Game offers families the Pie-Chart Model For Family Financial Discussions to open lines of communication. The pie-chart model is an excellent tool for explaining changes in the family's finances. Helping your teen understand the special circumstances can improve your son or daughter's feelings of security. If he or she is required to get a job to assist with finances, show your teen how this change will be reflected on the Playing Board-Spending Plan. Make sure your teen understands that the game has not been discontinued, but simply, that the resource base has changed. Let your teen take some personal responsibility. Their contribution can help them feel more secure in their changed situation.

Fill in the pie-chart on the following page with your current financial situation. Compare the pie-chart to your previous one. Show your teen both pie-charts to explain the changes and what you might expect from them. Use the pie-chart as a springboard to encourage your teen's questions.

Death

When a parent dies, a dependent teen often gets Social Security or pension or life insurance or even an inheritance that must be administered by another adult, a parent or a guardian, for the teen's future. The money generally isn't

---

Pie-Chart Model For Family Financial Discussions
Family Member Player _____

The pie represents 100% of your family's income. Slice the pie into percents to show how the family income is used for the points bulleted below:

- Costs of a Home

- Food and Entertainment

- Clothes and Education

- Transportation Costs

- Medical

- Vacation

- Emergencies, Savings, Investing

- Debt

- Charity

- Taxes

A blank copy of this worksheet is provided for your use in the appendix on page 313.

---

directly available to the teen until they reach the age of majority—no longer a minor. Sometimes this can have adverse consequences on a teen.

Problem

When teens know they will receive money due to a death, many feel entitled. Often this can lead to a cavalier attitude. Teens may come to conclude that their surviving parent or guardian can't tell them how the money should be spent, since they know it's theirs. Teens want nothing more than to be financially independent, which is to say, they want control of the resource.

Susan, a mother of three, lost her income-provider when her husband died of a heart attack. Aside from the emotional grief, she found herself facing a problem with her oldest son, who at that time was thirteen years old. Luckily, they had life insurance so she was able to pay off the house and meet baseline expenses. But, when her son learned that his mother received a monthly Social Security payment on his behalf, he wanted the money, every penny of it, put into an account in his name. Of course, she refused. She signed up for my course, wondering what she should do.

I advised her to start a Family Fund Contribution on his behalf, earmarking those funds from his Social Security payment, which was all she could afford, while insisting he then take on responsibility for certain monthly expenses, in his case, video games, DVDs, and snacks.

Once he realized he had some responsibility for covering his own expenses, he backed off from his initial stance of entitlement. They continued to have the occasional "showdown," but for the most part an air of cooperation returned to their stricken home.

Solution

The Real-Life Money Game encourages parents or guardians to set aside money received on behalf of a teen in a Rainy-Day Fund used only for emergencies. If resources are available, money could also be set aside in a trust account for future distribution. The money should *not* count in *The Real-Life* Money Game resource base. In other words, this money would *not* influence the Family Fund Contribution.

Help your son or daughter create a Playing Board-Spending Plan that is consistent with their spending patterns before the death. Stick with the plan, regardless of any windfall that results from sudden death. Set aside that windfall in an investment account. This will give your teen time to mature financially. Teens need to develop financial skills before they receive what will, to them, feel like lottery winnings. The money does run out if the resource is not properly managed. Teaching your teen money-management skills is the best preparation you could possibly give them for their future financial security.

• • •

The Real-Life Money Game's techniques and strategies can help stop damage caused by the three disruptive D's. Whether it's the undermining power-plays over money in a divorce, or significant changes in financial circumstances due to a disability or death, empowering your teen with financial skills will give your son or daughter the security needed to survive without feeling like their world is caving in. Most importantly, giving your teen the appropriate amount of financial accountability—emphasis on "appropriate"—instills them with a sense that they have control over something in their lives. Reinforce and maintain their self-sufficiency, while keeping in mind that it's a tricky balance.

Often in circumstances such as these, it's easy to put *too* much financial responsibility on your teen before he or she is ready. To counteract this, now more than ever, continue talking with your son or daughter at your regular monthly meetings. Keep the line of communication open. Use the Pie-Chart Model For Family Financial Discussions. When your teen knows what's going on, he or she doesn't have to speculate. They may not like what they hear, but teens value authenticity. It's been my experience that they'd rather participate in cooperative-resource management than have complete control taken away or dumped in their lap. Communicate. Cooperate. Keep to the plan.

Chapter Twenty-One
The Real-Life Money Game's Word on Worth

Often parents talk to their teens about *income*, but rarely do they talk about *worth*. To put the difference in simple terms, financial worth is what you own, less what you owe, and income is what you earn. Once parents learn to differentiate *worth* from *income*, a world of money possibilities will open up for their teens. Understanding financial worth helps teens embrace possibilities that go beyond frivolous spending or its converse, defensive hording. Teens can learn how to use their income for calculated risk-taking endeavors. For example, they might start putting resources into a car that, when they are able to drive, will enable them to pursue a teen business such as gardening or window cleaning. The long and the short of it is this: teens who think like risk-taking entrepreneurs discover how to *use* money to *make* money.

So what is net worth, really? And what is the ultimate goal?

In chapter one, families learn that a resource doesn't have to be finite. A financial resource can expand as needs and circumstances change. This is the scalable plan. Net worth, however, is a finite measurement, at a specific point in time, of the value of that resource. Up to this point your teen has been developing tangible financial skills to help him or her manage that resource. A net-worth calculation provides an overview—a realistic picture—of your teen's current financial situation. Thus, the goal of computing net worth is to assess the health of the financial resource on hand today to better pursue long-term financial goals in the future.

Income Versus Worth

Sound like a big job? Well, it's really quite simple. First, let's consider how you calculate net worth using *The Real-Life* Money Game's Word On Worth worksheet, shown on the following page, as the Greene family did.

The Real-Life Money Game's Word On Worth
Family Member Player _____ *Nathan Greene* _____

Add Together:

- How much you have in your "cash pockets" or your checking account | 19
- How much you have in your savings account | 453
- How much you have in your investment account
- How much you own:

  A bike | Bike | 150

  A car

  A computer | Computer | 250

  Other Personal Belongings

  Collectibles | Baseball cards | 100
- How much you own in a "Teen Business"
- Money owed you (what you've lent someone)
- Other

Total of What You Own | 972

Add Together:

- Money you owe
- Taxes you owe
- Other

Total of What You Owe | 0

Subtract the Total of What You Owe from the Total of What You Own to Get Your Financial Worth | 972

A blank copy of this worksheet is provided for your use in the appendix on page 319.

Using the results of the net worth calculation, the Greene family helped their fourteen-year-old son, Nathan, define one long-term financial goal. Their son loved cars. Though he couldn't drive his own yet, Nathan wanted to start a car-detailing business like my son, Michael. He'd had some experience washing cars at his uncle's dealership the previous summer. He'd also done some preliminary research to find out if neighbors would be willing to pay him to detail their cars. He told his parents he wanted to prepare a flyer to pass around to local businesses in the area who might have interested employees. In order to start the business, he needed money to purchase a power-vacuum, a car-buffer, and carpet-shampooing equipment for a total cost of approximately $250.

Reviewing each item on his net worth worksheet, together he and his parents considered his options. He could earn money doing odd jobs around the house until he had enough cash to buy the equipment. He could use a portion of his savings. He could sell his bike and baseball card collection. Or, he could borrow the money from his parents.

He didn't want to wait until he earned enough cash. That could be months away. He didn't want to use any of his savings as he was diligently setting this aside for his own car. He didn't want to sell his bike, since that was his only means of transportation, and he *loved* his baseball-card collection. He wasn't even sure that he could sell his bike for what he paid for it, nor was he sure how much someone would be willing to pay for his baseball cards. He felt certain he could make a go of the business, so he convinced his parents to loan him the money.

The Greenes thought the idea seemed sound, but they were hesitant. They knew he was taking a calculated risk that the business would work, and they didn't like the idea of their son borrowing money. But they agreed, as long as their son completed *The Real-Life* Money Game Borrowing Chart to establish the repayment terms and time limit for the loan. Within two months, Nathan would agree to pay for the equipment out of his Family Fund Contribution if the revenues from his business didn't. When their son agreed to the terms, the Greenes knew they had to let him try.

On the following page, let's consider how their son's net worth changes with this financial decision.

The Real-Life Money Game's Word On Worth
Family Member Player ____*Nathan Greene*____

Add Together:

- How much you have in your "cash pockets" or your checking account | 19
- How much you have in your savings account | 453
- How much you have in your investment account
- How much you own:

  A bike | Bike | 150

  A car

  A computer | Computer | 250

  Other Personal Belongings

  Collectibles | Baseball cards | 100
- How much you own in a "Teen Business" | Car-detail equip. | 250
- Money owed you (what you've lent someone)
- Other

Total of What You Own | **1,222**

Add Together:

- Money you owe | 250
- Taxes you owe
- Other

Total of What You Owe | **250**

Subtract the Total of What You Owe from the Total of What You Own to Get Your Financial Worth | **972**

A blank copy of this worksheet is provided for your use in the appendix on page 319.

Using what Nathan paid for the car-detailing equipment, his *cost,* as its value, the total of what he owns increases. Additionally, his net worth calculation decreases by what he owes to his parents, so his total net worth of $972 does not change. He has an opportunity to use money to make more, but he also risks decreasing his net worth if the business doesn't succeed. How much does he have at risk? Potentially $250 plus interest owing, less any money he could make if he were to sell the car-detailing equipment.

For two consecutive weekends, Nathan sat outside his local church parking lot and detailed church-goers cars while they were inside. He checked the pricing from other car detailing organizations, then set his price 25% lower, given his limited experience. He charged $75 per car. Within that time he had made enough to cover the cost of the equipment and to pay back his parents.

Let's consider, again, what Nathan's net worth statement looks like on the following page.

Since Nathan still owns the equipment, but paid off his parents, his total net worth has increased from $972 to $1,222. Originally, he'd told his parents that he wanted to use his business proceeds to save for his car and to invest, once he'd paid them back. But to his parents' surprise, their son was so excited with his entrepreneurial success, he took half his business earnings and bought used books, which he in turn sold for a small profit to retirement homes where residents had time to read, but little access to transportation or stores. This was a business decision he had the freedom to make as he was responsible for managing his own resource.

The net worth worksheet offers your teen an easy means of seeing the difference between income on an income worksheet versus net worth. I've found it best to help your teen calculate his or her net worth at least once every three to six months. Encourage your son or daughter to consider one long-range financial goal. Record the goal on *The Real-Life* Money Game Plan.

At the next net-worth review, use the results to compare two points in time. Ask thought-provoking questions that will help your teen think about his or her financial situation. Has the net worth increased or decreased? Why? Do you want to increase your assets? If so, how? By cutting spending? By saving money you received as a gift? By choosing investments with a greater rate of return? By starting a business?

The Real-Life Money Game's Word On Worth
Family Member Player   *Nathan Greene*

Add Together:

- How much you have in your "cash pockets" or your checking account | | 19
- How much you have in your savings account | | 453
- How much you have in your investment account
- How much you own:

    A bike | Bike | 150

    A car

    A computer | Computer | 250

    Other Personal Belongings

    Collectibles | Baseball cards | 100

- How much you own in a "Teen Business" | Car-detail equip. | 250
- Money owed you (what you've lent someone)
- Other

Total of What You Own | | **1,222**

Add Together:

- Money you owe
- Taxes you owe
- Other

Total of What You Owe

Subtract the Total of What You Owe from the Total of What You Own to Get Your Financial Worth | | **1,222**

A blank copy of this worksheet is provided for your use in the appendix on page 319.

Parents, please keep in mind it's the flexible nature of your teen's scalable plan that allows for entrepreneurial risk. That same *flexibility* may sometimes give you concern as you wonder whether your ambitious young entrepreneur will succeed or fail, but this is an important step toward financial maturity. And besides, your Family Fund Contribution won't change. You're off the hook.

Valuing the Resource

Calculating net worth, as you can see from the previous example, is fairly simple. The real difficulty lies in accurately valuing what your teen owns. How do you measure the value of a teen business, a signed portrait from a famous athlete, a sought-after but reworked old Mustang? Do you value your net worth at what you paid for each item? Or maybe what you could sell it for on eBay? How do you adjust the value for an asset's wear-and-tear?

Consider Conner's dilemma, looking back as a parent, in his attempt to make a long-range financial decision. Conner had just turned eighteen and graduated from high school. He decided to travel around Europe before pursuing college. Toward the tail-end of his travels, he found himself in Tehran and short on cash. He was enamored by the Persian rugs that were selling at that time for around $500, and he had heard through hear-say that the Shah had passed a law that would soon go into effect making it illegal to remove hand-woven tribal rugs from the country. Conner got to thinking that if this were to happen, those tribal rugs would immediately increase in value. He speculated that he could make enough money reselling the rug to further finance his travels. There would be no market for him in Iran, so he decided to ship the rug home to his father for re-sale in the United States. He risked half of the cash he had left to purchase a rug and ship it back home. His plan was to contact his father when he ran short of cash and ask him to sell it and wire the money back to the nearest American Express.

As it turns out, despite the Shah's ban, the US market was flooded with carpets. Conner had not given much consideration to what might happen to half his net worth if the speculation didn't work. He realized later that it was foolish to think he could support himself on the rug's eventual sale proceeds.

How realistic was his assessment of his value? How realistic was his long-range financial plan to sell the rug? Was this an appropriate use of his net worth, given the inherent nature of the risk? These are the important questions you and your teen need to consider when valuing net worth to promote risk-taking ventures.

Conner learned a lesson about the need to study the market before committing to risky speculation. You may want to caution your teen as well to consider the fickle nature of net worth that's based on the value of possessions. But, you also have the reassurance of knowing that, worst case scenario, they will only reduce the resource base they're working from. Unfortunate, but not tragic. And very possibly a good lesson to learn before life metes out harder lessons.

Chapter Twenty-Two
Keeping Score

. . . .

On that day at Toys "R" Us when Michael was twelve and *The Real-Life Money Game* was yet to be born, our unresolved argument left us with exactly two minutes to find the needed birthday present. Michael's baseball game was about to start. He continued to follow behind me, up one aisle and down the next. We hurried to "Games," the last aisle in the enormous warehouse-sized store. I suggested *The Game of Life* as a possible gift. Michael looked at me with a wry face that implied, "get real!" The big clock on the wall indicated time was up. Mustering the army sergeant's voice I absolutely hate, I barked, "Put the Nintendo game back!"

I listened to Michael mumbling under his breath, "I hate it when you…" as he stiffly turned back toward the video game section, and I thought, this is it. This is the last time.

From my experience, exercising the Golden Rule For Parents proved to be a far more effective posture than the militant screaming or the giving-in approach I used before playing *The Real-Life* Money Game with my son. I learned how to practice restraint. Michael developed independent thinking. I discovered that Michael was better able to rein in his own constant yearning after unsatisfied wants. Now that he was making the decisions, doing the thinking, he had a far better grasp of the value of money and the consequences of misusing it.

I was amazed to discover that within six months Michael's behavior did a complete about-face. I found him willing to be altruistic, more willing to save, hugely cautious and savvy about purchasing, occasionally frivolous, very giving to his friends, but also quick to get a "loan" payback, and always alert to new opportunities for earning money.

Perhaps more importantly, I discovered he was far more open to consider my guidance and to listen to my opinions. Sometimes Michael would follow them, but sometimes he'd politely decline with, "I appreciate your input, Mom, but I got it covered." Admittedly, it was hard for me to accept his occasional refusals to heed my opinion. In spite of my counsel, Michael would make mistakes, such as buying a poorly constructed toy that I knew was likely to break. A week later when the toy broke, I could have reacted with an "I told you so." But my restraint proved invaluable. I watched Michael carefully inspect subsequent toy purchases and learn from his mistakes.

If you, too, find yourself tight-lipped, tersely remonstrating with your never-satisfied, whining little beggars, you now have a choice. An option. Instead of engaging in an argument that will simply repeat itself, you can teach your teen *The Real-Life* Money Game.

By age seventeen, Michael has become an independent thinker and a savvy money manager. Michael is on his way to developing the financial skills he will need when he heads off to college. Best of all, since that day at Toys "R" Us, I haven't experienced a single showdown with Michael over money.

Scorekeeping Box Totals: Gauging Your Teen's Progress

No game would be complete without keeping score. The Scorekeeping Box, however, is not intended to identify winners and losers so much as to help you gauge your teen's progress. The Scorekeeping Boxes were introduced in parts one and two. Now we will look at the grand total Scorekeeping Box, which summarizes the key concepts learned in previous chapters. Based on the final point value earned by each teen-player at a given point in time, you can determine whether your teen is progressing at a pace you're comfortable with, or whether you need to make adjustments.

The Scorekeeping Box helps parents measure change or progress in their teen's money behavior over time. Point values identify player-level activities. Beginning-player-level activities score five points, intermediate-player-level activities score ten, and advanced-player-level activities score 20. You can use this point-value system, along with *The Real-Life* Money Game Plan Overview in chapter nine, to help you determine which activities would be appropriate for your son or daughter to practice at a given point in time.

Assist your teen in tallying up final scores. Fill in the point value for each of your teen's chapter activities.

Scorekeeping Box Totals
Family Member Player _____

Key Concepts	Activity Point Value	Date Activity Completed/Discussion Notes	Point Value Earned
Chapter 2 • **Who You Are and How You Fit Into *The Real-Life* Money Game**			
• Complete the Teen Player Profile Questionnaire.	5		
• Using the answers from the questionnaire as a guide, agree on one tangible money-management objective to achieve.	5		
Subtotal	**10**		
Chapter 3 • **What You Need to Play *The Real-Life* Money Game**			
• Gather the accessories.	5		
• Design a personal binder cover.	5		
• Organize the personal financial binder.	5		
• Open a Savings Account with ATM Card.	5		
• Open a Checking Account with a Debit Card.	10		
• Open an Investment Account.	20		
Subtotal	**50**		

Chapter 4   Where the Money Will Come From: Teen-Generated Income

- Complete the Activities Pie-Chart for both weekday and weekend.   5

- Identify available time to earn money.   5

- Earning: Get Paid for Household Task or Chore.   5

- Earning: Land a Job.   10

- Earning: Start a "Teen Business."   20

- Record money received during the month on the Income Worksheet.   10

Subtotal   **55**

Chapter 5   Where the Money Will Come From: Parent-Generated Income

- Record any allowance received on the Income Worksheet.   5

- Complete the Income Worksheet using current month's information.   5

- Complete the Expense Worksheet and agree on *selected* expenses to be paid.   10

- Project estimated expenses using the supplemental worksheet.   10

- Project estimated clothes expense on the supplimental worksheet.   10

- Follow the guidelines to determine a Rainy-Day Fund amount.   10

• Calculate the Family Fund Contribution and record the amount on the Income Worksheet.	20
Subtotal	**70**

Chapter 6 • Spending: The Mechanics

• Select Cash Pocket spending option.	5
• Select Savings Account and ATM Card spending option.	5
• Select Checking and Debit Card Account spending option.	10
• Select Investment Account spending option.	20
• Keep track of cash on hand.	5
• Balance the check register with the monthly bank statement.	10
• Keep a minimum balance in the bank or investment account.	20
Subtotal	**75**

Chapter 7 • *The Real-Life* Money Game Playing Board—A Spending Plan

• Transfer the information from the Income Worksheet onto the Playing Board-Spending Plan in column one under the heading "Income amounts I have projected at the beginning of the month."	5

- Transfer the information from the Expense Worksheet onto the Playing Board-Spending Plan column one under the heading "What I expect it to cost."   5

- Record any Rainy-Day Fund amount on the Playing Board-Spending Plan in column one.   10

- Add up column one income and fill in the total. Add up column one expenses and fill in the total. Calculate Total Income minus Total Expenses and fill in the amount on the Playing Board-Spending Plan in column one.   10

Subtotal   **30**

Chapter 8   *The Real-Life* Money Game Rules

- Learn and follow The Real-Life Money Game Rules.   5

- Understand the Golden Rule For Parents.   5

- Agree to what sanctions or consequences (penalty for noncompliance) might occur if the game is not played according to the instructions and the rules.   10

- Sign the general contract agreeing to the terms of The Real-Life Money Game.   10

- Agree to one subcontract that requires a long-term commitment.   20

Subtotal   **50**

Chapter 9 • *The Real-Life* Money Game Plan

• Agree on one general money-management skill-building goal.	5
• Review the specific steps to accomplish the goal.	10
• Discuss progress. If making progress toward the goal, continue following the detailed steps. If not, agree to modify the plan based on the initial efforts to achieve the goal.	20
Subtotal	**35**

Chapter 10 • Tracking *The Real-Life* Money Game Monthly Activity

• Transfer the information from the Income Worksheet onto the Playing Board-Spending Plan in column two under the heading "What I actually received during the month."	5
• Transfer the information from the Expense Worksheet onto the Playing Board-Spending Plan column two under the heading "What it actually costs."	5
• Record any Rainy-Day Fund amount in column two on the Playing Board-Spending Plan.	10
• Add up column two income and fill in the total. Add up column two expenses and fill in the total. Calculate Total Income minus Total Expenses and fill in the amount on the Playing Board-Spending Plan in column two.	10

- Compute the difference between column one and column two and record the amounts including the totals in column three.   20

Subtotal   **50**

Chapter 11   Saving: Playing It Safe

- Establish one short-term savings target for Saving For Now and set the money aside.   5

- Follow the Saving For Later instructions to calculate a long-term savings target, and set the money aside monthly.   10

- Commit a fixed percent of monthly income for Saving For (What Seems Like) Never, and set the amount aside.   10

- Fill in *The Real-Life* Money Game Three-Part Savings Plan: Now, Later, Never worksheet with three savings' targets and put aside money for all three.   20

Subtotal   **45**

Chapter 12   Giving: Is It Worse Than a Shot?

- Complete the "Who or What Matters Most to You?" exercise.   5

- Choose one cause or organization to contribute to on a regular basis.   10

- Choose one cause or organization to volunteer for on a regular basis.   10

- Choose one or more causes or
organizations to both contribute
to and volunteer for on a regular
basis.   20

Subtotal   **45**

Chapter 13 ● Borrowing and Lending: A Spendthrift's Nightmare or a Wise Money Manager's Hedge Against the Future?

- Complete *The Real-Life* Money
Game Borrowing Chart and follow the terms of the loan to pay it
back in a timely manner.   5

- Complete *The Real-Life* Money
Game Lending Chart and follow
the terms of the loan to receive
payments in a timely manner.   5

- Use a debit card, in lieu of a
credit card, on a regular basis.   10

- Apply for one major credit card
(available at age eighteen) and
use only for emergencies.   10

- Pay credit-card debt off monthly.   20

- Request a credit report and understand the importance of hav-
ing a credit history and rating.   20

Subtotal   **70**

Chapter 14 ● Investing: Creating More Resource

- Set aside a resource for investing
and note the amount on the Play-
ing Board-Spending Plan.   5

- Review the key investment terms.   5

- Compare the financial pages and the Internet to the stock listings and mutual listings symbols.   5

- Talk about how businesses operate in the economy.   5

- Discuss the fundamental principle of the stock market and key investment objective: Buy low and sell high.   10

- Calculate a company's market capitalization and classify it by size.   10

- Identify a company's characteristics as *income*, *value*, or *growth*.   10

- Discuss the key investment objective that non-correlating assets—companies whose share prices move in opposite directions in the stock market—reduce volatility by investing in a balance of asset classes called diversification.   10

- Talk about asset allocation, which means choosing where to put a resource whether in cash, stocks or bonds, and between a balance of companies by size and classification to diversify investments.   10

- Identify risk tolerance—the potential loss to accept in exchange for the gains sought.   10

- Calculate a desired rate of return and expect the highest rate of return at the identified level of risk.   10

• Choose a stock-market index as a standard for measuring the potential return on an investment.	10
• Review *general* investment alternatives available.	10
• Select *specific* investment alternatives using an active manager.	10
• Select *specific* investment alternatives using a passive manager.	20
• Select *specific* investment alternatives independent of a manager.	20
• Choose investments that offer the broadest range of access to asset classes to minimize risk and increase return.	20
• Track investment income on the Income Worksheet if used to pay Playing Board-Spending Plan expenses.	20
• Track investment income, gains, and losses, annually.	20
• Calculate realized and unrealized gains and losses on investments.	20
• Discuss the necessity to buy-and-hold investments rather than timing the market.	20
• Invest using Dollar-Cost Averaging.	20
• Invest using either a traditional IRA or a Roth IRA.	20
Subtotal	**300**

Chapter 15   Taxes: An Invisible Resource Depletion

- Discuss what a Social Security
  number is and why one is needed.   5

- Put a copy of the Social Security
  number in the personal financial
  binder and talk about the
  importance of safeguarding
  the information.   5

- Discuss how job earnings are
  reported and taxed. Look at a paycheck stub and understand how to
  complete federal Form W-4.   10

- Review how net profits from a
  "Teen Business" are taxed and
  how to report them to federal and
  to state governments.   10

- Show how *unearned* interest and
  dividend income and investment
  gains and losses are computed
  to determine federal and state
  taxes.   10

- Complete federal Form 1040-ES
  to pay quarterly estimated taxes.   20

- Prepare federal Form 1040 and
  any state tax forms to compute,
  report, and pay taxes owed.   20

Subtotal   **80**

Summary of Scores (Chapters 2 – 15)

Total Points Earned   **965**

Identifying Your Teen's Player Level

Player levels are based on the total points earned to date. Scores between 0-155 rank as beginning players; 156-505 rank as intermediate players; and 506-965 rank as advance players.

Why does it matter to know this? You probably wouldn't want to try to force-feed calculus to your fourth-grader. And by the same token, you probably don't want to go over investment spreadsheets with a teen who's still handling expenses out of cash pockets. Identifying a teen's player level, in other words, indicates what action families need to take. Advanced players may be encouraged to keep practicing the activities they've been doing—they are well on their way to winning *The Real-Life* Money Game and achieving financial independence.

Beginning Player	Intermediate Player	Advanced Player
0 – 155	**Beginning**	How exciting! You're just starting *The Real-Life* Money Game. Choose one or two more money skills for which you have not earned points and practice them.
156 – 505	**Intermediate**	Great progress! Review the key concepts and choose a more advanced skill to add to the money skills for which you've already earned points.
506 – 965	**Advanced**	Congratulations! Keep doing what you are doing. You're well on your way to winning *The Real-Life* Money Game and achieving financial independence.

• • •

Let's consider for a moment the key issue here. None of this scalable plan, none of these resource-management techniques, none of these practice exercises will make one iota of difference if you, the wary parent, are not willing to give up a modicum of control.

But, by ceding resource-management to your teen, are you really giving up control? For the short run, yes. You have to be willing to let the resource go. But our children are with us for so short a time. Before you know it, that teen is out the door and off to college and on into adulthood. What good can be done then by exercising tight-fisted control? Rather, by allowing your teen to take over management of key financial resources, by guiding them in this process, aren't you really establishing means by which your control—your influence— will extend far beyond their growing-up years? Aren't you in fact helping them acquire skills that will help you "control" disastrous behavior far beyond the formative years? Give a little now. Gain a lot later.

Appendix
Worksheets

Parent Player Profile Questionnaire..292

Parent Player Profile Answer Sheet 293

Teen Player Profile Questionnaire 294

Activities Pie Chart..295

The Real-Life Money Game Household Tasks and Chores 296

Jobs Areas For Teens 297

"Teen Business" Plan 298

Income Worksheet...299

Family Fund Contribution Questionnaire and Formula 300

Expense Worksheet...301

Estimated Projected Expenses 302

Estimated Projected Clothes Expense 303

The Real-Life Money Game Bank Reconciliation Worksheet 304

The Real-Life Money Game Playing Board Spending Plan 305

The Real-Life Money Game Contract...306

The Real-Life Money Game Plan 307

Savings Questionnaire...308

The Real-Life Money Game Three-Part Savings Plan: Now, Later, Never..................309

"Who or What Matters Most to You?" 310

The Real-Life Money Game Borrowing Chart 311

The Real-Life Money Game Lending Chart...312

Pie-Chart Model For Family Financial Discussions 313

Seven Deadly Sins: The Seven Most Common Financial Mistakes Parents Make.....314

Spending Habits Questionnaire 315

Financial Creativity Questionnaire 316

Four-Step Method For Problem Solving 317

Detailed Action Plan 318

The Real-Life Money Game's Word On Worth..319

Parent Player Profile Questionnaire
Family Member Player _____

Answer the following questions on the answer sheet provided using complete sentences and including the details.

Regarding your teen's money habits:

1. Have you ever discussed the subject of finances with your teen? If so, in what way?
2. How much money is currently available to your teen?
3. How would you describe how your teen handles money?
4. With regard to your teen's expenses, who typically pays for what?
5. How much money would you feel comfortable giving to your teen to manage?
6. What would be the primary reason your teen might want to learn money-management skills from you?

Regarding your current money habits:

7. Would you say you live within your means, or would you truly like to get spending under control?
8. Do you save money? If so, how do you use your savings? Do you use it to pay bills, or to make a major purchase or to take a family vacation, or do you leave it untouched?
9. How important is an emergency fund?
10. Are you saving for your teen's college? If so, how?
11. Are you saving for your retirement? If so, how?
12. Are you comfortable and confident using credit cards? (i.e. Do you pay them off monthly or do you keep a running balance for which you pay interest? Are you aware of the interest rate you pay?)
13. Are there reasons you consider using debt as worthwhile? If so, for what?
14. How do you feel about investing your money? What do you invest in?
15. How important is charitable giving to you and your family?

Identify your goals:

16. Why are you reading this book?
17. What is the primary tangible goal you hope to achieve by teaching your teen money-management skills?

From Chapter 2, Page 19

Parent Player Profile Answer Sheet
Family Member Player _____

Regarding your teen's money habits:

    1.

    2.

    3.

    4.

    5.

    6.

Regarding your current money habits:

    7.

    8.

    9.

  10.

  11.

  12.

  13.

  14.

  15.

Identify your goals:

  16.

  17.

From Chapter 2, Page 20

Teen Player Profile Questionnaire
Family Member Player _____

Ask your teen to answer the following questions regarding his or her own and parents' money habits. Answers should use complete sentences and include details.

1. How would you describe the way your parents handle money?

2. What would you like to learn most about managing money?

3. If you had money to manage, what would you want to do with it right now?

   • What things would you buy?

   • Would you save? How much? What for?

   • What things do you think you should be able to buy versus what things you think your parents should buy?

4. What are your future money goals?

   • Have enough to buy a _____

   • Save for _____

   • Give to _____

   • Invest in _____

   • Work for _____

From Chapter 2, Page 21

Activities Pie-Chart
Family Member Player _____

1. Make a separate list of the eleven activities noted on the Activities Pie-Chart worksheet.
2. Beside each one, assign an average daily amount of time your teen spends on this activity.
3. Divide the day into 100%. Now assign a percentage of that day to each activity and draw them into your circle as wedges of the pie, their relative size based on their percentage of the day.

- Sleep
- School
- Homework
- Extracurricular Activities
- Household Responsibilities
- Family Time
- TV
- Computer
- Job
- Volunteer Work
- Free time

From Chapter 4, Pages 34, 35

The Real-Life Money Game Household Tasks and Chores
Family Member Player _____

Household Chores:	Sunday	Monday	Tuesday	Wednesday	Thursday	Friday	Saturday	Amount Earned
Cooking								
Laundry								
Ironing								
Cleanup								
Garbage								
Beds								
Shopping								
Pet Care								
Yard								
Car Wash								
Other								
Financial Tasks:								
Sort Mail								
Pay Bills								
Filing								
Computer								
Research								
Total Due:								

From Chapter 4, Page 37

Jobs Areas For Teens
Family Member Player _____

- Athletic or Service Clubs
- Child and Daycare Assistant
- Computer Data Entry Assistant
- Department Store Inventory
- Entertainment: Movie Theaters, Fairs, Amusement Parks
- Factories and Industry
- Fast Food Restaurants
- Parks, Camps, and Recreation Facilities
- Small Business Retail Sales
- Sports: Lifeguard, Umpire, Golf Caddy, Assistant Coaching
- Tutoring
- Working at Parents' or Relatives' Business

Note other job interests or ideas:

From Chapter 4, Page 43

"Teen Business" Plan
Family Member Player _____

Organization Plan

Business Name and Description:

Product or Service:

Target Market/Primary Customers:

Rate or Price Charging:

Weekly Time Commitment:

Other Assistance Needed:

Financial Plan

Start-Up Capital and Available Sources:

Cash-Flow Projections:

Profit and Loss Statement:

Taxes Required:

Marketing Plan

Competition Within the Target Market:

Advertising:

Selling:

Implementation Plan

Establish and Set Up Base of Operation:

Contact Target Market/Primary Customers:

Analyze and Evaluate Results:

From Chapter 4, Page 45

Income Worksheet

Family Member Player _____   **Month:** _____

Date	Coins	Gifts	Earnings: Chores, Job, "Teen Business"	Allowance	Family Fund Contribution (Includes Rainy-Day Fund)	Savings & Investment	Savings & Investments Matched Funds	Borrowed Funds	Other Income	Week's Income
Week 1										
Week 2										
Week 3										
Week 4										
Total Income										

Chapter 4, Page 50; Chapter 5, Page 57; Chapter 7, Page 90; Chapter 10, Page 122

Family Fund Contribution Questionnaire
Family Member Player _____

1. How much money, if any, are you paying your teen?

2. Generally, how does your teen use the money?

3. Choose one thing you would like your teen to be responsible for paying.

From Chapter 5, Page 55

Family Fund Contribution Formula
Family Member Player _____

1. Compute your teen's current month's income using the Income Worksheet.
2. Calculate your teen's expenses using the Expense Worksheet.
   a. Record the expenses you are paying on your teen's behalf for the current or previous month.
   b. Record the expenses your teen is paying in the current or previous month.
3. Select expenses you want your teen to pay.
4. Compute a Rainy-Day Fund to set aside expenses for unanticipated costs.

Family Fund Contribution	= (	Expenses Teen Pays	+	Rainy-Day Fund	) –	Teen's Income
_____	= (	_____	+	_____	) –	_____

From Chapter 5, Pages 69, 70

Expense Worksheet

Family Member Player _____ **Month:** _____

Date	Food & Eating Out	Car Expense	Trans- portation	Enter- tainment	Books, Music, Movies	School Expense	Clothes & Accessories	Toiletries & Haircuts	Gifts Given to Family or Friends	Estimated Projected Expenses	Other Expenses	Week's Expenses
Week 1												
Week 2												
Week 3												
Week 4												
Total Expense												
Total Expense Teen Pays												

Chapter 5, Pages 59, 62; Chapter 7, Page 93; Chapter 10, Page 126

Estimated Projected Expenses
Family Member Player _____
From _____ To _____

Expense Item	Month Needed	Projected Amount

School Expenses:

- Tuition
- Special Events: Homecoming, Winter Ball, Sports Tournaments
- Music, Drama, Clubs
- Other

Car Expenses:

- Insurance
- Maintenance
- Repairs
- Other

Summer Activity Expenses:

- Camp
- Sports
- Vacation Spending Money
- Other

Other Expenses:

- Taxes

Total Projected Expenses

From Chapter 5, Page 65

Estimated Projected Clothes Expense
Family Member Player _____
From _____ To _____

Clothing Item	Inventory of What I Have	Description of What I Need	Month Needed	Projected Amount
• Coat				
• Shoes				
• Shirts/tops				
• Pants/shorts				
• Dresses/skirts				
• Underclothes				
• Accessories				
• Swimsuit				
• Special Occasion				
• Other				
Total Projected Expense				

From Chapter 5, Page 67

The Real-Life Money Game Bank Reconciliation Worksheet
Family Member Player _____
From _____ To _____

Step One:

- From your current month bank statement, write down the amount of money the bank shows you have in your account. Don't worry that the bank's date is different than your date. Write down the bank's ending balance here: _____

- Go to your check register. Put a check mark next to all the checks, and debit transactions in your check register that the bank shows on the statement. Add up all the outstanding checks and debit card transactions that have a circle by them and put the total here: _____

- In your check register, put a check mark next to all the deposits that the bank shows on the statement. Add up all the outstanding deposits that have a circle by them and put the total here: _____

Step Two:

- Take the ending bank balance from step one and subtract your total outstanding checks and debit card transactions from it; then add the total outstanding deposits and put the number here:

_____

Step Three:

- Update your check register by recording all the deposits you have made into your account through today's date. Write down your check register balance here:

_____

Step Four:

- Compare the number you computed in step two _____ with your check register balance in step three _____. If they are the same, congratulations! You have reconciled your check and debit card account register. This means that the cash balance you show today is correct.

- If the bank balance you computed in step two _____ is different than the check register balance you computed in step three _____, you will need to determine what the difference between them is and write it here _____.
  You will then need to go back through steps one through three to recheck your work for errors. Check also for the following: Recheck the addition in your check register balance or check to see if the bank charged any fees you have not yet recorded.

From Chapter 6, Pages 83

The Real-Life Money Game Playing Board-Spending Plan
Family Member Player _____ Month: _____

Income	Income amounts I have projected at the beginning of the month	What I actually received during the month	Difference between income I project in column one with the actual amount received in column two
• Coins • Gifts • Earnings • Allowance • Family Fund Contribution • Savings & Investment Income • Investments: Matched Funds • Borrowed Funds • Rainy-Day Fund • Other			
Total Income			

Expenses	What I expect it to cost	What it actually costs	Difference between expected cost in column one with the actual cost in column two
• Food & Eating Out • Car Expense • Transportation • Entertainment • Books, Music, Movies • School Expense • Clothes & Accessories • Toiletries & Haircuts • Gifts Given • Rainy-Day Fund • Other			
Total Expenses			
Total Income Minus Total Expenses			

From Chapter 7, Pages 91, 94; Chapter 10, Pages 124, 128, 130

The Real-Life Money Game Contract
Family Member Player _____
From _____ To _____

General Contract

The foregoing family members agree to play *The Real-Life* Money Game in accordance with the instructions and the rules. If any rules are broken or instructions not followed, these specified sanctions will be applied:

_____

_____

_____

Subcontract

The family members further agree to the special terms listed below:

_____

_____

Signed: _____ _____ _____

Date: _____ _____ _____

From Chapter 8, Page 105

The Real-Life Money Game Plan
Family Member Player _____
From _____ To _____

1. Identify at least one result/goal or tangible skill you wish to teach your teen.
2. List the steps your son or daughter can follow to accomplish the task.
3. Write down any notes with progress or items to be discussed at the scheduled meeting time.
4. Determine the time frame—the estimated period of time it will take to complete the goal—and write down the start and finish dates at the top of the worksheet.

Identify goal:

Detail tasks to accomplish the goal:

Discussion notes:

From Chapter 9, Pages 110, 114, 116, 117

Savings Questionnaire
Family Member Player _____

1. Why do you want your son or daughter to save?

2. How much, on average each month, would you like your teen to save?

3. How would you like your son or daughter to use his or her savings and when?

4. Choose one thing you would like your teen to be responsible to save for that might require up to six months? One to five years? More than five years?

From Chapter 11, Page 136

The Real-Life Money Game
Three-Part Savings Plan: Now, Later, Never
Family Member Player _____

For When	For What	Total Cost	Fixed Monthly Amount	Where: At What Rate
Now				
Later				
Never				
Total Monthly Savings				

From Chapter 11, Pages 138, 140, 143, 148

"Who or What Matters Most to You?"
Family Member Player _____

If you had some money to give, how would you most like to use it?

Why?

Determine How to Give: Money, Goods, A Gesture, or Volunteer Time	Decide How Often to Give: Per Week, Month, Quarter, Six-Months, or Year	Where to Give: List the Top Five Causes You Care About In Order of Priority	Name Specifically the Local or National Organization or the Cause

From Chapter 12, Page 152

The Real-Life Money Game Borrowing Chart
Family Member Player _____

What are you borrowing funds for?	
Is it a legitimate use of debt?	
Is there any other way you could come up with the money or only borrow some portion of the amount?	
How much are you borrowing and from what source?	
How will the debt be paid off—where will the money come from?	
When will the debt be paid off?	
What is the interest rate you will be paying and what will be the total cost of borrowing to you?	

From Chapter 13, Page 165

The Real-Life Money Game Lending Chart
Family Member Player _____

What are you lending funds for?

Is it a legitimate use for lending?

Is there any other way to come up with
the money besides a loan from you?

How much are you lending and to whom?

How will the loan to you be paid off—
where will the money come from?

When will the loan be paid off?

What is the interest rate you will be paid
and what will be the total income to you
for the loan?

From Chapter 13, Page 166

Pie-Chart Model For Family Financial Discussions
Family Member Player _____

The pie represents 100% of your family's income. Slice the pie into percents to show how the family income is used for the points bulleted below:

- Costs of a Home

- Food and Entertainment

- Clothes and Education

- Transportation Costs

- Medical

- Vacation

- Emergencies, Savings, Investing

- Debt

- Charity

- Taxes

From Chapter 17, Page 226; Chapter 20, Page 265

Seven Deadly Sins: The Seven Most Common Financial Mistakes Parents Make With Their Teens
Family Member Player _____

1. **Overly Excessive: The Free Handouts**
   Action to Take:

2. **Overly Strict: Never Enough Money**
   Action to Take:

3. **Secrecy: "My teen knows nothing about our finances."**
   Action to Take:

4. **The Cyclical Nature of Negative Presumption: Never Good Enough**
   Action to Take:

5. **Saying Too Much: The "I told you so!" Syndrome**
   Action to Take:

6. **Saying Too Little: The Fallacy of Sink or Swim**
   Action to Take:

7. **Money for the "Goods": Pressure to Perform**
   Action to Take:

From Chapter 17, Page 236

Spending Habits Questionnaire
Family Member Player _____

1. List the five most important things to spend money on between now and the end of the month.

2. How much money do I need to spend on each?

3. How much money do I have left on hand?

4. If I'm short money, how can I adjust the dollar amounts listed for each item to make up the shortfall? What items could I eliminate?

From Chapter 18, Page 242

Financial Creativity Questionnaire
Family Member Player _____

1. Look around you for opportunities to make money. Ask yourself what your business community, church, or environment needs to develop a viable money-making idea.

2. Identify and interview local entrepreneurs. What do they do? How did they get started?

3. How might you add or improve on a simple business idea?

4. How might you increase the resource base?

5. How could you create a demand or market for your money-making idea?

From Chapter 18, Page 246

Four-Step Method For Problem Solving
Family Member Player _____

1. **The Problem:** Come up with a statement of the problem that both you and your teen agree on.

2. **The Tangible Skill Required:** Choose one tangible money-management skill required to address the problem.

3. **The Intangible Result:** Choose one intangible money-management skill you wish to achieve with your teen.

4. **The Workable Solution:** Identify and write down both parents' and teen's needs. Make a list of possible solutions. Choose solutions that get both parents and teen's needs met and eliminate the rest.

Parents' Needs	Teen's Needs

List of Possible Solutions:

Ultimate Solution:

From Chapter 19, Pages 251, 256

317

Detailed Action Plan
Family Member Player _____

Solution Start Date:

Solution End Date:

Detailed Action Plan:

Was your son or daughter happy with the results?

Did the commitment prove too difficult to carry out for either parent or teen?

Is the tangible skill being learned?

Is the problem being resolved? If not, why not? What changes can you make to the original solution to promote success?

Has the problem changed such that you need to go through the Four-Step Method For Problem Solving again?

From Chapter 19, Page 258

***The Real-Life* Money Game's Word On Worth**
Family Member Player _____

Add Together:

- How much you have in your "cash pockets" or your checking account
- How much you have in your savings account
- How much you have in your investment account
- How much you own:

    A bike

    A car

    A computer

    Other Personal Belongings

    Collectibles

- How much you own in a "Teen Business"
- Money owed you (what you've lent someone)
- Other

Total of What You Own

Add Together:

- Money you owe
- Taxes you owe
- Other

Total of What You Owe

Subtract the Total of What You Owe from the Total of What You Own to Get Your Financial Worth

From Chapter 21, Pages 270, 272, 274

319

Index
Play *The Real-Life* Money Game With Your Teen

A

Accessories, 11, 23-30, 211-212, 279

Active investment manager, 185-192

Activities Pie Chart, 33-36, 51, 212, 219, 226

Advanced-player level, 12, 278

Age of majority, 265

Age-old conflict, 31

Agreement, 11, 104-106, 257, 263

Alcohol, 102

Allowance, 31-32, 53-58, 212

American Dream, 246

American Institute of Philanthropy, 156

American Savings Education Council, 141

AmeriCorps, 158

Ameritrade, 203

Arguments, 9, 104, 250

Arm's-length, 176

Asset
allocation, 172, 178-180
classes, 179, 187
wear-and-tear, 275

Authors, 186

Automated Teller Machines (ATM), 77

Available time, 212, 219

B

Babysitting, 46-50

Back-end load, 175

Bank
account, 23-29, 75-82, 212-215
reconciliation worksheet, 79-83, 209, 243
cut-off date, 82
statement, 77-84

Bank Savings Account With ATM Card, 23, 28

Bankruptcy, 161

Beginning-player level, 12, 278

Behaviors, 5, 12-14, 110, 171

Benchmark, 71

Beneficiary, 28

Better Business Bureau, 156

Bill-paying jobs, 38

Binders
personal financial, 23-26

Book's Promise, 14

Borrowing, 13, 48, 99, 162-164, 219, 222-225, 271

Broker, 185-189, 209

Buffett, Warren, 186

Bureau of Labor Statistics, 71, 227

Butler, Samuel, 106

Buy-and-hold, 187-188

Buyer's remorse, 239, 243

C

Calculator, 23, 26

Capital
gains, 201
losses, 201

Capitalistic economy, 174

Car
expense fund, 25, 43, 59-62, 72, 76, 92-94, 101, 106, 118, 126-129, 135, 164, 227, 259, 261-264
insurance, 17, 38, 43-44, 61, 72, 76-77, 227, 249, 253-259, 262
maintenance, 43, 227, 253
purchase/payment, 17-18, 38, 76, 104, 142, 164, 209
title, 106
wash, 37-38
detailing, 271-274

Carbon copy, 29, 80

Carroll, Lewis, 106

CASA (National Center on Addiction and Substance Abuse), 102

Case-study families
Delaney, 66, 233
Greene, 221, 269-274
Horowitz, 262-263
MacLean, 66, 147-148, 221, 232, 259-260
Sanchez, 32, 38-40, 63, 72, 81, 106, 117-118, 146-154, 167, 225-243, 259
Williamson, vii, 3, 7-13, 34-39, 47-55, 63-68, 71, 75, 78-82, 94-95, 100-108, 113-119, 123-129, 130, 142-156, 163, 180-182, 187, 192-193, 197-202, 208-210, 217-223, 227-232, 242-250, 271-277
Wilson, 17-18, 27, 39, 49-50, 56-69, 88-118, 122-128, 135-162, 189-222, 239-241, 249-258

Cash
balance, 78-82, 179, 230, 243
pocket, 26-28, 75-78

Cell phone, 135-136

Certificate of deposit (CD), 183

Certified
  Financial Planner (CFP), 185
  Public Accountant (CPA), 185
Chamber of Commerce, 202
Charitable
  giving, 13, 19, 129, 151-156, 265
  organization, 100-103, 156
Checkbook, 3, 11-12, 23, 82, 156
Checking
  account, 5, 11, 13, 23, 26, 28-30, 75-86, 214, 243-244, 279
  fees, 28, 81, 230, 243
Child support, 264
Chores worksheet, 36-39, 212
Church, 10, 100-101, 151, 156, 228, 273
Cigarettes, 102
Clear-sheet protectors, 25-26
Closing price, 175-176, 188
Clothes
  expense fund, 7-9, 59-66, 115-116, 213, 223-227, 232
  shopping, 7, 9, 33, 66, 223-224, 232
Co-sign, 28-29, 162-163
Co-workers, 42
Coins, 24, 32, 49-50, 57, 90, 122, 212
Collaborator, 7
Collateral, 106
Collection, 271
College
  education fund, 9, 19, 26, 135, 144-146, 164, 190-191
  financial planning, 144-146
  entry-age, 4, 161
Columbia University, 102
Communication, 16-17, 97, 217, 264, 267
Community service agencies, 157-158

Company
  abbreviations, 174-175
  classifications, 178
  revenues, 174, 176
  size, 177-180, 193
  stock, 174-180, 187, 192-193, 201
Competitors, 174
Compliance, 104
Compound, 135, 141, 171
Computer, 25, 33-35, 37-38, 48, 103, 135-136, 163-164, 247, 270
Congress, 4
Consequences of
  borrowing, 164
  mistakes, 171, 231, 277
  overspending, 232
  running out of money, 99
Consultant, 48, 327
Consumer, 161
Contract
  negotiations, 205-209
  renegotiation, 205-209
  subcontract, 104-108
Control
  transferring control of money, 6-10, 78, 109, 234-235, 261
Cooking, 37
Correlation, 163
Cost
  basis, 61, 64, 113, 188, 197
  comparison, 38
County, 199, 202
Credit
  card, 4, 11-13, 26-30, 79-80, 97, 161-169
  crisis, 161
  history, 163-164
  limit, 7, 162
  rating, 164
  record, 60, 79-80, 163
  card company, 162

Cumulative scorekeeping box, 216
Currency, 31, 53, 211
Custodian account, 28
Customers, 44, 161
Cyclical Nature of Negative Presumption, 220, 228-230, 235

D

Deadlines, 111
Death, 261, 264-266
Debit
  card account, 5, 11, 13, 23, 26, 28-30, 75-86, 162-168, 214, 243, 279
  payments, 162-163
  transactions, 26, 79-85, 243
  statements, 26, 162
Debt
  payments, 162-163
  repayment, 167, 214, 245
Decision-making, 7, 10, 12, 230, 235
Deduction, 200, 202
Delayed gratification, 5, 14, 109, 113, 141, 230
Dependent, 200, 264
Detailed Action Plan worksheet, 252, 257
Disability, 261, 263-266
Discipline, 9, 102, 220, 230
Discounted commission, 193
Discretionary
  choices, 9, 31, 94, 223-224, 232, 260
  costs, 223-224
  expenses, 9, 31, 63, 94, 100, 102, 131, 210, 223, 260
  money, 8-9, 31, 63, 94, 97, 100, 102, 131, 210, 223-224, 232, 260

Discussion, 15, 30, 40, 55, 63, 99, 198, 204, 253, 279
Disney World, 39
Disposable personal income, 161
Disruptive circumstances
  death, 205
  disability, 205
  divorce, 205
Diversification, 172, 177-179, 193
Dividend, 48, 175-176, 204
Divorce, 261-266
DJIA (Dow Jones Industrial
  Average), 182
Dollar-Cost Averaging, 188
Donate, 154, 157
Down payment, 180-181, 189, 209
DRIP (Direct Investment Plan),
  184
Drugs, 103
Dual-step parenting, 261

E

Early-learning, 26
Earning, 5-7, 10-13, 32-47, 51,
  56-57, 75-78, 112, 164, 191-
  193, 197-204, 211-216, 218-
  219, 225, 250, 259-260, 273
Economy, 174, 178
Education, 3, 141, 164, 227, 265,
  327
Emergency fund, 19, 68
Emotional accounting, 255
Empirical data, 186
Employee, 197
Employment, 40
Empower, 263
Entitlement, 250, 266
Entrepreneurial
  risk, 10, 246, 273, 275
  spirit, 10, 246
  success, 273
Equifax, 168

Equity fund, 184
Estate tax planning, 202
Estimated Projected
  Clothes Expense worksheet,
    66, 115-116, 213
  Expenses, 59, 62, 64, 66, 92,
    126, 213
Ethics, 235
Evaluate
  Investment Alternatives, 172,
    185
  Results, 101, 172
Ex-capital gains distribution, 175
Excess
  funds, 97, 100-101, 129, 131,
    210, 216
  revenues, 176
Excise tax, 199
Exemption, 200
Expense
  actual, 121-132
  Expenses Your Teen Pays,
    54-73
  worksheet, 58-73, 93, 125-127,
    131-132, 213-215
Experian, 168
Extracurricular activities, 33-35

F

Fama, Eugene F., 186
Family Fund Contribution (FFC)
  Formula, 7, 56
  Questionnaire, 55
FDIC (Federal Deposit Insurance
  Corporation), 183
Fear, 2, 27, 115, 118, 254
Federal Form
  1040, 197-204
  1040ES, 197-204
  Schedule C, 200
  W-4, 198-199, 204

Financial
  Creativity Questionnaire, 246
  dream, 171, 180-181, 186, 246
  history, 193
  independence, 2, 4, 6, 78, 223,
    245, 247, 253, 289, 327
  literacy, 2, vii-viii, 4, 327
  plan, 3-4, 6-9, 12, 112-113,
    121-129, 207-216, 218-219,
    223-225, 227, 235, 245,
    262-264, 266-267, 269-276,
    289
  planning goal, 144
  responsibility, 6, 171, 253,
    262, 267
  skills (see Money-
    management skills)
  tasks, 33, 37, 40, 104, 211-212,
    219
Financiers, 245, 247
Finite
  measurement, 269
  quantity, 8
Fiscal, 243
Fixed
  costs, 68, 218, 223, 227
  income, 13, 55, 218, 227
Flexibility, 2, 8, 10-11, 26, 36, 38,
  70, 89, 211, 252, 275
Flexible scalable plan, 8, 118
*Foundation of Finance: Portfo-
lio Decisions and Securities
Prices,* 186
Four-Step Method For Problem
  Solving, 250-251, 255, 259-260
Free Handouts, 220-221, 235
French, Dan W., 186
Frugal, 222, 246
Fundamentals, 7, 207
Funding shortfalls, 99
Fundraiser, 8
Future date, 143

G

Generating Income, 33, 131, 207, 217

Generation Y, 4, 64

Generosity, 151, 153, 222, 244

Getty, J. Paul, 2

Gifting, 203

Gifts, birthday and holiday, 32-33, 63-64, 154, 212, 259

Giving, 4-7, 11, 13, 19, 25, 101, 109, 129, 151-159, 217-219

Glossary of investment terms, 172-173

Golden Rule For Parents, 106-107, 213, 231, 235, 241, 277

Good-enough, 243

Grades, 54, 233, 235

Grandparents, 32, 56

Great American icon (athletic shoes), 239

Greenspan, Alan, vii

Growth
company, 178, 193
stocks, 178, 193

Guardian, 28, 264-265

Guidestar, 157

Gut level, 6, 98, 140, 158, 211, 231

H

Hands-off, parenting, 106, 237

Hands-on, 1, 3-4, 109, 140, 237, 245

Harris Interactive Poll, 54

Hazards of debt, 161

Hoarding, 10

Homelessness, 157-158

Homework, 33-35, 113

Honest, 231, 255

Household
chores, 13, 31-33, 36-39, 49, 104, 113, 123, 212, 219
contributions, 33, 36, 104
costs, 225
funds, 7, 9, 13, 32, 49, 101, 123, 212, 219, 262
jobs, 36, 38-39, 212, 225, 254
tasks, 13, 32-33, 36-39, 49, 104, 212, 219

I

Identity theft, 103

Illegal
expenditures, 97
substances, 102

Impoverished, 224

Impulse purchase, 154

Income
family, 226-227, 264-266
sources, 5, 7, 31-32, 49, 53, 72, 75, 172, 212
stocks, 47, 178, 201
tax, 13, 24, 189, 197-202, 204, 215, 218
versus worth, 269-274
worksheet, 31-51, 53-73, 89-95, 121-132, 189, 211-216, 242

Incorporated, 32

Independent
financial consultant, 327
investment advisor, 186
sector, 151
thinker, 278

Index
fund, 123, 194
stock market, 173, 182
tabs, 23-26, 76, 123, 165-166

Individual retirement account (IRA), 13, 190-191, 194, 209, 219

Information access advantages, 164

Inheritance, 264

Insufficient funds, 80

Insurance
car, 17, 38, 43-44, 61, 72, 76-77, 227, 249, 253-259, 262
home, 226
life, 264-265
policies, 38

Intangible skills
job, 40, 212
money-management, 4, 6, 12, 109, 255
result, 5-6, 12, 214, 250-251, 254-255
delayed gratification, 5, 14, 109-113, 141, 230
differentiating wants from needs, 14, 109-113
independent thinking, 14, 109-113
personal responsibility, 14, 109-113
problem solving, 14, 109-113
self-confidence, 5-6, 14, 40, 109-113
self-discipline, 14, 109-113, 229
self-motivation, 6, 14, 109-113, 234, 235
strong work ethic, 14, 109-113
valuing assets, 14, 109-113

Intermediate-player level, 12, 278

Internal Revenue Service (IRS), 76, 203

Internet
café, 44
purchases, 17, 97, 202
research, 13, 38, 103, 202
safeguards, 103
websites, 174, 177

Intervene, 239, 241-243

Interview, 15, 115

Inventory, 47, 66

Investment

  accountant, 28-29, 75, 80

  Account Information

    Checklist, 28

  advice, 201

  alternative, 185

  basics, 147, 172

  bond, 174-177

  classifications, micro, 177

  classifications, mid, 177

  classifications, large, 177

  classifications, small, 177

  firm, 190

  Five Steps to Investing, 172,

    191-194

    Step One, 172

    Step Two, 174

    Step Three, 180

    Step Four, 185

    Step Five, 187

  income, 47-48, 171-195, 197-

    204, 212-215

  institution, 13, 28, 80-82, 190

  matched funds, 50, 57, 90,

    122, 144, 172

  noncorrelating securities, 178

  options, 26, 28, 75, 86, 129,

    181, 185, 214

  performance, 177-178, 182

  portfolio, 177, 186, 188, 193

  products, 174, 178, 185-186

  research, 13, 80, 185, 209

  risk, 171-172, 178-181, 187,

    189-191, 193

  sales, 197

  spreadsheets, 289

  statement, 80-82, 127, 162,

    188, 209, 215

  strategy, 144, 172, 177, 180,

    182, 185, 187-188, 193

  terms, 16, 172, 174, 176, 181

  transactions, 26, 81-82, 201,

    209

Investment manager

  active, 185-192

  passive, 185-192

J

Job

  income, 5, 13, 31-51, 90,

    101,122, 197-204, 211-212,

    217, 249-260, 263-264, 269

  Job Areas For Teens, 40-43,

    212

  performance, 36, 38

  search, 40, 164, 202

Judgment, 106, 230-231, 235

Jump$tart Coalition, vii, 4

K

Keep Track of Your Cash, 81

Keeping Score, 12, 18, 30, 51,

  72-73, 86-87, 95, 108, 118-119,

  131-132, 150, 159, 168-169,

  194-196, 203, 204

Key Investment Objectives, 215,

  219

Kiddie tax, 200

L

Labor laws, 40-44, 212

Large-cap

  companies, 177, 193

  funds, 193

Learn to Earn: The Beginner's

  Guide to Investing, 186

Legal age requirements, 203

Lending

  chart, 164-166

  institution, 13, 163

  funds, 7, 13, 89, 129, 131, 164-

    167, 219

Level of maturity, 148

Life insurance, 264-265

Lifeguard, 17, 115, 254, 257

Line of communication, 267

Living Expenses, 146

Local Taxes, 44, 202

Long-term financial

  decision, 271, 273, 275

  goal, 216, 269, 271, 273

  plan, 216, 269, 273, 275

  retirement, 273

Lottery, 266

Lynch, Peter, 186

M

Magic For Dummies, 107

Mailing envelopes, 25

Margin, 142

Marijuana, 102

Market

  capitalization formula, 193

  performance, 177-178, 182

  value, 175, 177-178, 187-188,

    275-276

Master business license, 41

Match

  donors, 157

  funds, 9, 79, 101, 146, 172,

    262

Mature, 14, 266

Merrill Lynch, 209-210

Methodology, 11, 33, 53, 101

Microsoft

  Investor Relations, 193

  profits, 193

  stock price, 193

  Xbox, 244

Middle-class, 158

Minimum

  age, 7, 28, 162

balance, 7, 28, 162-163, 243
fund, 7, 56, 163
Minor, 178, 202, 259, 265
Mistakes teens make, 239-245
Mix of varying-sized companies, 177
Mixed messages, 255
Money
    Clip, 23-24
    Equals Opportunity, 8
    gurus, vii
    habits, 15-16, 19, 144, 158, 167, 219, 227, 242, 245, 247, 261
    order, XXX-XXX
    priorities, 8, 15-17, 34-35, 77, 155, 218
Money-making opportunities, 245-246
Money-management
    foundation, 263
    goals, 1, 12, 19
    problem, 6, 94, 109, 251, 254-255, 260, 263
    process, 12, 220, 260
    skills, 3-6, 12-19, 31-33, 40, 47, 97, 101-102, 104, 109-111, 118, 212-216, 217-218, 220-225, 227-228, 232-237, 239-247, 253-255, 260, 266, 269-276
Mortgage, 163, 180, 226
Motivation, 44
Mutual fund abbreviations, 174-175

N

NASDAQ Composite Index, 182
NASDAQ-AMEX Market Group, 192-193
National Center on Addiction and Substance Abuse (CASA), 102

Negative cycle of presumption, 228
Negotiate, vii, 8, 217, 234
Net asset value (NAV), 175
Net Chg, 175
Net long-term capital
    gain, 201
    losses, 201
Net profits, 197, 200, 204
Net self-employment income, 202
Net-worth, 269, 273
Never Enough Money, 220, 235
Never Good Enough, 220, 228, 235
New York Stock Exchange (NYSE), 192
New York Times, 161
News headlines, 2, 161
Newspaper carriers, 202
Nintendo, vii, 277
No load – no sales commission, 175
Non-correlating
    companies, 178-179, 193
    securities, 178
Non-taxable
    retirement fund, 191
Noncompliance, 213, 250
Noncorrelating, 178
Nonprofit
    groups, 156
    organization, 7, 156, 158
Number-crunching, 129

O

Object of The Real-Life Money Game, 6, 109, 212
Online
    credit reports, 168
    investment resources, 174, 185-186, 192
    services, 28, 64, 157, 162

tax resources, 202
transfers, 79, 85
One Up on Wall Street, 186
Order of priority, 152, 217-218, 237
Original investment, 180-181, 193
Over-scheduled, 111
Overdraft, 7, 28, 162, 239, 243
Overly
    Excessive, 220, 235
    Strict, 220, 222, 235
Ownership share, 174, 180

P

Paid household tasks, 212
Paid jobs, 36, 208
Paperless society, 80
Parent
    co-sign, 162
    generated income, 53-73
    generation, 225
    oft-asked questions, 31
    Player Profile Questionnaire, 15-16, 19, 212
    power, 261
Part-time job, 39, 81, 259
Passive investment manager, 185-192
Patience, 239, 245, 247, 260
Paycheck, 26, 197, 199, 202, 204
Paycheck stub, 204
Payday, 39
Payday-loan, 161
Payroll, 199, 202
PE The price/earnings ratio, 175
Peer Pressure, 98, 250
Pension, 264
Percent, 4, 8, 13, 18, 54, 107, 129, 147, 244
Percentage of income, 199
Percentage of the day, 34-35

Percentage terms, 175, 181

Percentages, 33, 226

Percentages of daily activities, 33

Percents, 265

Personal binder cover, 30, 279

Personal Financial Binder, 24-26, 30, 68, 76, 123, 165-166, 202-204, 210, 212, 279

Personal Financial Literacy, vii, 4

Personal Identification Number, 77

Personal responsibility, 6, 40, 109, 207, 211, 222, 234-235, 255, 264

Philanthropic, 154, 158

Pie chart

    Activities, 33-36, 51, 212, 219, 226

    Asset Allocation, 179

    Average Federal Tax Rates, 198-199

    Pie-Chart Model For Family Financial Discussions, 226-227, 235, 264-267

Player Profile Questionnaire, 15-19, 23, 212, 245, 247, 279

Player-level

    advanced, 12, 278

    beginning, 12, 278

    intermediate, 12, 278

Playing Board-Spending Plan, 11, 29, 89-95, 121-132, 208-217

Pocketmoney, 55

Point-value system, 278

Pool money, 7

Portfolio

    analysis, 186-188

    decisions, 186-188

    of investments, 177, 186-188, 193

Positive Cycle of Presumption, 229

Practicing, skill-building, viii, 48, 106, 217, 220-221, 247, 289

Pre-established parameters, 218

Predictability, 178

Presumptions, 228-229

Principles of compounding, 141

Prioritizing time, 33, 40

Probability, 187

Problem-solving, 99, 210

Process-oriented solution, 234

Profitable companies, 178

Profits, 176, 178, 190, 193, 197, 200, 204

Projected Clothes Expense, 64-66, 115-116, 213

Projected Estimated Expenses, 59-64, 92, 121, 126, 213

Proper use of credit, 161

Psychologists, 36

Punishment, 233

Punitive measure, 10

Purchase price, original, 76, 139, 149, 154, 181

Purchase receipts, 78-80

Purse, 23-24, 26

Q

Questionnaires, 17-18

Quicken, 203

R

Rainy-Day Fund, 54-57, 68-70, 99-100, 213, 266

Rate of return, 141-143, 171-172, 177, 179-182, 186, 193, 273

Real-Life Money Game (see *The Real-Life* Money Game)

Receipt, 75-76, 81, 230

Reconcile

    checking-account statement, 127

    investment statement, 127

Record-keeping, 27, 39, 79

Recurring pattern of failure, 228, 235

Recycling, 44

Refund of tax, 197

Reliable Pocket, 23-24

Relief fund, World Trade Center, 156

Religious institutions, 156

Research, 13, 37-38, 48, 64, 80, 103, 185, 202, 209, 247, 271

Resistance/Noncompliance, 250

Resolving conflict, 249, 251, 253, 255, 257, 259

Resource

    management, 3, 129-130, 254, 267

    renewable, 2-3

Retail price, 244

Retirement

    account, 190

    age, 190

Revenues, 174, 176, 202, 271

Rewards, 39, 139, 211

Right-of-passage, 29

Risk

    identified level of, 181

    of substance abuse, 102

    tolerance, 180-181, 193

    risk-taking, 4, 10, 36, 102, 161, 171-196, 246, 271-276

Rivalry, 250

Roth Individual Retirement Account (Roth IRA), 13, 190-191, 194, 209, 219

Rules

    Golden Rule for Parents (see Golden Rule for Parents)

    Rule One, 97-99, 242

    Rule Two, 97

    Rule Three, 97, 102

    Rule Four, 97, 103

Rule Five, 97
Rule of 72, the, 142

S

S&P 500, 182
Safekeeping, 69
Salary, 147
Sales tax, 202
Sanctions, 97, 213
Saving, 137-150
    For Now, 139
    For Later, 140
    For (what seems like) Never, 146
Savings
    account, 11, 23, 26, 28, 30, 75-79, 86, 101, 125, 163, 210, 214, 261, 266, 270, 279
    base price, 142
    concepts, 217
    goal, 102-103, 118, 143, 146-147, 210, 262, 264
    questionnaire, 136
Save Now For Some Total Future Amount, 143
Saying Too Little, 220, 235
Saying Too Much, 220, 235
Scalable financial plan, 3, 6, 207, 252
Schedules, 38
School Expense, 59, 62, 92, 126
School lunch, 60, 63, 153
Scorekeeping (see keeping score)
Secrecy, 220, 226, 235
Securities, 25, 47, 171-196, 200-204
Securities and Exchange Commission (SEC), 183
Security and Portfolio Analysis: Concepts and Management, 186

Self-
    awareness, 229
    confidence, 5-6, 40, 109
    disciplined, 229
    employment, 44, 198, 202
    fulfilling prophecy, 228
    motivation, 6, 109, 234, 235
    reliance, 33
    sufficiency, 267
    worth, 229
Semi-annual, 16, 77
Seven Deadly Sins, 217, 220, 234-235, 237
Seven financial habits of successful teen financiers, 245, 247
Seven Most Common Financial Mistakes Parents Make With Their Teens, 220, 235
Shareholders, 176
Shares Outstanding, 177
Shelter, 158
Shift income, 200
Shopping, 7, 9, 33, 37, 66, 77-78, 98, 103, 106, 223, 232
Short-fall, 77
Short-term, 13, 139, 201, 219, 234-235, 263
Showdown, vii-viii, 266, 278
Sibling Rivalry, 250
Silence, 106, 231
Single-parenting, 261
Sink-or-swim, 233
Sins (see Seven Deadly)
Skills In Order of Priority, 217, 237
Social security
    number, 200-202, 204
    payment, 265-266
    Social Security Administration, 201
    tax, 197-199, 201
Solution, viii, 234, 250-252, 254-255, 257, 259-260, 263-264, 266

Special circumstances, 68, 154, 261, 263-265, 267
Spending Habits Questionnaire, 242
Spending options, 26, 28, 75, 86, 214
Spending Plan (see Playing Board Spending Plan)
Spending priorities, 16-17, 77
Spending-mechanic option, 72, 76, 219
Spending-plan funds, 13
Spending-plan parameters, 89, 98-99, 153
Spirit of entrepreneurship, 9-10, 246
Spreadsheet, 38
Standard & Poor's 500 (S&P 500), 182
State
    governments, 204
    income tax, 202
    labor laws, 40, 44
    law, 203
    of residence, 28
    State of Washington, 327
    taxes, 198-199, 202-204
Statistics, 53-54, 71, 227
Steps
    Step-by-step instructions, 142, 149, 207
    Step One, 82, 172, 208, 211, 252
    Step Two, 174, 213
    Step Three, 61, 82, 111, 179-180, 185, 214
    Step Four, 111, 185, 215
    Step Five, 187, 215
    Steps For Investing, 219
Stinginess, 222
Stock
    fund abbreviations, 174-175
    market, 171-196

index, 182
price volatility, 178
quote, 175
single company, 177, 193
Stockholders, 177
Strong work ethic, 6, 40, 109, 234
Students, 3-4, 47, 153, 158, 161,
    167, 225, 229, 240-241
Subjective items, 63
Substance abuse, 102
Successful teen financiers, 242-
    247
Summary of Scores, 288
Summer
    camp, 135-136
    job, 113-115
Supply-and-demand, 176
Surveys, 141, 161
Symbol, 193
System of organization, 23

T

Tabs, 25
Tangible money-management
    skills, 4, 53, 58, 133, 213, 217,
    251-254
Tax
    annual basis, 197
    concepts, 199
    consequences, 215, 218-219
    estimated payment vouchers,
        203
    expense, 13, 198, 215
    gains/losses, 188-190
    gift, 202
    identification number, 200
    income tax, 197-204
    information, 103, 201, 203
    investment income, 200-201
    job earnings, 199, 202
    labor, 40, 44
    rates, 198-199

return, 13, 76, 197-200, 202-
    203
sales, 142
slice, 198-199
Social Security, 197-204
standard deduction, 200
tax-deferred retirement
    account, 190-191
Taxpayers, 201
Teaching Skills In Order of Prior-
    ity, 217
Teen
    borrowing, 164
    income sources, 32, 49
    labor laws, 40-41
    Player Profile Questionnaire,
        15-17, 212, 245, 247, 279
    available hours, 44
    available time, 212, 219
    check register, 82
    current financial situation,
        269
    current income, 56
    current money habits, 245
    expenses, 19
    financial system of organiza-
        tion
    future well-being, 4
    income, 5-7, 31-51, 53-56, 75,
        212
    jobs, 40-43, 212
    personal financial binder, 24,
        26, 76, 212
    philanthropy, 151
    risk tolerance, 180
    scalable plan, 275
    social security number, 200
    dream, 191
    financial independence, 327
Teen business
    eBay, 46, 103, 275
    plan, 44-47, 212
    value of, 275

Television, vii, 33-35, 58, 98, 153
The Real-Life Money Game
    Bank Reconciliation Work-
        sheet, 80-82, 127, 209, 243
    Borrowing Chart, 164-165,
        271
    Debt Rules, 167-168, 214, 219
    Five-Step Instructions, 207-
        211, 213, 215
    Household Tasks, 37-39, 212
    Income Worksheet *****
    Plan, 2, 1, 11-13, 68-69, 106,
        109-111, 113, 115-119, 171,
        181, 198, 209, 213-216,
        273, 278
    Plan Overview, 12-13, 111,
        118, 216, 278
    Playing Board-Spending Plan,
        11, 29, 89-95, 121-132,
        208-217
    Rules, 1, 97, 99, 101, 103, 105,
        107, 213
    Three-Part Savings Plan, 137-
        138, 150, 214
    website, 7
    Word On Worth, 269-276
Theft, 103
Thought-provoking questions,
    222, 273
Three disruptive D's, 261, 266
Three-Part Savings Plan, 137-
    138, 150, 214, 219
Throw-away-society, 241
Ticker symbol, 193
Timeline, 180, 257
Tracking The Real-Life Money
    Game Monthly Activity, 121,
    123, 125, 127, 129, 131
Trans Union, 168
Transfer funds, 29, 80
Treasury Department, vii, 4
True tax cost, 197
Trust account, 266

Tuition, 146, 225
TurboTax, 203

U

U.S. Department of Labor, 41
Ultimate goal, 29, 148, 151, 197, 269
Ultimate solution, 251, 255
Uncooperative, 38
Undermining power-plays, 266
Uniform Gifts to Minors Act (UGMA), 28
Uniform Transfers to Minors Act (UTMA), 28
Unplanned Expenses, 54, 56, 68
Unpredictable, 176
Unused capital loss, 201
Upper-middle, 144
Utility stocks, 178

V

Vacation, 19, 39, 72, 115, 208, 227, 265
Value companies, 178
Value of possessions, 276
Values, 2, 5, 8, 15, 36, 71, 110, 229, 252, 278
Valuing assets, 6, 109
Verifiable information, 76, 187
Veto power, 97, 100
Video, 55, 63, 266, 277
Visionaries, 246
Visual, record-keeping, 27, 34, 76-77, 80, 129, 141
Vol 100s, 175
Volatility, 178-179
Volunteer
    resources, 156-157
    volunteerism, 33-35, 158, 233

W

W-2, 199
W-4, 198-199, 204
Wall Street Journal, 161, 174, 192
Wallet, 7, 23-24, 26, 209, 221, 232
Warren Buffett Way, The, 186
Washington Post, 161
Wear-and-tear, 275
Websites
    www.bls.gov, 71, 227
    www.collegeboard.com, 146
    www.collegesavings.org, 146
    www.dol.gov, 41
    www.econsumer.equifax.com, 168
    www.ed.gov, 146
    www.experian.com, 168
    www.fafsa.ed.gov, 146
    www.finaid.org, 146
    www.finance.yahoo.com, 203
    www.guidestar.org, 157
    www.irs.gov, 202-203
    www.networkforgood.org, 157
    www.quicken.com, 203
    www.reallifemoneygame.com, 47, 186
    www.savingforcollege.com, 146
    www.smartmoney.com, 203
    www.tdameritrade.com, 203
    www.transunion.com, 168
    www.turbotax.com, 203
Weeks Hi Lo, 175
Who Or What Matters Most, 151-152, 159, 214, 219
Why Teach Teens About Savings, 135
Willing buyer, 176
Willing seller, 176
Win/win solutions, 249-260
Windfall, 266

Winning Strategies
    For Parents, 217-237
    For Teens, 239-247
Wise Giving Alliance, 156
Withdrawals, 5, 79-80, 82, 190
Withholding, 198-199
Workable solution, 234, 250-252, 255, 257, 260
Worksheets, 24, 60, 64, 94, 164, 215, 291
Worth, 7, 9-12, 39, 61, 171-177, 190, 216, 234, 254-255, 269-276

X

X and/or e Ex-cash dividend, 175
Xbox, 244

Y-Z

Yard maintenance, 226
Year-end, 25, 189
Year-to-date (YTD), 175
Yellow-highlighting pen, 63
Yield, 175
Youth Volunteer Corps, 158